Standard Guide to US World War II

TANKS & ARTILLERY

by Konrad F. Schreier Jr.

Front cover photo courtesy Patton Museum of Cavalry & Armor
Back cover inset photos courtesy Thomas Berndt

Published by

**krause
publications**

700 E. State Street • Iola, WI 54990-0001

Library of Congress Catalog Number: 93-80696
ISBN: 0-87341-297-4
Printed in the United States of America

Contents

Dedication

This book is dedicated to the memory of the late Col. George B. Jarrett, U.S. Army Ordnance Department (1902-1974).

Col. Jarrett was both my friend and mentor. He introduced me to many senior U.S. Army Ordnance Department officers and civilians with whom I discussed the materiel in this book and its history.

Col. Jarrett was closely associated with the U.S. Army Ordnance Museum at Aberdeen Proving Grounds, Maryland, from the 1930s until his death. He was its director from 1946 until his retirement from active duty with the U.S. Army in 1966.

I could not have written this book without Col. Jarrett's several decades of patiently answering my questions about U.S. Army ordnance materiel and its history. His many loans of publications, documents and photographs relating to this were invaluable.

Konrad F. Schreier, Jr.

Introduction

This is a guide to as well as a history of the tanks and artillery used by the U.S. Army in World War II. The "materiel," World War II U.S. Army for "equipment," described is primarily that actually used in combat, or that which is otherwise of importance or special interest.

The nomenclature is the familiar form used in the U.S. Armed Forces in World War II. However, it does not necessarily conform to the more complicated form such as artillery designations by both cannon and carriage model numbers which was used for support and supply purposes in World War II.

The language, dimensional notations, abbreviations, etc. are those used in the U.S. Army in World War II.

Although most of the materiel described was created by or for the U.S. Army, some, such as the LVT tracked landing vehicles invented for the U.S. Marine Corps, were not. However, the U.S. Army had a major role in designing and supplying all of it.

During World War II, the basic ordnance materiel used by the U.S. Marine Corps was all standard U.S. Army issue supplied by the U.S. Army.

Information on much of the materiel described is scattered and difficult to access. This book is intended to supply identification and information on it before it becomes lost in the mists of time and history.

Chapter 1
The Stuart Light Tanks

The Stuart light tank was the first American-designed and built ground combat weapon battle tested in World War II. Stuart light tanks went into action with the British 8th Army in the North African desert before the United States entered the war. The small group of U.S. Army technicians with them was delighted to observe their success, but it did not surprise them. The Stuart was the product of development begun decades before its first fight.

The U.S. Army's Stuart light tanks — the M2A4, M3 series and M5 series — were the result of developments dating back to the 1920s. They were the first U.S. Army tanks to include a number of key design elements, which contributed to the success of all U.S. Army tanks and related vehicles in World War II.

U.S. Marine Corps Light Tanks M2A4 advancing into action on Guadalcanal in 1942.

Left to right are a Light Tank M2A4, a Light Tank M2A3 and a Cavalry Combat Car M1 light tank in a 1939 demonstration at Aberdeen Proving Grounds. The M2A4 replaced both the M2A3 and M1 with a single model with a 37mm cannon and heavier armor, and it was the only one of the three models used in combat.

One of these elements was the U.S. Army's rubber-bushed tank track developed in the early 1930s. This track, which still contributes to the success of U.S. Army tracked combat vehicles, replaced the easily worn "dry pin" hinged tank track links with a pin in rubber bushings, allowing the track links to flex without friction or wear. When the first rubber-bushed pin tracks were tested about 1932, their life was several times that of dry pin tracks. The rubber-bushed track pin system was developed by the U.S. Army Rock Island Arsenal and Timken Bearing Co.

Another important element introduced in the Stuart light tank was the unique U.S. Army volute spring suspension for the tank's road wheels. A volute spring is a bar coiled on edge like a clock spring with one end the inner coil and the other end the outer coil. A volute spring is much more powerful than any leaf, coil or torsion bar spring taking up the same space. The volute spring road wheel bogie for a pair of road wheels was a very compact unit.

Another unique American development was a power train with a compact engine in the rear of the tank, with the transmission and track cross-drive in the bow of the tank. When this power train was

U.S. Army Light Tanks M3 advancing along a road in North Africa in 1942.

developed in the 1930s, it used a modified air-cooled radial gasoline aircraft engine, which was one of the most compact engines used in World War II tanks.

All these American-developed features were developed in the first M2 series light tanks produced in the mid-1930s. The early models were too lightly armed and armored for use in combat in World War II, but they were among the fastest and most reliable tanks of the period.

In 1939, the U.S. Army adopted the last of the M2 series light tanks: the Light Tank M2A4. This model was armed with a high

Late model U.S. Army Light Tanks M3A1 coping with mud in the Pacific Theater of War in 1944. The apparently stuck tank did make it through the mud hole!

velocity 37mm gun firing the same ammunition as the new U.S. Army 37mm antitank gun, and its armor was adequate for early World War II.

Although less than 400 M2A4s were built, some of them saw combat in the defense of the Philippines in 1941-1942, and they did a good job until shortages of their 37mm gun ammunition and spare parts put them out of action. A few of them also saw action in the Pacific Theater of War in 1942 and 1943, long after they had been replaced by an improved model.

In July 1940, the U.S. Army had an improved model of the M2A4 designated the Light Tank M3, however, due to the urgent need for tanks, it was not completely phased into production until March 1941. The one major difference between the M2A4 and M3 was that the M3 suspension was redesigned to make the rear track wheel into road wheel instead of its being an idler wheel off the ground as it was in the M2A4. This improved the M3's mobility by extending the track's ground contact. Both tanks were armed with the high velocity 37mm gun.

The Light Tank M3 first saw combat in North Africa in mid-1942 as Lend-Lease military assistance materiel with the British Army. When the British tankers first saw the M3, they were very skeptical because of its unique American design. It looked nothing like any other tank in their war, and they had yet to be combat tested.

In training, and later in combat, the M3 quickly proved a very capable tank. Its ability to sustain speeds of 20-30 miles per hour astounded the British tankers, who were used to both their and their enemy's tanks moving at 10-20 miles per hour. The tanks with which they were familiar required new tracks every 500 miles or so and frequent major mechanical repair; the M3 could often go more than 1,000 miles on a set of tracks without any major mechanical work. The British were so impressed with the M3 that when they named it, as they did with all their tanks, they used the name of a very famous American cavalry general, Confederate Gen. Stuart. This was the first U.S. Army tank with a name.

By August 1941, enough changes had been made in the M3 for it to be redesignated the Light Tank M3A1. These changes included a new turret without the original turret's cupola and an

U.S. Army Light Tanks M5 passing through a town in northern France in July 1944.

This photo taken in Italy in 1944 shows a Light Tank M3A3 on the left and a Medium Tank M4 on the right, giving an excellent comparison of the relative size of the two vehicles.

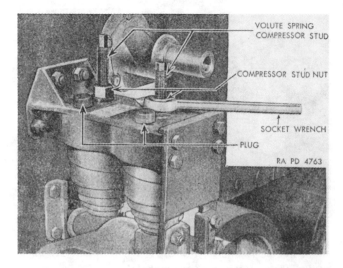

This picture shows the volute spring as used in the bogie suspensions of all U.S. Army M3 and M5 light tanks.

elevation stabilizer unit for the 37mm gun to make its fire-on-the-move more accurate. As well as being powered by an air-cooled radial gasoline engine, some 500 M3A1s used a radial air-cooled diesel engine to meet the U.S. Marine Corps requirement as well as alleviate the shortage of gasoline engines. During production, a welded hull and turret were phased in to replace the original riveted types.

In August 1942, a major change in the M3's hull created a new model designated the M3A3. The new hull featured a one-piece sloped armor hull front, which was a major improvement over the original stepped hull front. When production of the M3A3 was phased out in 1943, production of the M3 Stuart tanks was completed with some 13,539 having been built: 5,881 M3s, 4,261 M3Als and 3,427 M3A3s. M3s were used by the U.S. Army until the end of World War II.

The last model Stuart, the Light Tank M5, was developed to overcome a serious production problem. As soon as the United States entered the war the demand for air-cooled radial engines for

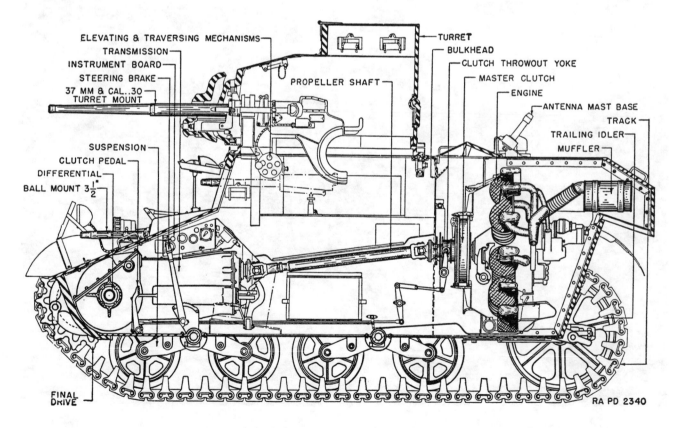

This cross-section drawing of the U.S. Army Light Tank M3 shows the arrangement used in all M3 and M5 light tanks.

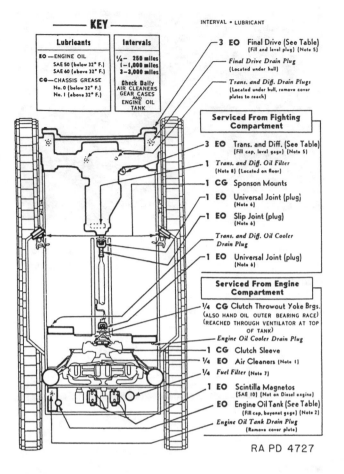

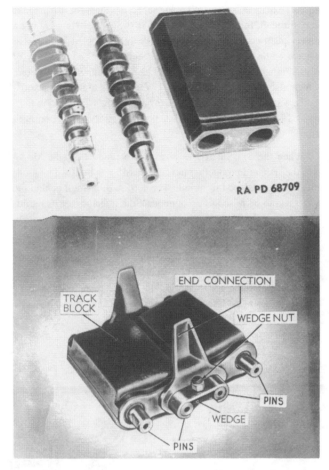

This lubrication chart for the Light Tank M3 shows the power train arrangement used on all M3 and M5 light tanks.

Above is a rubber block track link with the link pins with their rubber bushings, and below are two of these links as assembled to make the track. This rubber bushed tank track design was used on all U.S. Army World War II tanks and related vehicles built on tank chassis.

The U.S. Army 40-ton Tank Recovery Unit M25 "Dragon Wagon" transporting two Light Tanks M5. The M25 was extensively used in 1944-1945 for this and other heavy transport purposes.

aircraft expanded so much it made supplying them for use in tanks very difficult. In February 1942, an M3Al Stuart modified to use a power plant consisting of two Cadillac liquid-cooled V-8 passenger car engines as a common power unit was tested as a way of overcoming the power plant shortages. Although this system, which also used General Motors Hydramatic automatic transmissions, was adopted by the U.S. Army as the Light Tank M5 in February 1942, the urgent need for tanks delayed its production until almost 1943.

When the M5 Stuart was phased into production, the M3A3 was the standard production model. The M5 was built with a modification of its sloped front hull: The portion of the hull behind the turret had to be raised to accommodate the radiators for its liquid-cooled engines. The M5 Stuart was phased out of production in late 1943 after some 7,000 had been built.

While the Stuart was considered an obsolescent combat tank by the end of 1943, it was used for combat operations and as a training vehicle until the end of World War II. In Europe, it was considered useful as a fast full-tracked scout and reconnaissance vehicle.

A U.S. Marine Corps Light Tank M3A3 with a heavy flame thrower in place of its 37mm gun in action in the Pacific Theater in 1944.

RA PD 45946

The U.S. Army Light Tank M3A1. This is a late production example with an all-welded hull and turret and without the sponson machine gun provisions.

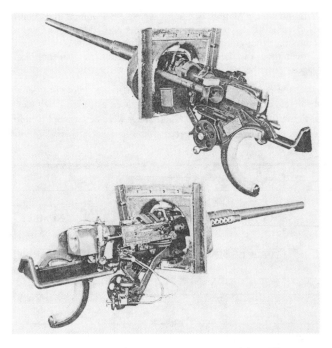

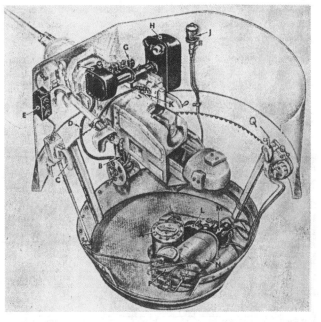

This is the basic combination gun mount with a 37mm gun and .30 Browning Machine Gun M1919 as used in all U.S. Army M2A4, M3 and M5 light tanks. This is an early model; the later model differed.

This is the 37mm combination gun mount gyro stabilizer as used in the U.S. Army M3 and M5 light tanks. It stabilizes the mount in elevation only and is hydraulically operated. The elements are: (A) collector ring, (B) disengaging switch, (C) flexible shaft, (E) control box, (F) gear box and mounting bracket, (G) cylinder and piston, (H) gyroscope control, (J) reservoir, (K) recoil switch, (L) master switch, (M) hydraulic pump, (N) pump electric motor, (P) hydraulic traverse pump, (Q) hydraulic traverse motor.

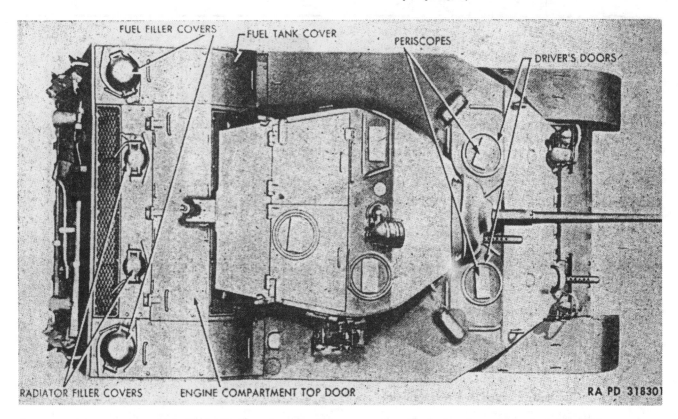

Top view of the U.S. Army Light Tank M5. Note the typical pioneer and mechanical tools on the back of the vehicle.

In the Pacific, it was used to fight Japanese tanks until the end of the war. The Stuarts were kept in use because they were mechanically reliable and easy to maintain.

Of the number of experimental Stuart conversions made to motor gun, howitzer and mortar carriages, only one, the 75mm Howitzer Motor Carriage M8, was ever adopted. A number of Stuarts, particularly in the Pacific Theater, were modified to mount flame throwers; however, no standard model was ever officially adopted.

In the field, a number of Stuarts were field modified into "command vehicles" by removing their turrets and adding more radio communications equipment. When the Cullen Plow was developed to overcome the hedgerow problem encountered in northern France, a number of Stuarts were outfitted with them.

At the end of World War II, the Stuart tanks were considered obsolete. Although they continued to be used as training vehicles, particularly with the National Guard, they were never employed in combat by the U.S. Armed Forces after 1945.

Light Tanks M2A1, M3 and M5 Series

TS15,30,51, 70,88,107,1 27,145,158, 172,191	FIGHTING DIMENSIONS (AVERAGE)				CONSTRUCTIONS				ROAD SPEED	NUMBER
MODEL	WEIGHT	LENGTH	WIDTH	HEIGHT	HULL	TURRET	ENGINE	TRANS- MISSION	(MAX)	BUILT
M2A4	23,000 lbs.	14 ft., 6 in.	7 ft., 4 in.	8 ft., 8 in.	Riveted	Riveted	Wright	Manual	25 mph	375
M3	27,400 lbs.	14 ft., 10-3/8 in.	7 ft., 4 in.	8 ft., 8 in.	Riveted	Riveted or Welded	Wright	Manual	31 mph	5,311
M3 (Diesel)	27,400 lbs.	14 ft., 10-3/8 in.	7 ft., 4 in.	8 ft., 8 in.	Riveted	Riveted or Welded	Guiberson	Manual	31 mph	500
M3A1	28,500 lbs.	14 ft., 10-3/8 in.	7 ft., 4 in.	7 ft., 6-1/2 in.	Riveted or Welded	Cast or Welded	Wright	Manual	31 mph	4,410
M3 A1 (Diesel)	28,500 lbs.	14 ft., 10-3/8 in.	7 ft., 4 in.	7 ft., 6-1/2 in.	Riveted or Welded	Cast or Welded	Guiberson	Manual	31 mph	211
M3A3	31.750 lbs.	14 ft., 10-3/8 in.	7 ft., 4 in.	7 ft., 6-1/2 in.	Welded	Cast	Wright	Manual	31 mph	3,427
M5	33,000 lbs.	14 ft., 3-3/4 in.	7 ft., 4-1/2 in.	7 ft., 6-1/2 in.	Welded	Cast	Twin Cadillac	Automatic	40 mph	2,074
M5A1	33,000 lbs.	14 ft., 3-3/4 in.	7 ft., 4-1/2 in.	7 ft., 6-1/2 in.	Welded	Cast	Twin Cadillac	Automatic	40 mph	4,736

NOTES: Armament: Main Gun: 37mm Tank gun M6 in combination mount with a coaxial cal. .30 Browning Machine Gun M1919A4 (for 37mm gun data, see 37mm Antitank Gun M3). M3A1, M3A3 and M5 have power gun elevation stabilizer and turret power traverse.

Additional Armament: 2 cal. .30 Browning Machine Guns M1919A4, one in pintle mount on turret and one in ball mount in bow of hull. M2A1s and some M3s had 2 cal. .30 Browning Machine Gun M1919A4 mounted to fire forward in the sponsons on either side. When these fixed guns were proven useless in combat in North Africa, existing ones were removed and provisions for the mount were removed with existing gun ports being covered with an armor patch.

ENGINES: Wright: Radial air-cooled gasoline 7-cylinder Model W-670, 668 cu. in. rated at 242 hp at 2,400 rpm (also made by Continental Motors).

Guiberson: Radial air-cooled diesel 9-cylinder Model T-1020, 1,021 cu. in. rated 220 hp at 2,200 rpm.

Twin Cadillac: V8 liquid-cooled gasoline engines Model series 42, each 210 cu. in. rated 110 hp at 3,400 rpm.

TRANSMISSIONS: M2A1 and M3 series: Manual five speeds and reverse.

M5: GM "Hydramatic" automatic type.

CREW: 4.

OTHER VEHICLES BUILT ON STUART CHASSIS:

75mm Howitzer Motor Carriage M8 built on M5A1 Stuart chassis and hull.

A U.S. Army Light Tank M5 with a Cullen hedgerow Plow under a camouflage net in northern France in late 1944. Note the five-gallon gas cans hanging on the sides of the tank and the bed rolls and spare bogie wheel on its glacis plate.

The U.S. Army Light Tank M2A3. This is either a very early production unit or one of the prototypes.

The U.S. Army Light Tank M3.

The U.S. Army Light Tank M3A3.

The U.S. Army Light Tank M5A1. Note the bump on the rear of its hull for the liquid-cooled Cadillac engines' radiators and the removable sand shields over the top of the suspension. These shields could be used on any M3 or M5 light tank in desert conditions.

Chapter 2
The Grant and Sherman Medium Tanks

Every credible authority agrees that the U.S. Army Sherman medium tank was one of the most important and successful weapons of World War II. Fifty years after the end of the war, a few Shermans and their variants can still be found in military use! This remarkable vehicle was the end result of a U.S. Army requirement for a medium tank dating back to the 1920s.

In 1938, the U.S. Army Rock Island Arsenal began to design and build a series of new prototype medium tanks to meet the still unfulfilled requirement. The first of these experimental prototypes used the tracks, suspension and power train of the M2 light tank modified for the larger vehicle. When this prototype proved to be unsatisfactory in many respects, a series of prototypes with many improvements and a more powerful power plant were built and tested. The last of these was considered satisfactory, and in August 1939 it was ordered into production as the Medium Tank M2.

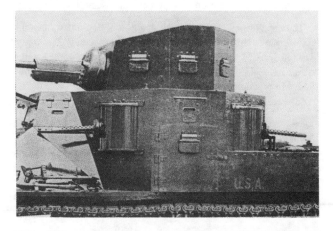

This closeup of the upper central hull of a Medium Tank M2 shows the unique casemate-mounted cal. .30 Browning machine guns, a feature of the design which proved completely unsuccessful.

The M2s rendered good service as training vehicles until very heavy usage wore them out by the end of 1942.

In order to build the number of medium tanks required for the rapidly expanding National Defense Program, a new source for mass production of the M2 mediums was sought. In August 1940, the U.S. Army placed a contract to build 1,000 M2s and a new factory to build them with Chrysler Motor Company. When Chrysler President Kaufman T. Keller was preparing the project, he found

Medium Tanks M2A1 on maneuvers in 1941. This model was never used in combat, but its power train, suspension and tracks were the prototypes for those of the M3 Grant and M4 Sherman medium tanks.

The M2 medium used improved and enlarged rubber-bushed tracks, volute spring suspension and a power train based on the M2 light tank design. The rest of the tank was an unusual design with a high boxy hull with casement-mounted .30 cal. Browning Machine Guns M1919A4 in each of its corners and topped with a turret mounting a 37mm gun with a coaxial Browning .30 cal. M1919A4 machine gun. From August 1939 through August 1941, Rock Island Arsenal built over 224 M2 medium tanks.

From their introduction, the M2 mediums proved rugged and mechanically reliable vehicles, but U.S. Army observation of the latest European tanks showed they were unsuitable for combat use.

This experimental modification of an M2 medium tank built in 1939, mounting a 75mm Pack Howitzer M1, was the prototype for the 75mm gun mount in the Grant M3 medium tank. The cupola on top of the hull includes a meter-long optical range finder and a cal. .30 Browning Machine Gun.

that the U.S. Armored Force Board's medium tank requirement called for one armed with a 75mm gun, and that the U.S. Army Ordnance Department tank engineering people had already mocked up a wooden prototype. It was quickly decided that Chrysler's new Detroit Tank Arsenal would produce this new model.

This began the involvement of the American automobile industry in the U.S. Army's World War II tank program, and the era of the mass produced assembly line tanks began. This resulted in all U.S. Army tank series being built with a high degree of parts and assembly interchangeability, particularly in things like tracks, suspension, turrets, drive trains and gun mount assemblies.

The capabilities of the American automobile industry as tank producers were demonstrated when the first of the new 75mm gun Medium Tank M3s rolled out of the Chrysler Detroit Tank Arsenal on April 1, 1941, just nine months after the project began! By June 1941, M3 mediums were being delivered in quantity.

The Medium Tank M3 was an upgraded version of the M2 model. Its design — with a turret mounted 37mm gun on top and a 75mm gun in a sponson in the right front corner of its hull — was the result of the fact that the U.S. Army Ordnance Department tank engineers had yet to complete the development of turret-mounting a 75mm gun suitable for a medium tank. From its introduction, the M3 was considered an interim model to be replaced with an improved model with a turret-mounted 75mm gun.

The formal roll-out of the first U.S. Army Medium Tank M3 built by Baldwin Locomotive Works. The two cal. .30 Browning Machine Guns in the fixed mounts on the right side of the glacis plate were not used in combat by the U.S. Army. (Baldwin Locomotive Works photo)

The formal roll-out of the first U.S. Army Medium Tank M3 built at the Chrysler Corp.-operated U.S. Army Detroit Tank Arsenal. (Chrysler Corp. photo)

Altogether, six models of the M3 series medium tank were produced, but only the original M3 model was produced in quantity, and it was the standard U.S. Army model. The original M3 had a riveted armor hull and a cast 37mm gun turret. It was powered by the Wright air-cooled radial gasoline engine Model R-975, a modified aircraft power plant. The M3 model accounted for some 80 percent of the M3 series production. The other five models were primarily production trials of power plant and hull construction methods.

The first Medium Tanks M3 to see combat were ones sent to the British under Lend-Lease. Despite the obviously clumsy position of the 75mm gun in the right front corner of the hull, it immediately proved successful in combat in the summer and fall 1942 battles in the North African desert.

The British gave the M3 medium tank its two names. A version built with a 37mm gun turret specially designed to meet British requirements was called the Lee for the famous Civil War general, and the standard U.S. Army model, which they also received, was named the Grant for another famous Civil War general. The tank named Grant was the one the U.S. Army used.

The first U.S. Army M3 Grants to see combat were with armored units with the invasion of North Africa in November 1942, which came to the fight from bases in the British Isles. They

were reasonably successful in action; however, the U.S. Army did not use M3 Grants as combat tanks after the end of the North African Campaign in 1943.

Some M3 Grants were still in use as U.S. Army training vehicles until the last were withdrawn in 1944. Beginning as early as 1942,

On the right is a U.S. Army Medium Tank M3, on the left a U.S. Army Medium Tank M4. They are being refueled at a "gas station" at a U.S. Army training command post in 1942.

This U.S. Army Medium Tank M3 — the interim model 75mm gun with a muzzle counterweight — was photographed in North Africa in late 1942 after running 1,376 miles under combat conditions. The fact that the tank is still serviceable is typical for U.S. Army tanks of the M3-M4 types.

A U.S. Army Medium Tank M3 on a Truck-Trailer, 45-ton, Tank Transporter M19 using a Diamond T truck, 12-ton, 6x4, M20 in the California Desert Training Center in 1942. This was the first U.S. Army tank transporter.

This is one of a very limited number of U.S. Army Medium Tanks M3 deployed in the Pacific Theater of Operations in late 1942 or early 1943.

Two U.S. Army Tank Recovery Vehicles M31 in operation in Italy in 1944. These were rebuilt Medium Tanks M3, and they used the top 37mm gun turret as their crane base. Note the door in place of the 75mm sponson gun, which has a dummy cannon.

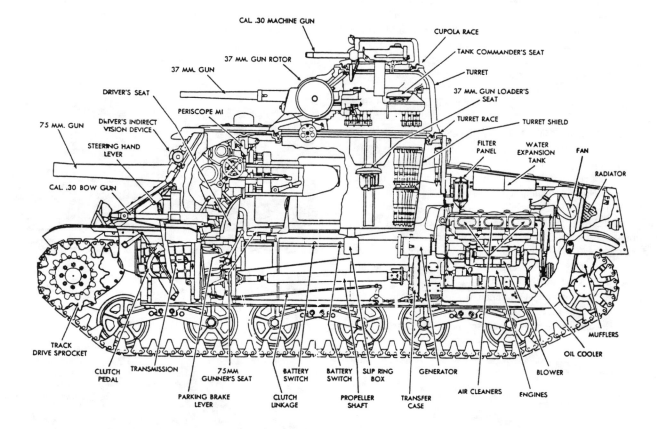

CAL .30 MACHINE GUN
37 MM. GUN ROTOR
37 MM. GUN
DRIVER'S SEAT
PERISCOPE MI
DRIVER'S INDIRECT VISION DEVICE
75 MM. GUN
STEERING HAND LEVER
CAL .30 BOW GUN
CUPOLA RACE
TANK COMMANDER'S SEAT
TURRET
37 MM. GUN LOADER'S SEAT
TURRET RACE
TURRET SHIELD
FILTER PANEL
WATER EXPANSION TANK
FAN
RADIATOR
MUFFLERS
OIL COOLER
BLOWER
ENGINES
AIR CLEANERS
GENERATOR
TRANSFER CASE
PROPELLER SHAFT
SLIP RING BOX
BATTERY SWITCH
BATTERY SWITCH
CLUTCH LINKAGE
75MM GUNNER'S SEAT
PARKING BRAKE LEVER
TRANSMISSION
CLUTCH PEDAL
TRACK DRIVE SPROCKET

Cross section of a typical U.S. Army Medium Tank M3 (an M3A5).

A U.S. Army Medium Tank M3 converted into a Tank Recovery Vehicle M31 being tested as a bridge emplacing vehicle in Italy in 1944.

A U.S. Army Medium Tank M3 converted into a Full-Track Prime Mover M33 towing the barrel-recoil assembly of a U.S. Army 8-inch gun M1 in Italy in 1944.

M3 Grants were being converted for other uses. In 1942 and 1943, a substantial number were converted into full-track Tank Recovery Vehicles M31 by removing the 37mm gun from the turret and replacing the 75mm gun with a dummy cannon, and adding a heavy lift crane, heavy-duty winch, and other equipment for battlefield tank recovery work. Others were converted into prime movers for heavy and super-heavy field artillery weapons as full-track Prime Movers M33 by removing the 37mm gun turret and replacing the 75mm gun with a dummy cannon and adding a heavy-duty winch and other special support equipment for artillery service.

The U.S. Army had classified the M3 Grant as Substitute Standard in October 1941 before it had used it in World War II. It was made Limited Standard in April 1943, and Obsolete in April 1945. The M3 Grants converted for other uses were retained until the end of World War II, and the rest were scrapped with their reusable parts

A U.S. Army Medium Tank M3A1. Only a few of these were built as test of casting complex armor hulls in one piece.

and assemblies being salvaged. Despite this, some — such as the ones the British used in the Burma Campaign, which ended in May 1945 — remained in combat use until the end of World War II.

Although the last M3 Grant was produced in December 1942, work on engineering its replacement had begun before it had gone out of production. A mock-up of the new model had been completed by May 1941, and the prototype Medium Tank T6 was under test in the summer of 1941. The new model with its 75mm gun in a turret was adopted in October 1941, and the British immediately christened it the Sherman. Pilot production of the M4 Sherman was actually already under way, and it was relatively easy to phase into production as many of its critical parts, including its basic bottom hull, power train, suspension and tracks, all were the same as the M3 Grant's.

This is a late production U.S. Army Medium Tank M3A5 built with the same 75mm gun as the Medium Tank M4 and without the side doors of earlier M3 series tanks. This model was used for Lend-Lease military assistance only.

The M4 Sherman was produced at some eighteen facilities with a number of phased-in modifications and improvements through its production from 1941 to 1945. In addition, many went through major depot rebuilds and were factory "remanufactured"; many which received this sort of work incorporated parts from more than one model and/or variation. By 1944, U.S. Army Ordnance Department publications stated the M4 is "produced simultaneously by different manufacturers, the various models differ from each other principally in their engines." Of course this is an oversimplification which does not take into account the many changes and modifications over the production.

One special feature all U.S. Armed Forces Shermans and most other U.S. World War II tanks had was a power traverse mechanism for the turret. They also had a gyroscopic main gun elevation stabilization system. These combined to make firing the main gun while moving more effective.

The M4 Sherman and all other U.S. Army tanks were equipped with an FM communications radio system unique to the U.S. Armed Forces in World War II. This system could be patched into any local field artillery fire control and direction system to allow the tank's main gun to fire as field artillery. All U.S. World War II tanks had the required azimuth and elevation controls to permit their use as field artillery weapons, and they were frequently called on to fire field artillery missions.

A very early production U.S. Army Medium Tank M4A1 with the fixed cal. .30 machine gun mounts in the glacis plate, eliminated very ealy in production and never used in combat.

Late manufacture U.S. Army cast hull Medium Tanks M4A1 in action in the Philippines in mid-1944. These have the one-piece cross drive housing and improved glacis armor.

U.S. Army Medium Tanks M4A3E8 in Germany in 1945. Note the 76mm gun used on the M4A3E8 is equipped with a muzzle brake while those used on other M4 series tanks are not.

A U.S. Army Medium Tank M4A3E2, assault model, rearmed with a 76mm gun in action in Germany in the spring of 1945.

Late model U.S. Army welded-hull Medium Tanks M4 firing a field artillery mission in France in late 1944.

Late model U.S. Army welded-hull Medium Tanks M4A3 with 76mm guns firing a field artillery mission in Italy in late 1944.

From the time of its introduction, the M4 Sherman demonstrated outstanding speed and maneuverability. Its reliability and ease of maintenance, even with the 30-cylinder Chrysler "Multibank" engine, was outstanding compared to most other tanks built in World War II.

Even today, the ability of a World War II M4 Sherman to run as far as 2,500 miles on a set of tracks and bogie wheels without major maintenance remains as good as any other tank ever built.

Despite its proven capability at its introduction, many changes and modifications were phased into M4 Sherman production during World War II and were often applied during remanufacture or major overhauls. Some of these involved the tracks and suspension.

Early production M4 Shermans used the same track and suspension as the M3 Grants. In late 1942, a new bogie assembly — which replaced the original track return wheel at the top of the

This picture of an upgraded U.S. Army welded-hull Medium Tank M4 series was taken in a U.S. Army Ordnance Department facility in England in 1944 to show the modifications incorporated at the depot. These include a new style mantle for the 75mm gun, applique armor on the sides and over the old style vision ports, and track widening "duck bill" track connectors.

This upgraded early model U.S. Army welded-hull Series Medium Tank M4 in action in France in the summer of 1944 has applique armor on its hull sides, turret front corners, and over its early type vision ports. It is also equipped with a Cullen hedgerow plow on its bow.

An upgraded early model U.S. Army welded-hull Medium Tank M4 series in action in France in late 1944. This tank has applique armor plates on its hull side. The officer in the foreground is Gen. George S. Patton, the U.S. Army's foremost World War II tank general.

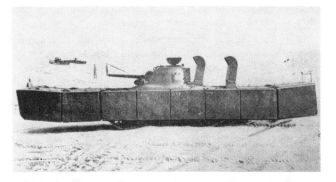

A U.S. Army Medium Tank M4 equipped with the pontoon flotation unit used in several operations in the Pacific Theater of Operations. This unit depended on the tank's tracks for water propulsion.

This photo, taken in northern France in the summer of 1945, shows U.S. Army Ordnance Department personnel installing a Cullen hedgerow plow on the nose of a late model cast hull 76mm gun U.S. Army Medium Tank M4A1.

A U.S. Army Medium Tank M4 series with a flame thrower replacing the main gun as used by the U.S. Marine Corps in the Pacific Theater of Operations in 1944-1945.

A U.S. Army Medium Tank M4 series re-equipped with a flame thrower in place of the bow cal. .30 machine gun and with a bumper bar to push down jungle growth used by the U.S. Marine Corps in the Pacific Theater of Operations.

These track widening "duck bill" track connectors were installed on many U.S. Army Medium Tanks, M4 series and related vehicles from late 1943 on to improve their mobility in mud, sand and similar difficult conditions.

assembly with a combination of a relocated return wheel and return skid plate — was phased into production.

In 1943, a new, wider center guide track was designed to replace the original edge guided track, and a new bogie assembly was designed for the new track. The new Horizontal Volute Spring Suspension, HVSS, and wide track were phased into production in 1944. The improved system enhanced the M4 Sherman's overall mobility, and it was retrofitted to many M4 Shermans and related vehicles in late World War II and after the war.

By 1942, improvements in the M4 Sherman's hull and armor design were being made. One of the first was a new one-piece front cross drive housing, which replaced the original three-piece type inherited from the M3 Grant design in late 1942. This unit both improved the armor protection and was easier to manufacture, and it was frequently retrofitted to remanufactured M4 Shermans.

Beginning in early 1943, troops in the field in North Africa began adding "applique" armor to M4 Sherman; this added armor was soon being applied to them by U.S. Army Depots. Pieces of armor plate were welded to the hull and/or turret where they would afford improved protection. The most used applique armor was on the hull sides to protect the crew spaces. Although some M4 Shermans were fitted with extra armor on the hull front plate in the field, this could seriously affect the balance of the tank by making it nose heavy, and it was never officially done or recommended.

The original M4 Sherman hull front "glacis" plate was sloped at 56° and had crew vision provisions projecting to its front. In early 1944, the slope of the glacis plate was changed to 47°, and

the crew vision provisions were moved off it to the top of the hull with periscopes replacing the original vision slots. This change improved the overall armor protection and simplified hull manufacture. When many older M4 Shermans were remanufactured or given depot major overhauls, an applique piece of armor was often welded over the original crew vision ports, and hatches with vision periscopes were installed in the top of the hull.

In 1943, the original narrow movable shield portion of the main gun coaxial gun mount was widened to give better protection, and this change was another incorporated when older M4 Shermans were remanufactured. At about the same time, the turret casting was enlarged to give additional space in its rear portion.

As a result of these changes, along with a number of less important ones, it became very difficult to sort out the various model M4 Shermans since the basic model designations were seldom changed or added to designate them. The U.S. Army Ordnance Department's attempt to overcome this problem by referring to M4 Shermans by the year model of their manufacture was futile because of the extensive retrofitting done in remanufacturing and/or major overhauling. By the end of World War II, it had become impossible to tell just what variation an M4 Sherman actually was without looking at it, and it took a considerable effort after the war to sort them out.

As improvements were phased into M4 Sherman production, many early models were converted for other uses. Beginning in late 1943, one conversion was to Track Prime Movers M34 for heavy and super-heavy field artillery weapons. These had a winch,

This U.S. Army Medium Tank M4 shows sandbag defense against German shaped-charge Panzerfaust weapons installed in late 1944 and 1945 when these were encountered in northern Europe. Many other type of defenses against these weapons were used including timber and wire fencing.

A U.S. Army Medium Tank M4 series converted to a Tank Recovery Unit M32 series with its lifting boom stowed and a fording vent for its engine installed.

A U.S. Army Medium Tank M4 series equipped with a British Flail Mine Exploder. The U.S. Army only made very limited use of this unit since German mines blew the flail chains off frequently.

crane, and other equipment added to make them suitable for field artillery use, and the turret was removed and replaced with a lightly armored box with a machine gun mount. Another conversion was the Tank Recovery Vehicle M32 series. These got a powerful winch, a crane and other provisions for battlefield recovery of damaged tanks. This proved a very successful modification, and it was used by the U.S. Army long after World War II.

There were also a number of attachments developed for the M4 Sherman. Late in the war, a number were fitted with bulldozer kits to be used as armored combat bulldozers. These were first improvised in the field from existing crawler tractor bulldozer kits, and late in the war special versions were manufactured for the purpose (see the chapter on the armored bulldozer).

A number of devices used to modify the M4 Sherman into a mine-clearing tank (to make paths in mine fields without being blown up) were developed. Several types of "mine rollers" were tested in combat in the European Theater of war. The British-developed ground beating "flail" mine exploder was also combat-tested.

These devices were extremely cumbersome, and, although they often worked, all were too easily damaged by the mines and never considered really practical.

In Italy, under fire, stripped-down Sherman tanks were used to move ditch crossing bridges into position. However, these "bridging tanks" proved awkward and unsatisfactory in use. A number of devices, including special pontoons, were experimented with in an attempt to make the M4 Sherman into an amphibious tank, but none were successful.

However, kits which allowed the M4 Shermans to "wade" through water up to the top of the turret were developed and proved useful. These were used in landings in both France and on Pacific islands. Once ashore, this "fording equipment" was stripped from the tank as soon as possible.

In the field, specifically in the Pacific Theater, flame throwers were added to the M4 Sherman's armament. In some of these field modifications, regular U.S. Army Chemical Warfare Service "infantry" flame throwers were installed in the tank's bow machine gun mount, and in others experimental heavy flame throwers were installed, replacing the tank's main gun in the turret. Although these tank flame throwers proved very useful in combat, none were adopted or standardized during World War II.

A number of rocket launchers for the M4 Sherman were tested to increase the shock effect of the tanks in offensive

A U.S. Army Medium Tank M4 series equipped with a Mine Exploder T1E1 in action in northern Europe in the winter of 1944-1945.

A U.S. Army Medium Tank M4 series equipped with a Mine Exploder T1E3 crossing a pontoon bridge in northern Europe in the spring of 1945. GIs nicknamed this unit the "Aunt Jemima" for the famous pancake mix of the time.

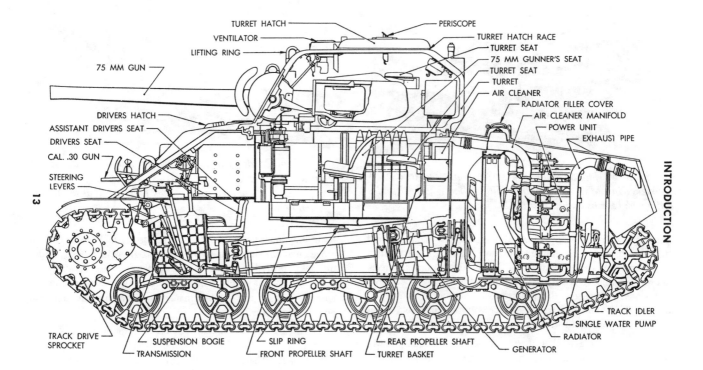

Cross section of a typical U.S. Army Medium Tank M4 series (M4A4).

actions. Two — a 4.5-in. multiple launcher and a 7.2-in. multiple launcher which mounted on the tank's turret — were adopted and used in combat with some success. (See chapter on rocket artillery).

One very effective field expedient device developed for the M4 Sherman was the Cullen Hedgerow Plow (also used on Stuart light tanks). When trying to drive over a hedgerow, a tank's lighter belly armor was exposed. The Cullen Hedgerow Plow, invented by Sgt. Curtis G. Cullen, added teeth capable of tearing holes in the European hedgerows. Structural steel salvaged from German beach defenses along the French coast was used in their construction.

The U.S. Army primarily used only those models of the M4 series Sherman powered by either the Wright radial air-cooled gasoline engine or the Ford liquid-cooled V-8 engine. The M4 Shermans with other engines were primarily used to supply Allied Nations, which received them as Lend-Lease military assistance. The U.S. Marine Corps, however, did receive and use a limited number powered with the twin liquid-cooled GMC diesel power plant. The U.S. Armed Forces always had first choice of any American materiel produced, and they were always supplied with what they required before any materiel was offered as Lend-Lease.

When the last World War II model M4 Shermans were issued in 1944-1945, practically all of them went to the U.S. Army. This included the special limited production M4A3E2 "assault tank," which was loaded with several tons of extra armor and equipped with a special lower-geared drive to carry it.

Except for a few samples sent to the British, the U.S. Army got all the M4 Shermans built with the improved HVSS track and suspension. These "Easy Eight" Shermans proved the best of the M4s built, and many existing Shermans with the old suspension and tracks were rebuilt with the HVSS track and suspension after World War II.

A U.S. Army Medium Tank M4 series converted to a Tank Recovery Unit M32 series using its boom to lift the turret assembly out of a late production U.S. Army Medium Tank M4 series.

The U.S. Army Medium Tank M4A3E8. (Chrysler Corp. photo)

A U.S. Army Medium Tank M4 series converted to a Tank Recovery Unit M32 series with its boom deployed and lifting a U.S. Army Light Tank M5.

The U.S. Army Medium Tank M4 series as built with the cast front welded rear "hermaphrodite" hull. Most M4s with this hull construction were used as Lend-Lease military assistance.

U.S. Army Medium Tank M4 series equipped with the British Duplex Drive Flotation Unit. It got its name from the propeller and rudder system applied to the rear of the tank. The U.S. Army found the unit was much too easily swamped in heavy surf, and made very little use of it.

The U.S. Army Medium Tank M3A3E2, assault model, as built with the 75mm gun.

The U.S. Army 40-ton Tank Recovery Unit M25 "Dragon Wagon" loading a U.S. Army Medium Tank M4A1. The M25 was extensively used to move tanks and other very heavy cargo in 1944-1945. (Pacific Car & Foundry Co. photo)

The M4 Sherman tank was not a single model, but a large family of similar model tanks. They, and the related vehicles built on their chassis, unquestionably made a large contribution to the Allied victory in World War II. Everybody, even former enemies, considered its superior mechanical qualities and excellent speed and mobility the best of any tank used in the war.

Grant and Sherman Tank Main Guns

The main gun armament of the M3 Grants and M4 Shermans was critical to their combat effectiveness, and they went through considerable development.

When the M3 Grant was designed in late 1939, it was to be armed with a 75mm gun similar to the 75mm Tank Gun M3 adopted later. This 75mm gun was designed to fire standard U.S. Army 75mm field gun ammunition with the same ballistics as the U.S. Army's 75mm modernized "French 75" field gun.

When the U.S. Armored Force Board tested the prototype M3 Grants in early 1941, they objected to the long barrel of the 75mm gun because it projected from its sponson mount well past the front of the left track and tangled with trees and brush when charging through them. It was feared this could damage the gun and its mount in combat. As a result, the barrel of the 75mm gun was shortened 16-5/8 inches so it would not extend past the track. This "short" gun was adopted as the 75mm Tank Gun M2 and put in production for the M3 Grant tank.

When the British had observed tests of the M3 Grant and asked for them under Lend-Lease, they had the original long gun. When they got their first M3 Lee versions of the M3 Grant, they were armed with the standard short 75mm Gun M2 as the M3 Grant. The British observed that the short 75mm M2 gun had a muzzle velocity of 1,850 fps, 200 fps less than the longer gun originally tested, and this was a 10 percent reduction in power they could not afford to lose. They requested their M3 Lees be equipped with the original longer 75mm gun.

The U.S. Army Ordnance Department Tank Engineering Division agreed with the British request, and immediately put the long gun into production. In July 1941, the longer 75mm Tank Gun M3 was adopted; it had the same barrel length as the original long gun and the same 2,050 fps muzzle velocity as the standard 75mm field gun.

During the transition from the M3 Grant to the M4 Sherman in 1941-1942, the M3 75mm tank guns were in short supply, and both models had to be equipped with the M2 75mm gun to get them into the hands of troops. When either an M3 Grant or an M4 Sherman with a gun mount for the M3 75mm gun was armed with an M2 75mm gun, a counterweight had to be installed on the M2 gun to compensate for the loss of weight in its cut-off muzzle. This oddity actually saw use in combat in North Africa, but the M2 guns were replaced with M3 guns as quickly as possible.

All the Shermans built in 1941, 1942 and much of 1943 were armed with the 75mm tank gun M3. However, beginning in late 1942, reports from combat troops in the field in North Africa repeatedly said the M4 Sherman needed a more powerful, higher velocity gun. Development of a 3-in. gun for the M4 Sherman was authorized. The project began to adapt the 3-in. Tank Gun M7 used in the 3-in. Gun Motor Carriage M10 tank destroyer and Heavy Tank M6 to a mount which would fit the existing M4 Sherman turret, but the 3-in. M7 gun was too large and heavy to make this possible.

This led to the designing of a new lightweight, high-velocity 76mm gun which fired the same projectiles as the 3-in. gun from a new cartridge case. This gun was adopted in mid-1943 as the 76mm Tank Gun M1.

The new 76mm tank gun was the first U.S. Army gun in the 76mm gun caliber, and it fit in a combination mount similar to and interchangeable with the one used for 75mm guns in the M4 Sherman's turret. The new 76mm tank gun was actually ballistically superior to the 3-in. gun originally proposed, and it fired new High Velocity Armor Piercing (HVAP) ammunition, which could destroy the German Panther and Tiger tanks.

Unfortunately, the introduction of the new 76mm gun-armed M4 Shermans was delayed by production difficulties. Once it was available in late 1943, many new M4 Shermans were equipped with it, and it was retrofitted in many when they were either remanufactured or given major overhauls. However, due to persistent shortages of both the 76mm gun and its ammunition, M4

Shermans with the original 75mm gun were still in wide use at the end of World War II.

In 1943, it was also decided to arm M4 Shermans with 105mm howitzers so they could be used as support artillery with armored forces in the same role as the 105mm Howitzer Motor Carriage M7 "Priest." This was easily done by modifying the barrel of the standard 105mm Howitzer M2 to fit a mount very similar to and interchangeable with the standard M4 Sherman 75mm gun combination mount, and it was issued as the 105mm Howitzer M4 in 1944. The ballistics of the M4 Sherman tank 105mm Howitzer were identical to those of the standard 105mm Howitzer M2.

The above main weapons were the only ones used to arm U.S. Army M3 Grant and M4 Sherman tanks in World War II.

A 1944 production M4A3 Sherman with a 76mm gun.

A late production U.S. Army Medium Tank M4A3 equipped with fording vents for its engine. A single vent was used on the M4 and M4A1.

A Medium Tank M2A1 being demonstrated at Aberdeen Proving Ground for the Army Ordnance Association meeting in the fall of 1941.

MODEL: Medium Tanks M2 and M2A1

WEIGHT: Fighting: M2; 38,000 lbs.; M2A1: 47,000 lbs.

DIMENSIONS: Length: 17 ft., 6 in.; Width: 8 ft., 6 in.; Height: 9 ft., 4 in.

ARMAMENT: Main gun: 37mm gun M6 in mount with coaxial cal. .30 Browning Machine Gun M1919A4. 8 additional cal. .30 Browning Machine Guns M1919A4: 1 in each of 4 upper hull casemate mounts, 2 fixed mounts in hull front glacis, 2 in pintle mounts on turret.

ENGINE: Wright air-cooled 9-cylinder radial model R975, 973 cu. in. rated; 350 hp at 2,100 rpm.

TRANSMISSION: Manual

NORMAL ROAD SPEED: 26 mph max.

MODELS: M2 (vertical-sided turret) 126 built; M2A1 (slope-sided turret) 98 built

NOTE: Used as training vehicle only.

CREW: 6.

A typical standard U.S. Army Medium Tank M3.

MODEL: Medium Tank M3

WEIGHT: Fighting: 60,000 lbs.

DIMENSIONS: Length: 18 ft., 6 in. Height: 10 ft., 3 in. Width: 10 ft., 3 in.

ARMAMENT: 1-75mm Tank Gun M2 in sponson mount; Traverse: 14 degree R&L; Elevation: +19.2 degrees, -7.8 degrees; 1-37mm tank gun M6 in turret in combination mount with cal. .30 Browning Machine Gun M1919A4; 3-cal. .30 Browning Machine Guns M1919A4, 1 in turret cupola turret and 2 fixed in hull front.

ENGINE: Wright Air Cooled 9-cylinder radial model R975, 973 cu. in. rated 340 hp at 2,400 rpm.

TRANSMISSION: Manual 5-speed and reverse.

NORMAL ROAD SPEED: 26 mph max.

CREW: 6.

NOTE: The 2-cal. .30 machine guns in hull front were removed prior to combat use, and their ports were plugged.

MODEL DIFFERENCES: The Medium Tank M3 was the standard production model used by the U.S. Army in combat. A total of 4,942 were built, including about 600 "Lees" with a special 37mm gun turret to meet British requirements. M3 production ended in December 1942.

In addition to the M3, there were five other models built. Their total production was 1,784. They are:

M3A1: A limited production test of a cast armor upper hull. Three hundred were built and used as test or training vehicles only.

M2A2: A production test built with an all-welded hull. Twelve were built and used as test vehicles only.

M2A3: A welded-hull limited production model powered with twin liquid-cooled GMC diesel motors, Model 6-71. A total of 322 were built with a small number going to the U.S. Marine Corps as training vehicles and the rest to Lend-Lease.

M3A4: A riveted-hull model powered by the Chrysler liquid-cooled 30-cylinder gasoline "multibank" engine. The 109 built were used as test and/or training vehicles and/or for Lend-Lease.

M3A5: A riveted-hull limited production powered by twin GMC liquid-cooled diesel engines. A total of 591 were built with a few going to the U.S. Marine Corps and the rest for Lend-Lease.

Other Production Vehicles Built On the Medium Tank M3 Chassis:

105mm Howitzer Motor Carriage M7 "Priest"
155mm Gun Motor Carriage M12 "King Kong"
Cargo Carrier M30 (for the 155mm Gun Motor Carriage M12)

MODEL	FIGHTING WEIGHT	DIMENSIONS (AVERAGE)			HULL CONSTRUCTION	ENGINE (2)	TRANSMISSION (3)	NORMAL ROADSPEED (MAX.)
		LENGTH OVER TRACKS	HEIGHT	WIDTH				
M4	67,000 to 70,000 lbs.	19 ft., 4 in.	9 ft., 0 in.	8 ft., 7 in.	Welded	Wright	Manual	24 mph
M4A1	67,000 to 70,000 lbs.	19 ft., 2 in.	9 ft., 0 in.	8 ft., 7 in.	Cast	Wright	Manual	24 mph
M4A2	70,000 to 72,800 lbs.	19 ft., 5 in.	9 ft., 0 in.	8 ft., 7 in.	Welded	Twin GMC Diesel	Manual	29 mph
M4A3	68,400 to 71,100 lbs.	19 ft., 5-1/2 in.	9 ft., 0 in.	8 ft., 7 in.	Welded	Ford	Manual	26 mph
M4A4	71,900 lbs.	19 ft., 10-1/2 in.	9 ft., 0 in.	8 ft., 7 in.	Welded	Chrysler Multibank	Manual	25 mph
M4A3E2 (4)	82,000 lbs.	19 ft., 5-1/2 in.	9 ft., 0 in.	8 ft., 7 in.	Welded	Ford	Manual	22 mph
M4 HVSS (1)	72,500 lbs.	19 ft., 10-1/2 in.	9 ft., 0 in.	9 ft., 8 in.	Welded or Cast-Welded	Wright	Manual	24 mph
M4A3HVSS (1)	73,400 to 74,000 lbs.	19 ft., 10-1/2 in.	9 ft., 0 in.	9 ft., 8 in.	Welded	Ford	Manual	26 mph

NOTES:

(1): HVSS M4s were built with Horizontal Volute Spring Suspension and wide center guide track. A total of 3,825 were built with this modification in 1944-1945, and a significant number more were remanufactured with it during and after the end of World War II.

(2): M4s were manufactured with four different non-interchangeable engines as follows:

WRIGHT: A 9-cylinder radial air-cooled gasoline engine Model R975 (also built by Continental Motors), 973 cu. in. rated 400 hp at 2,400 rpm. Approximately 18,066 were built with this engine primarily for U.S. Army use.

TWIN GMC DIESELS: Each a 6-cylinder liquid-cooled Model 6-71, 425 cu. in. rated at 180 hp at 2,100 rpm. Approximately 9,507 produced for Lend-Lease except for a small number for the U.S. Marine Corps.

FORD: A liquid-cooled gasoline V-8 Model GAA, 1,100 cu. in. rated 500 hp at 2,600 rpm. Approximately 9,507 produced with this engine primarily for U.S. Army use.

CHRYSLER MULTIBANK: A liquid-cooled 30-cylinder engine made by combining five 6-cylinder gasoline automobiles engines with a common power output. A total of 1,253 cu. in. rated 425 hp at 2,850 rpm. Approximately 7,499 built with this engine for Lend-Lease.

(3): TRANSMISSIONS: All 5-speed forward and reverse manual.

(4): The M4A3E2 was a special limited production model with extra heavy armor. A total 254 built for use in the European Theater of War by the U.S. Army. A number had their original 75mm guns replaced with 76mm guns before they were used in combat.

ARMAMENT: The main armament of all M4s was a cannon in coaxial mount with a cal. .30 Browning Machine Gun M1919A4. In addition, a cal. .30 Browning Machine Gun M1919A4 was provided in a ball mount in the bow. All U.S. Army M4s were equipped with a cal. .50 Browning Machine Gun M2-HB in a pintle mount on the turret. Prototype and early production M4s had a pair of fixed cal. .30 Browning Machine Guns M1919A4 in a fixed mount in the bow, which were deleted as useless before combat use.

The cannon production assembled in M4 factory production were:

75mm Gun M3: Approximately 44,000 as built.

76mm Gun M1: Approximately 6,465 as built.

105mm Howitzer M4: Approximately 4,180 as built.

However, due to gun and mount interchangeability, many M4s otherwise armed were retrofitted with the 76mm Gun M1 during remanufacture and/or major overhauls during and after World War II.

CREW: 5.

Other Production Vehicles Based On The M4 Series Tank Chassis:

3-in. Gun Motor Carriage M10 (tank destroyer)

90mm Gun Motor Carriage M36 (tank destroyer)

155mm Gun Motor Carriage M40

8-in. Howitzer Motor Carriage M43

An early production cast hull U.S. Army Medium Tank M4 with the three-part cross drive housing.

An early production U.S. Army welded-hull Medium Tank M4 series with the three-piece cross drive housing.

An intermediate production U.S. Army Medium Tank M4 series with a welded hull and one-piece cross drive housing.

A very late production welded-hull U.S. Army Medium Tank M4A3 with a 105mm howitzer and track assembly with track widening "duck bill" track connectors and semi-sand shield skirts.

Chapter 3
The Chaffee and Pershing Tanks

During World War II, the U.S. Army introduced the M24 Chaffee light tank and the M26 Pershing heavy tank. Both were very advanced designs for their time, and they established basic principles which still influence armored fighting vehicle design.

The development of the M24 Chaffee began with a U.S. Armored Force Board requirement for a 75mm gun armed light tank, which originated as a result of observations of combat in North Africa in 1942. A preliminary test was done by mounting a 75mm gun developed for use in aircraft in a modified 75mm Howitzer Motor Carriage M8 built on the chassis of the M5 Stuart light tank. This aircraft 75mm gun fired the same ammunition as the 75mm gun used in the M4 Sherman medium tank. Tests proved that, while a light tank could successfully mount a 75mm gun, the Stuart light tank was too small to do it practically.

The project then concentrated on a new 75mm gun armed light tank being developed by the U.S. Army Rock Island Arsenal and the International Harvester Company. It quickly became evident

U.S. Army troops preparing to move a U.S. Army Heavy Tank M26 across a river on a pontoon barge in Germany in early 1945.

U.S. Army Heavy Tank M26 being demonstrated in late 1944. This tank, which was the basis of a series of U.S. Army medium tanks from the 1940s to the 1970s, saw only limited service in World War II in 1945.

A U.S. Army Heavy Tank M26 in march order with its turret reversed so its long 90mm gun could be supported on a "crutch" on the rear of the vehicle.

that this Light Tank T7 project was not going to produce the 75mm gun armed light tank required. The problem was that the T7 weighed as much as a medium tank, and it was smaller and inferior to the M4 Sherman medium tank. Although the T7 was standardized as the Medium Tank M7, it was a redundant design, and it was never put in production.

At the same time, another project to develop a 75mm gun armed light tank, the Light Tank T24, showed promise. The T24 was a project of the Cadillac Division of General Motors and U.S. Army Ordnance Department tank engineers associated with the production of the M5 Stuart light tank. In April 1943, they were authorized to construct experimental prototypes of their 75mm gun armed Light Tank T24, and the first prototypes were delivered in October 1943.

The T24 was armed with the same lightweight 75mm aircraft gun that had been tested on the modified 75mm Howitzer Motor Carriage M8. It also used the twin Cadillac V-8 motors, Hydramatic automatic transmission and power train of the M5 Stuart

light tank. The hull and turret, however, were newly designed using welded armor construction, and were somewhat larger than those of the M5 Stuart. They were also much lighter in weight than the cast hull and turret of the T7.

The T24 also used a new center guide track and a torsion bar suspension, which gave it a much improved ride. The U.S. Army had been working on torsion bar tank suspensions since the mid-1930s, and U.S. Army Ordnance Department Chief of Research and Development not only advocated them, but he had invented a system of torsion bar suspension in the mid-1930s. By the time the T24 project was under development, the difficult problem of manufacturing the long twisting torsion bar springs which ran across the bottom of the tank's hull had only recently been perfected.

From its first trials, the T24 tested out a superior light tank in practically every respect. Its 40,000-pound fighting weight met the basic light tank criteria of World War II. The T24 was ordered into limited production in late 1943.

Field trials proved the T24 was very sucessful in all respects, and it was adopted as the Light Tank M24 in July 1944. By that time, a large number had already been built as the T24 was being phased into production to replace the M5 Stuart.

The M24 was appropriately named for U.S. Army Gen. Adna R. Chaffee, a pioneer in the use of tanks in the U.S. Army's Armored Force. It first went into action in Italy in 1944, and immediatly proved itself in combat. It not only had excellent mobility under field conditions, but its ability to sustain speeds up to 35 mph on a reasonably good surface was outstanding. Its 75mm gun was a proven weapon.

In all, some 4,731 M24 Chaffees were built during World War II. Before the war ended, the U.S. Army had begun replacing all its M3 and M5 Stuart light tanks with the M24 light tank, and it served long after World War II.

The mechanically reliable and rugged chassis of the M24 Chaffee was the basis for several self-propelled artillery weapons developed in World War II. The first was the 40mm Gun Motor

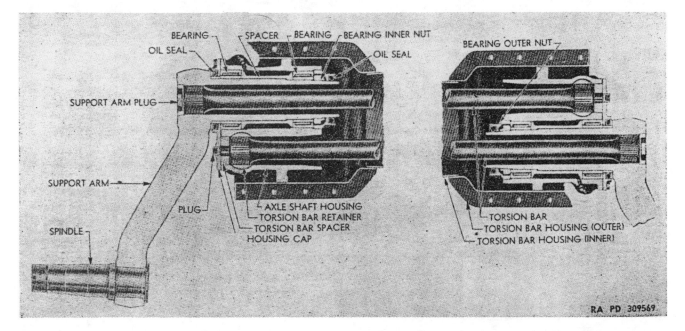

The torsion bar suspension as used on the U.S. Army Heavy Tank M26 and U.S. Army Light Tank M24. The spindle on the support arm shown on the left side supports the road wheel, which the track runs on.

The International Harvester-built U.S. Army Medium Tank M7. This 1942 tank began as a project to produce a 75mm gun armed light tank, which got completely out of hand. It was a complete failure, and, although it was adopted, it was never put in production.

A U.S. Army Light Tank M24 in action in northern Europe in early 1945. Although the M24 saw service in Italy, northern Europe and the Pacific Theater of Operations in late 1944 and 1945, it arrived in the hands of troops so late in the war that its use was limited.

Carriage M19 mounting twin Bofors automatic antiaircraft guns. The M19 was never deployed overseas since Allied air superority made its use unnecessary by the time it was available.

The 105mm Howitzer Motor Carriage M37 developed to replace the 105mm Howitzer Motor carriage M7 "Priest" was another self-propelled weapon developed too late for use in the war. The 155mm Howitzer Motor Carriage built on the M24 Chaffee chassis was another unit developed to meet a World War II requirement, but it was not adopted until May 1945, too late to see use in the war.

As the M24 Chaffee was developed as an improved replacement for the M5 Stuart light tank, the M26 Pershing began as a project to develop an improvement on the M4 Sherman medium tank. This project was begun in 1942 to produce an improved medium tank with a more powerful gun, better armor, a lower silhouette and an improved power train, suspension and tracks. This led to a long development series of many T20 medium tanks, and very limited production of them for field trials was authorized.

However, while these prototypes had demonstrated many possible improvements by early 1943, none were adopted for production. The requirement for M4 Sherman tanks was too urgent to

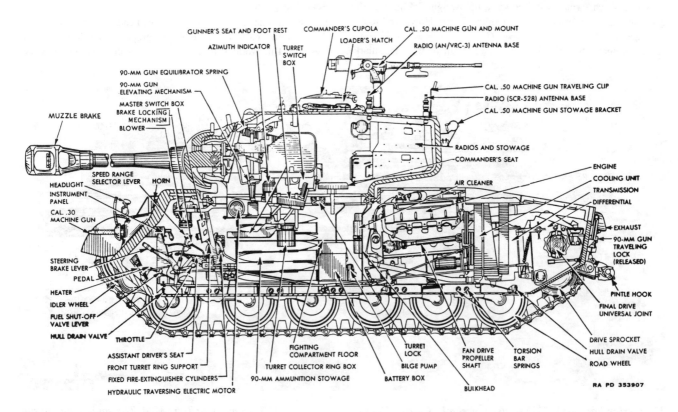

A cross section of the U.S. Army Heavy Tank M26.

allow the introduction of a new model to interfere with its production.

By late 1943, the need for a 90mm gun armed tank better able to fight the Germans' Panther and Tiger tanks reached the point that a requirement for one was issued. By this time, the T25 with a horizontal volute spring suspension and the T26 with a torsion bar suspension were under test.

In September 1943, limited production of the T26 with the torsion bar suspension was ordered because this model gave a better ride than the T25. The T26 had a fighting weight of about 92,000 pounds, and it was a heavy tank by U.S. Army World War II classification.

The T26 incorporated many features developed in the T20 series prototypes. It used a torsion bar suspension with a new wide center guide track, a new rear cross drive power train with a "Torquematic" fluid drive automatic transmission, and an improved Ford V-8 Model GAA gasoline engine. Its 90mm Tank Gun M3, which fired standard U.S. Army 90mm gun ammunition, could cope with the German Panther and Tiger tanks. Its heavy cast armor hull and turret gave excellent protection against German tank and antitank gun fire.

The First T26s, officially Medium Tanks T26El, reached the European Theater of Operations in January 1945, and were first used in combat there in February. The only other World War II combat they saw was on Okinawa in the Pacific Theater of War in May 1945.

In May 1945, the T26El was officially adopted as the Heavy Tank M26. By then it was a combat proven vehicle, and some 2,350 were built in 1944 and 1945. They remained in service with the U.S. Army long after the war.

In 1945, work was begun on experimental self-propelled 8-in. guns and 240mm howitzers mounted on modifications of the M26 Pershing chassis as super heavy self-propelled artillery weapons. Although a number of prototypes were built, they were too large and heavy to be practical, and their development was dropped after World War II.

RA PD 347020

Light Tank M24.

MODEL: Light Tank M24

WEIGHT: Fighting: 38,750 lbs.

DIMENSIONS: Length: 16 ft., 3 in. over hull. Height: 8 ft., 1 in.; Width: 9 ft., 4 in.

CANNON: 75mm Tank Gun M6. Mount includes co-axial cal. .30 Browning Machine Gun M1919A4. RANGE: 13,600 yards max., 1,000 yards antitank. Ammunition: Fixed HE, AP, APC, Canister and Chem. smoke. Projectile Weight: 13 to 15 lbs. Traverse: 360 degrees. Elevation: +15 degrees, -10 degrees

ADDITIONAL ARMAMENT: 1-cal. .50 Browning Machine Gun M2-HB in pintle mount on turret, 1-cal. .30 Browning Machine Gun M1919A4 in hull bow mount.

ENGINE: Common output twin Cadillac series 42 V-8s, 210 cu. in. rated, 110 hp at 3,400 rpm each.

TRANSMISSION: Hydramatic "Automatic" type.

NORMAL ROAD SPEED: 35 mph max.

CREW: 4.

Heavy Tank M26.

MODEL: Heavy Tank M26

WEIGHT: Fighting: 92,000 lbs.

DIMENSIONS: Length: 20 ft., 9-1/4 in. over tracks. Height: 9 ft., 1-3/8 in.; Width: 11 ft., 6-/14 in.

CANNON: 90mm Tank Gun M3; mount includes co-axial cal. .30 Browning Machine Gun M1919A4. RANGE: 21,400 yards max., 1,000 yards. antitank. Ammunition: Fixed HE, APC, HVAP and Chem. smoke. Projectile Weight: HE: 23.4 lbs., HVAP: 16.8 lbs. Traverse: 360 degrees, Elevation: +20 degrees, -10 degrees.

ADDITIONAL ARMAMENT: 1-cal. .50 Browning Machine Gun M2-HB in pintle mount on turret; 1-cal. .30 Browning Machine Gun M1919A4 in hull bow mount.

ENGINE: Ford V-8 model GAF, 1,100 cu. in. rated at 2,600 rpm, 500 hp.

TRANSMISSION: Torquematic "automatic" type

NORMAL ROAD SPEED: 20 mph. max.

CREW: 5.

Chapter 4
The Locust Airborne Tank and Heavy Supertank

The Light Tank M22 "Locust" was intended for use in airborne operations, and the Heavy Tank M6 "Supertank" was the most heavily armed and armored tank of its day. Both these tanks made a significant contribution to the Allied victory in World War II without ever firing a shot in combat. Their highly publicized existence caused the enemy considerable consternation, and they diverted resources to counter their perceived threat.

The requirements for the M22 Locust and M6 Supertank were adopted in May 1941 before the United States entered World War II. The M6 Supertank was the first to get prototype vehicles built.

The M6 supertank was a joint project of the U.S. Army Ordnance Department Tank Engineering Division and the Baldwin Locomotive Works to build the Heavy Tank T1. It was to be as big, heavy and well armed as any tank the U.S. Army was aware of at the time.

U.S. Army intelligence knew about two foreign heavy tank programs at the time: the 50-ton JS-l "Stalin" being built by the USSR and the experimental 45-ton tank being developed by the Germans. The Germans had used obsolescent heavy tanks in their invasion of Norway in 1940, and the one they were working on became the Tiger. The Germans had encountered the Stalins in their 1941 invasion of the Soviet Union.

The U.S. Army Heavy Tank T1 was to counter the threat of enemy heavy tanks. It was a 126,000-pound monster armed with a 3-in. gun. Using as much existing U.S. Army tank technology as possible, the designers gave it a cast armor hull and turret. Its wide track was derived from a double-width M3 Stuart light tank track, as was its suspension. A Wright 900 hp air-cooled radial engine powered it.

The power train was the largest single problem with the heavy T1. After experiments with several types, including a manual transmission and an electric drive derived from diesel-electric railroad locomotives, a "fluid drive" automatic type was eventually used in most of the production. The power train experiments for the T1 never developed a completely satisfactory system; however, they did lead directly to the successful power train of the U.S. Army Heavy Tank M26 "Pershing" of late World War II.

The last prototype in the T1 series was standardized in May 1942 as the Heavy Tank M6, and U.S. Army public relations gave it the name "Supertank." It was already in very limited production.

There were, however, serious problems in using the 63-ton M6 Supertank. The U.S. Army Quartermaster Department did not have the equipment needed to ship and land it overseas. The U.S. Army Corps of Engineers field and pontoon bridging equipment was not

On parade at the Baldwin Locomotive Works in late 1941 are, left to right, a U.S. Army Light Tank M3, a U.S. Army Heavy Tank M6 and a U.S. Army Medium Tank M3. (Baldwin Locomotive Works photo)

This is the 1942 production version of the U.S. Army Heavy Tank M6. It shows the 3-in. gun mount with its coaxial 37mm gun, the twin caliber .50 Browning Machine Gun bow mount, and the twin track and suspension derived from production U.S. Army tanks of the time.

The enemy, however, did not know that the decision not to use the M6 Supertanks in combat had been made, because it was a pretty well kept military secret until 1944. U.S. Army intelligence evaluations reported the existence of the M6 Supertank was a factor in the German decision to commit resources to the production of their PZKW-V Tiger heavy tank, which could have been better expended in producing the more effective PZKW-VI Panther medium tank. In the opinion of most World War II U.S. Army authorities, this alone made the M6 Supertank program a success even if it never produced a tank used in combat.

Like the M6 Supertank program, the M22 light airborne tank program never produced a tank used in combat, but the program also made a contribution to the Allied victory. The requirement for the M22 Locust grew out of the successful German use of airborne forces in early World War II. It was a joint project of the U.S. Army Ordnance Department Tank Engineering Division and the Marmon-Herrington Corp., with considerable advice from the U.S. Army Air Force and U.S. Army Airborne Forces Command.

Marmon-Herrington was formed in 1931 by automobile manufacturer Walter C. Marmon and ex-U.S. Army automotive engineer Col. Arthur W. Herrington to design and build all-wheel-drive

capable of supporting it, and they reported the roads and bridges in overseas areas where the U.S. Army would fight couldn't support it either.

However, the U.S. Army Armored Force Board raised the most crucial objection to the M6 Supertank. They said, in no uncertain terms, that two faster and more maneuverable M4 Sherman medium tanks would be more effective in combat than one M6 heavy tank. As a result, the U.S. Army Ground Forces Command made the decision that the M6 Supertank would not be committed to combat.

In all, only eighty M6 Supertanks were built between 1942 and 1944. While they were the centerpieces of many U.S. Army public relations programs, none were ever sent overseas. In fact, no armored unit was ever equipped with them, and only a few were issued to tank training centers for "orientation purposes."

A few more were used for test programs such as mounting 90mm, 105mm and 4.7-in (120mm) guns on tanks. The majority were placed in storage in U.S. Army tank storage depots where they remained until they were scrapped shortly after the end of World War II.

This U.S. Army Heavy Tank M6 has been fitted with a new turret mounting an experimental 105mm gun. In 1942-1943, the M6 was extensively used for experimental testing of tank guns from 90mm to 120mm.

This war bond poster featuring a U.S. Army Heavy Tank M6 crushing a passenger car is an example of how the M6 was widely used as a wartime public relations tool in 1942, although the U.S. Army Ground Forces had already decided the M6 would not be used in combat.

This public relations photo of a U.S. Army Light Tank M22 (Airborne) was widely circulated in 1943 despite the fact that the U.S. Army Airborne Command had no practical way of delivering the vehicle for use in combat.

conversions of commercial trucks and tanks. The company built its first very small, light tanks in 1935. It sold them in the commercial arms export trade, and the U.S. Marine Corps bought a handful. Marmon-Herrington was the only commercial tank manufacturer in the United States in the 1930s.

The U.S. Army and Marmon-Herrington originally worked together on the production of 240 Model CTLS-4TAC machine gun armed eight-ton tanks for China in 1941-1942. When it proved impossible to deliver these tiny tanks to China, the U.S. Army took them as the Light Tank T16. A few were used in Alaska early in the war, and the rest were sent to places such as Mexico and South America as military assistance training vehicles. The T16 light tank used much technology, such as tracks, suspension and power trains, adapted from the U.S. Army Stuart M3 light tank of the time.

The Marmon-Herrington commercial Model CTLS-4TAC light tank purchased by the U.S. Army as the Light Tank T16. The T16 did not meet U.S. Army requirements. It was originally intended as military assistance for China under Lend-Lease but could not be delivered, so a number were issued to U.S. Army units in Alaska and elsewhere.

The U.S. Army Ordnance Department selected Marmon-Herrington to build the airborne light tank as soon as the requirement was issued in May 1941. The first prototype Light Tank (Airborne) T9 was delivered in the fall of 1941, and, after considerable development work, it was placed in limited production in 1943. The T9, named the Locust by U.S. Army public relations, was a 16,000-pound tank with many features, including its tracks, suspension and power train, similar to that of the standard U.S. Army M3 Stuart light tank. To accommodate its very small size, its power plant was a modified Lycoming six-cylinder horizontally opposed air-cooled aircraft engine. Its total armament was a standard U.S. Army 37mm tank gun in a coaxial mount with a cal. .30 Browning Machine Gun M1919A4. At the time the first T9 Locusts were built, the United States had yet to produce a plane or glider that could carry one. By 1943, there were experimental planes and gliders that could carry it under test and development, but none were in production.

The U.S. Army adopted the T9 as the Light Tank M22 (Airborne) in September 1944, long after it was recognized it would never be committed for combat. The 830 M22s built were always classified Limited Standard by the U.S. Army.

From mid-1942 through the end of World War II, the U.S. Army often featured M22 Locusts in public relations demonstrations of its airborne forces. Information was released showing how it could be carried into combat by such aircraft as a Boeing B17 Flying Fortress heavy bomber or the Douglas C54 Skymaster four-engine transport plane, and this was done experimentally. There was also a cargo glider under development, which could carry one. Unfortunately, by the end of World War II, the U.S. Army Air Forces still had not adopted a plane or glider that could do the job practically.

The enemy, however, firmly believed the M22 Locust would be used with U.S. Army airborne troops. In places such as northern France, the Germans deployed troops and weapons in areas where they thought they would be used, and this caused them to hold back forces that otherwise might have been used against the June 6, 1944 D-Day landings.

The Japanese also anticipated encountering the M22 Locust in operations, but they never did.

In evaluations, the U.S. Army authorities said the M22 Locust, like the M6 Supertank, had been a valuable program because it had caused the diversion of enemy troops and materiel. The evaluations also indicated the M22 Locust would probably have been a disaster in combat because it was so lightly armed and armored. They were disposed of very soon after World War II.

A Marmon-Herrington built U.S. Army Light Tank M22 (Airborne) with a Marmon-Herrington commercial light tank CTMS-1TB2. The CTMS is about the same size as a U.S. Army Light Tank M3, and this one is armed with an experimental twin 37mm gun mount. This photo was probably taken in 1942.

A U.S. Army Light Tank M22 (Airborne) disembarking from a U.S. Army Air Force experimental Fairchild XC82 cargo plane in 1945. The U.S. Army Air Force had no operational aircraft capable of delivering an M22 in combat in World War II, but it did run widely publicized experiments of doing so by hanging one under a cargo plane — such as the Douglas C54 — in late 1944 and 1945.

RA PD 43321

Heavy Tank M6.

MODEL: Heavy Tank M6

WEIGHT: Fighting: 126,500 lbs.

DIMENSIONS: Length: 25 ft., 0 in. over tracks; Width: 10 ft., 2-1/2 in.; Height: 9 ft., 10 in.

CANNON: 3-in. tank gun M7 and 37mm tank gun M6 in combination mount. Range: 3-in. gun: 16,100 yards max; 1,000 yards antitank; 37mm gun; 12,850 yards max, 500 yards antitank. Ammunition: 3-in. gun Tank, AT, AA gun series; 37mm; M3 Tank-AT gun series.

ADDITIONAL ARMAMENT: Twin cal. .50 Browning Machine Guns M2-HB in bow mount; 2-cal. .30 Browning Machine Guns M1919A4, one in bow mount, one on turret.

ENGINE: Wright: Air-Cooled 9-cylinder radial model 9-200, 1,823 cu. in. rated 775 hp at 2,300 rpm.

TRANSMISSION: Torquematic "Automatic" Type.

NORMAL ROAD SPEED: 22 mph max.

CREW: 6.

Light Tank M22.

MODEL: Light Tank M22 (Airborne)

WEIGHT: Fighting: 16,000 lbs. without crew.

DIMENSIONS: Length: 12 ft., 11 in.; Height: 5 ft., 8-1/2 in.; Width: 7 ft., 3-3/4 in.

CANNON: 37mm tank gun M6; mount includes co-axial cal. .30 Browning Machine Gun M1919A4. Range: 12,850 yards max, 500 yards antitank. Ammunition: Fixed HE, AP, APC and Canister, M3 Tank AT gun series only. Projectile Weight: 1.5 to 2 lbs. Traverse: 360 degrees; elevation: +30 degrees, -10 degrees.

ENGINE: Lycoming horizontal 6-cylinder opposed air-cooled model 0-435-L, 434 cu. in. rated 162 hp at 2,800 rpm (mounted horizontally).

TRANSMISSION: Manual 4 speeds forward and reverse.

CREW: 3.

Chapter 5
Tank Destroyers

The tank destroyer was a unique, often misunderstood, and often misused U.S. Army concept for a highly mobile self-propelled antitank gun. The tank destroyer, which placed an antitank gun on a motor vehicle, was conceived when the German "Blitzkrieg" overwhelmed the French and British in May 1940. Although they were never considered completely satisfactory in combat, they did do a great deal of useful work in World War II, and then disappeared soon after it was over.

The U.S. Army classified tank destroyers as Motor Gun Carriages along with its self-propelled artillery. What distinguished a tank destroyer was that it had a gun primarily intended for use as an antitank gun. All tank destroyer guns also had the necessary aiming provisions to allow them to fire as field artillery weapons.

Tank destroyers had thinner armor than tanks, and they had open top turrets while tank turret tops were armored. Being lighter in weight than tanks, tank destroyers were considerably faster than tanks. The tank destroyer was intended to use tactics of stealth, concealment, speed and hit-and-run, and, when used this way, they performed their missions adequately. Unfortunately, tank destroyers looked like tanks, and they were sometimes misemployed as tanks. They proved vulnerable to enemy fire and suffered badly.

However, despite acknowledged drawbacks, tank destroyers made a significant contribution to the Allied World War II victory, particularly in the defeat of the Germans.

The first vehicle the U.S. Army used to test the tank destroyer was the 75mm Gun Motor Carriage M3. It consisted of a modernized World War I French 75mm field gun mounted in a modified M3 armored half-track. When this half-track self-propelled 75 was adopted in November 1941, it had already been field tested in maneuvers.

Although the half-track-mounted 75 was designed as a mobile self-propelled field gun, when it first saw action in North Africa in late 1942, it proved reasonably effective against enemy armor.

U.S. Army 3-in. Gun Motor Carriages M10 tank destroyers being used at the Southern California Desert Training Center in late 1942.

A U.S. Army 3-in. Gun Motor Carriage M10 tank destroyer in action in Italy in 1944.

A rear view of the U.S. Army 3-in. Gun Motor Carriage M10 showing the counterweights on the back of the turret required to balance the gun and the pioneer tools carried by all U.S. World War II tanks.

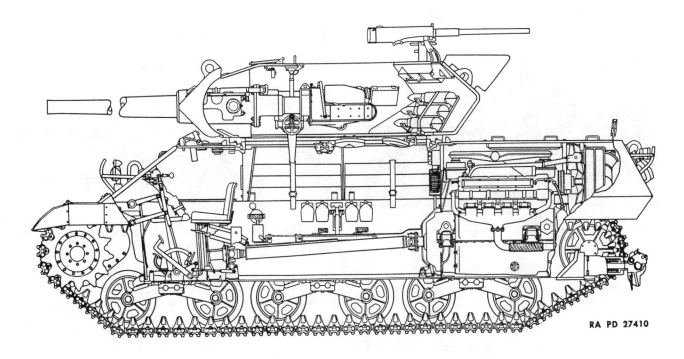

RA PD 27410

A cross-section of a typical U.S. Army 3-in. Gun Motor-Carriage M10 (M10A1)

A U.S. Army 37mm Gun Motor Carriage M6 tank destroyer. When these vehicles were being salvaged in 1943-1944, a number of the large gun shields were retrofitted on 37mm antitank guns for use in the Pacific Theater of Operations.

A prototype U.S. Army 90mm Gun Motor Carriage M36 at a press demonstration in 1944.

U.S. Army 90mm Gun Motor Carriages M36 rolling into action in northern Europe in late 1944.

However, improved tank destroyers soon became available, and it reverted to its intended role as a self-propelled field gun. (See half-track self-propelled artillery.)

With an urgent requirement for a tank destroyer for training, the U.S. Army adopted the 37mm Gun Motor Carriage M6 in February 1942 as an interim solution. This tank destroyer consisted of a modified 37mm antitank gun with a large light armor shield mounted in the back of a modified, but completely unarmored, three-quarter-ton Dodge Weapons Carrier light truck.

A number of these 37mm M6 tank destroyers were committed to the invasion of North Africa in November 1942, and they proved to be practically useless against enemy armor. They were withdrawn from combat use, but they continued in service as training weapons until declared obsolete in January 1945. By that time, practically all of them had disappeared from U.S. Army use.

In February 1942, another tank destroyer was constructed to meet a British Lend-Lease requirement. This was a 57mm American-built British-designed antitank gun mounted on a half-track designated the 57mm Gun Motor Carriage T48. Only 50 were built, and

these disappeared after the British handed them to the Soviet Union before ever using them. (See half-track self-propelled artillery).

In April 1942, U.S. Army intelligence and observer reports led to a new requirement for a much more powerful tank destroyer. This one would mount a modified 3-in. antiaircraft gun capable of dealing with practically any enemy tank of the time. Since the requirement was very urgent, the design and development program went forward very quickly, and the new tank destroyer was adopted as the 3-in. Gun Motor Carriage M10 in September 1942, and it was immediately put in production.

The 3-in. M10 used the chassis and power train from an M4 Sherman medium tank, with a new very simple and distinctive light armor top hull and a new open-top turret mounting a 3-in. Tank Gun M7. Although this was a very quickly designed vehicle, it proved very successful when it first went into action in North Africa in 1942, and it was used for the rest of World War II.

The 3-in. M10 proved to be very easy to manufacture and was built on a "build until told to stop" basis. Long before the "stop" order came through after some 7,000 had been built, all the U.S.

Top view of the U.S. Army 3-in. Gun Motor Carriage M10 tank destroyer showing the open top turret.

A U.S. Army 76mm Gun Motor Carriage M18 "Hellcat" tank destroyer in northern Europe in late 1944.

A late model U.S. Army 76mm Gun Motor Carriage M18 "Hellcat" tank destroyer with the 76mm gun used in the U.S. Army Medium. Tank M4A3E8 in action in Germany in early 1945.

Army's existing and projected future requirements for the 3-in. M10 had been far exceeded, and most of the production was being placed in depot storage. Production stopped in November 1943, and other uses were found for the excess units.

The first came in early late 1943, when the U.S. Army finally decided to deploy its super heavy field artillery: the 8-in. Gun M1 and the 240mm Howitzer M1 . Unfortunately, the high speed tractors required for these guns were not in production, and modified M3 Grant medium tanks were already being used to pull them. The 3-in. M10 was modified by removing the turret and adding a powerful winch, air compressor and other equipment required by artillerymen, and it became the Full Track Prime Mover M35. The M35s remained in service until they were replaced by the high-speed artillery tractors after World War II.

Around the end of 1942, a requirement was initiated to mount a tank version of the standard U.S. Army 90mm antiaircraft gun in a tank destroyer. Other higher priority projects caused the project to move very slowly, but by the end of 1943, a 90mm tank gun turret for the 3-in. M10 had been developed and tested. It was already in production when it was adopted as the 90mm Gun Motor Carriage M36 in June 1944.

The 90mm M36 tank destroyer first saw action in northern Europe shortly after D-Day in July 1944. Its 90mm gun proved capable of dealing with any German tank.

A very late production U.S. Army 90mm Gun Motor Carriage M36 with an armor cover for the open top turret and armed with the same 90mm gun used in the U.S. Army Heavy Tank M26. This model was not used in combat in World War II.

In all, some 1,122 3-in. M10s were converted to 90mm M36s in 1944-1945. When the projected requirement for 90mm gun tank destroyers exceeded the number of 3-in. M10s available for conversion, a quick solution to the projected shortage was designed. A new open-top 90mm gun turret for a standard M4 Sherman medium tank was designed and adopted as the 90mm Gun Motor Carriage M36BI. Only 187 of these were built, and they were delivered too late to see action in World War II.

The limited production U.S. Army 90mm Gun Motor Carriage M36B1 built on the hull and chassis of the late U.S. Army Medium Tank M4A3. The turret has the counterweight on the rear of its turret used on all M36 tank destroyers. This model was not used in combat in World War II.

In early 1943, the U.S. Army Tank Destroyer Command initiated a new requirement for a lightweight high-speed tank destroyer armed with the same 76mm tank gun developed for the M4 Sherman medium tank. This requirement was met in July 1943 by the adoption of the 76mm Gun Motor Carriage M18, adapted from existing experimental and developmental light armored vehicles. The 76mm gun M18 was quickly named the "Hellcat," and to this day it remains one of the most outstanding armored fighting vehicles ever built.

The M18 Hellcat was to all intents and purposes a completely new production design. It was lightly armored, and it used a center guide track, torsion bar suspension and an automatic transmission. It was powered by a 400 hp radial air-cooled engine, which gave the 20,000 pound fighting weight vehicle the highest horsepower to weight ratio of any full-tracked armored vehicle of its day. As a result of its advanced design and high horsepower, the M18 Hellcat was, and still is, probably the fastest full-tracked armored combat vehicle ever built. Most World War II tanks had top speeds of no more than 30 mph, and the governed top speed of the M18 Hellcat was 55 mph! It could sustain road speeds of as much as 45 mph! When the first M18 Hellcats were being tested in the United States, they terrified many an American motorist driving at the wartime national speed limit of 35 mph as they flew past them. M18 Hellcats equipped with experimental tracks attained speeds of as much as 75 mph! This was arguably the highest speed ever attained by a full-tracked armored vehicle, but it was so hard on the M18 Hellcat that it was of no military value.

The M18 Hellcat went into action in Europe in the summer of 1944, and quickly proved it was probably the best tank destroyer of all. Its great speed not only got it into action in very short time, but it made it very difficult for enemy guns to hit it. In July, the 630rd Tank Destroyer Battalion's M18 Hellcats reported knocking out fifty-three German tanks, including Panthers and Tigers, and fifteen German self-propelled guns with the loss of only seventeen of their M18s. Many other units equipped with M18 Hellcats reported similar outstanding records, and the German tankers were terrified of the speedy vehicles.

A total of 2,507 M18 Hellcats had been built when the U.S. Army's requirements for them was filled and production was stopped in October 1944.

Although the M18 Hellcat was retained by the U.S. Army long after all other tank destroyers had been discarded, it never saw combat after World War II.

A number of other vehicles based on the M18 Hellcat chassis were built and tested, but only one ever got past the experimental stage of development. It came to be after the U.S. Army Armored Force Board saw the M18 Hellcat perform and suggested it be made the basis for a high-speed personnel carrier and gun tractor. To test this suggestion, the U.S. Army Ordnance Department removed the turret and part of the hull top plate from a couple, and fitted them with seats for a driver and eight passengers. In June 1944, the production of some 500 of these was authorized as the Armored Utility Vehicle M39.

Although few, if any, M39s saw combat use in World War II, they proved the idea was sound. They were the first full-track armored personnel carriers built for the U.S. Army, and they remained in service long after World War II.

Troops dismount from a U.S. Army Armored Utility Vehicle M39 armored personnel carrier based on the hull and chassis of the U.S. Army 76mm Gun Motor Carriage M18 "Hellcat" tank destroyer. This vehicle was not used in combat in World War II.

A U.S. Army Full-Track Prime Mover M35, built by removing the turret from a U.S. Army 3-in. Gun Motor Carriage M10 tank destroyer, in action pulling the barrel of an 240mm Howitzer M1 in Italy in late 1944.

On the left is a U.S. Army 76mm Gun Motor Carriage M18 "Hellcat" tank destroyer, on the right a U.S. Army 3-in. Gun Motor Carriage M10. The guns on these two vehicles are of equal power.

Top view of the U.S. Army 76mm Gun Motor Carriage M18 "Hellcat" tank destroyer showing its open top turret.

RA PD 45619

37mm Gun Motor Carriage M6.

MODEL: 37mm Gun Motor Carriage M6

WEIGHT: Fighting: 7,350 lbs.

DIMENSIONS: Length: 14 ft., 10 in. Height: 6 ft., 10-3/4 in. Width: 7 ft., 3 in.

ARMAMENT: Modified 37mm Antitank Gun M3. Range: 12,850 yards max., 500 yards antitank. Ammunition: Fixed HE, AP, APC and Canister for 37mm M3 tank — AT gun series only. Projectile weight: 1.5 to 2 lbs.

TRAVERSE: 360 degrees, elevation +15 degrees, -10 degrees.

CHASSIS: Modified Truck, Weapons Carrier 3/4-ton 4x4 (Dodge model WC-52) with winch. Engine: Dodge model T214, 230.2 cu. in. Rated 76 hp at 3,200 rpm. Transmission: 4-speed and reverse with 2-speed transfer case. Winch capacity: 5,000 lbs. max.

NORMAL SPEED: 55 mph. max.

CREW: 4.

RA PD 45568

3-in. Gun Motor Carriage M10 and M10A1.

MODEL: 3 in. Gun Motor Carriage M10 and M10A1

WEIGHT: Fighting: M10: 66,000 lbs.; M10A1: 64,000 lbs.

DIMENSIONS: Length: 19 ft., 7 in. over track and hull. Height: 8 ft., 1-1/2 in. Width: 10 ft., 0 in.

CANNON: 3-in. Tank Gun M7 in open top turret. Mount includes co-axial cal. .30 Browning Machine Gun M1919A4. Range: 16,100 yards max., 1,000 yards anti-tank. Ammunition: fixed HE, AP, APC, canister and chem. smoke. Projectile weight: 13 to 15.5 lbs. Traverse: 360 degrees. Elevation: +19 degrees, -10 degrees.

ADDITIONAL ARMAMENT: 1-cal. .50 Browning Machine Gun M2-HB in pintle mount on turret.

BASIC CHASSIS: M-10: Medium Tank M4A2 with twin GM model 671 diesel engines with common output. M10A1: Medium Tank M4A3 with Ford V-8 model GAA engine.

NORMAL ROAD SPEED: 30 mph max.

CREW: 5.

RA PD
347097

90mm Gun Motor Carriage M36 and M36B1.

MODEL: 90mm Gun Motor Carriage M36 and M36B1

WEIGHT: Fighting: M36: 62,000 lbs.; M36B1: 68,000 lbs.

DIMENSIONS: Length: 20 ft., 2 in. over hull and tracks. Height: 8 ft., 10 in. Width: M36: 10 ft., 0 in.; M36B1: 8 ft., 8-1/2 in.

CANNON: 90mm Tank Gun M3 in open top turret. Mount includes co-axial cal. .30 Browning Machine Gun M1919A4. Range: 21,400 yards max., 1,000 yards anti-tank. Ammunition: Fixed HE, APC, HVAP and chem. smoke. Projectile weight: HE: 23.4 lbs., HVAP: 16.8 lbs.

TRAVERSE: 360 degrees. Elevation: +20 degrees, -10 degrees.

ADDITIONAL ARMAMENT: M36 and M36B1: 1-cal. .50 Browning Machine Gun M2-HB; M36B2: 1-cal. .30 Browning Machine Gun M1919A4 in bow mount.

BASIC CHASSIS: M36: Rebuilt 3-in. Gun Motor Carriage M10A1; M36B1: Medium tank M4A3. Both use Ford V8 model GAA engine.

NORMAL ROAD SPEED: M36: 30 mph max.; M36B1: 26 mph max.

CREW: 5

ADDITIONAL MODELS: (Late production not used in combat in World War II) 90mm Gun Motor Carriage M36B1: Built on hull and chassis of late Medium tank M4A3. 90mm Gun Motor Carriage M36B2: As M36 with same 90mm gun as Heavy Tank M26 and armor turret cover.

RA PD 347074

76mm Gun Motor Carriage M18.

MODEL: 76mm Gun Motor Carriage M18

WEIGHT: Fighting: 40,000 lbs.

DIMENSIONS: Length: 17 ft., 4 in. over hull and tracks. Height: 8 ft., 0 in. Width: 9 ft., 2 in.

CANNON: 76mm Tank Gun M1 in open top turret. Mount includes co-axial cal. .30 Browning Machine Gun M1919A4. Range: 16,100 yards max., 1,000 yards anti-tank. Ammunition: Fixed HE, APC, HVAP, cannister and chem. smoke. Projectile weight: 14.5 to 15.5 lbs.

TRAVERSE: 360 degrees. Elevation: +19-1/2 degrees, -10 degrees.

ADDITIONAL ARMAMENT: 1-cal. .50 Browning Machine Gun M2-HB in pintle mount on turret.

ENGINE: Wright air-cooled model R975 radial rated 400 hp at 2,400 rpm.

TRANSMISSION: Hydramatic "Automatic" type.

NORMAL ROAD SPEED: 45 mph. max.

CREW: 5.

RA PD 347144

Armored Utility Vehicle M39.

MODEL: Armored Utility Vehicle M39

WEIGHT: Fighting: 35,000 lbs.

DIMENSIONS: Length: 17 ft., 4 in. Height: 5 ft., 11 in. Width: 9 ft., 2 in.

ARMAMENT: 1-cal. .50 Browning Machine Gun M2-HB on antiaircraft ring mount.

ARMOR: 1/2 in. max., 1/4 in. min.

ENGINE: Wright air-cooled model R975 radial rated 400 hp at 2,400 rpm.

TRANSMISSION: Hydramatic "Automatic" type.

NORMAL ROAD SPEED: 45 mph. max.

CREW: Driver and 8 passengers.

Chapter 6
Armored Half-Tracks

The U.S. Army's armored half-track was one of the most widely used and distinctive vehicles of World War II. Like other famous American motor vehicles, such as the Jeep, three-quarter-ton Dodge Weapons Carrier and GMC 2-1/2-ton 6x6, the half-track wasn't perfected until about 1940. However, its basic concept of a highly mobile motor vehicle with steering wheels in front and short tracks in back dated back to World War I.

The half-track was invented in Imperial Russia about 1914 by Alexander Kegresse, a chauffeur of the Imperial household. During World War I, a number of cars and trucks were fitted with his half-tracks. At the onset of the 1917 Communist Revolution, Kegresse fled from Russia and then joined the French Citroen automobile company to continue the development of his half-track.

The U.S. Army purchased and tested several Citroen-Kegresse half-tracks between 1925 and 1930, and found they worked quite well. In 1930, the U.S. Army purchased a license to build half-tracks.

This 1941 photo shows GIs out on a demonstration ride in an early production Half-Track Personnel Carrier M3.

The James Cunningham automobile company and the U.S. Army Rock Island automotive engineering division combined to develop the half-track. By the mid-1930s, they had perfected several "half-track adapters," which could be installed in place of the rear wheels on conventional automotive chassis. During the last half of the 1930s, a number of these were tested, and several were built in very limited numbers. The half-track adapter proved very useful in improving cross-country vehicle mobility.

In 1939, the U.S. Army adopted the armored open-top 4x4 Scout Car M3, and one of these was modified to use a half-track adapter. This armored half-track performed very well, and it had the distinct advantage of being very easy to mass produce. It was also a very inexpensive armored vehicle.

The U.S. Army tested the half-track adapter with both linked tracks like those of a tank and a "rubber-band" track consisting of

a rubber-encased steel wire cable, both based on original Kegresse systems. The U.S. Army adopted the rubber-band half-track track, and it was very successfully used on all World War II U.S. Army armored half-tracks.

In 1941, the U.S. Army standardized the Half-Track Car M2 and Half Track Personnel Carrier M3. Both were based on the Scout Car M3, and they were very similar in appearance. The M2 and M3 armored half-tracks were originally built by White Motor Co. on a heavy-duty truck chassis. They also were produced later by the Autocar Company and Diamond-T Motor Company. They all used the White engine, power train and chassis.

During World War II, several modifications were made in the M2 and M3 armored half-tracks. Several variations of headlights and black-out lights were used. Early M2 and M3 armored half-tracks used a track machine gun mount running around the inside of the top of the hull on which pintle mounts for cal. .30 or cal. .50 machine guns could be placed where desired. Then a number were built with an assortment of post and bracket mounts for cal. .30 or .50 machine guns. Neither of these systems proved very satisfactory, and in late 1942 a new ring mount in an armored box over the co-driver's seat was adopted, and this system was used for the rest of World War II.

The basic armored half-track proved to be a very flexible machine. They were used as motor carriages for a number of light field artillery and light antiaircraft artillery weapons. In addition to being used as armored personnel carriers, they were often used as armored cargo and ammunition carriers under enemy fire. A num-

This 1941 photo of an early production Half-Track Personnel Carrier M3 shows the rear door.

U.S. Army half-tracks "w/Winch," with winch, in depot storage in England in early 1944. The letter "S" following the U.S.A. serial number on the hood indicates these vehicles have received a major overhaul and are ready for issue.

A U.S. Army M3 series half-track on the march in a town in northern Europe in late 1944. This half-track is equipped with a winch and appears to be carrying a full infantry squad and their equipment.

This U.S. Army Half-Track Personnel Carrier used by Gen. George S. Patton at the California Desert Training Center in 1942 has an armor top cover and sand shields over the half-track assemblies, which are typical of the many modifications done by troops in the field.

ber were used as prime movers for antitank guns and light field artillery weapons. A number were fitted as armored field ambulances complete with the obligatory red cross markings.

While all armored half-tracks came with a canvas top, these were seldom used in combat situations. In the field, a few were fitted with armored tops to afford protection from enemy air attack. A number were also field-equipped with screen tops to deflect attempts to throw hand grenades into them.

Troops using half-tracks liked them. Even though it was light, their armor was reassuring since it stopped most shell fragments and small arms fire. They were also very reliable and mechanically simple, which made maintenance and repair easy.

The great utility of the armored half-track caused other Allies to request them under Lend-Lease military assistance. To fill this demand, the U.S. Army brought International Harvester into the program as a second supplier in 1942. International produced a distinctive model based on their own truck engine, power train and chassis.

The International half-tracks were the M5 and M9 models, and these were practically identical for all intents and purposes. They looked nearly identical to the White M2 and M3 models and were almost the same size and weight. However, the M5 and M9 half-track bodies had rounded rear corners while the rear corners of the M2 and M3 were square. Most were built with a .50 ring mount for a cal. .50 machine gun in an armored box over the co-driver's seat, and, like the M2 and M3, this could be and sometimes was

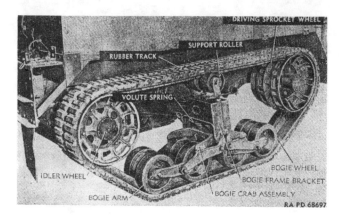

The half-track assembly used on all U.S. Army World War II half-tracks. Its rear idler wheel is on the left; its front-drive wheel is on the right.

removed and replaced with other machine gun mounts in the field when it interfered with the use of the armored half-track.

In the field, there was practically no difference in the performance, reliability or ease of maintenance between the M2, M3, M5 or M9 armored half-tracks. The tires, tracks, half-track adapters, and many other parts and assemblies of the various models were, in fact, interchangeable.

Many M2, M3, M5 and M9 half-tracks were built with doors in the rear of the bodies when these were appropriate. While most half-tracks were built with the front roller assembly to overcome ditches and other obstacles, as much as a third of the production was built with a powerful winch in place of the front-mounted roller. Winch-equipped half-tracks were primarily intended for U.S. Armed Forces' use. All half-tracks were also built with a towing pintle hitch for trailers, field artillery weapons and the like.

Although the U.S. Army primarily used the M2 and M3 half-tracks, they also used limited numbers of the M5s and M9s. In all, some 41,200 armored half-tracks of all models were built in World War II, and were rated very successful vehicles. However, the armored half-track only served in the U.S. Armed Forces after World War II until it could be replaced with full-tracked armored vehicles designed to fill the same requirements.

A U.S. Army Half-Track Personnel Carrier M3 on a river patrol in the Pacific Theater of Operations in early 1944.

This Half-Track Car M3A2 w/winch, with winch, shows the cal. .50 machine gun mount above the co-driver's seat and the pintle-mounted cal. .30 machine gun mounts on the rear of the body.

A U.S. Army Half-Track Car M2 w/Winch, with winch. Note the five-gallon gasoline can, ax, toolbox and vehicle cover as well as the exhaust pipe projecting through the half-track assembly. This photo was probably taken in early 1943.

U.S. Army Half-Track Cars M3A2 in a town in northern Germany in late 1944.

Armored Half-Track Models

These are basic models of the U.S. Army armored half-track as they were manufactured. Many of these were modified and/or received additional equipment after manufacture at depots and by units in the field to meet special requirements. The best way to distinguish the models is by the armament provisions on them. The data on the related models listed will be found in the chapters in which they are listed.

White Motor Company Models
These were also built by Autocar Company and Diamond-T Motor Company.

Half-Track Car M2	The original model with a skate rail machine gun mounting system around the top of the hull. **RELATED MODELS:** 81mm Half-Track Mortar Carrier M4.
Half-Track Car M2A1	As Half-Track Car M2 but with ring mount for cal. .50 machine gun above co-driver's seat and brackets on sides and rear for machine gun mounts.
Half-Track Personnel Carrier M3	Similar to Half Track Car M2 but 10 in. longer body and rear access door. Has pedestal mount for machine gun in rear body compartment. **RELATED MODELS:** cal. .50 Multiple Motor Gun Carriage M13, cal. .50 Multiple Gun Motor Carriage M16, Multiple Gun Motor Carriages M15 and M15A1 (chassis and cab only), 57mm Gun Motor Carriage T48, 75mm Gun Motor Carriage M3, 75mm Howitzer Motor Carriage T30, Half-Track 81mm Mortar Carrier M21 and 105mm Howitzer Motor Carriage T19.
Half-Track Personnel Carrier M3A1	As Half-Track Personnel Carrier M3 but with cal. .50 machine gun ring mount above co-driver's seat and side and rear brackets for pintle machine gun mounts.
Half-Track Car M3A2	A standardized production model replacing all earlier M2 and M3 half-track models. Similar to Half-Track Personnel Carrier M3A1 with cal. .50 machine gun ring mount above co-driver's seat. Interior of hull provided with fastening provisions for a wide variety of post-manufacture equipment installation.

International Harvester Co. Models

Half-Track Personnel Carrier M5	IHC equivalent of White M3. **RELATED MODEL:** cal. .50 Multiple Gun Motor Carriage M17.
Half-Track Personnel Carrier M5A1	IHC equivalent of White M3A1.
Half-Track Car M9A1	IHC equivalent of White M2A1.

NOTE: The principal difference between the M2 series and M3 series and the M5 series and M9 series is the length of their bodies from the door to the rear end. M2 series and M9 series bodies are 98-in. long while M3 series and M5 series bodies are 108-in. long. However, the basic chassis of the M2 series and the M3 series are identical as are those of the M5 series and M9 series.
U.S. Army Ordinance data states the M3 series and M9 series often have rear body doors while the M2 series and M5 series usually do not.

A Half-Track Personnel Carrier M3A1 in action in the Pacific Theater of War in late 1944.

A U.S. Army M3 series half-track ambulance in service in northern Germany in late 1944. Note that the required red crosses have been painted on this vehicle.

64

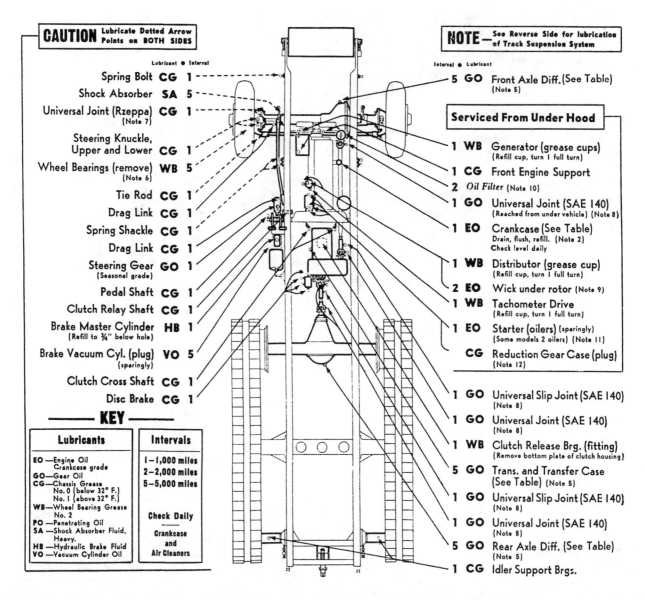

Lubricant ● Interval

Spring Bolt	CG	1
Shock Absorber	SA	5
Universal Joint (Rzeppa) (Note 7)	CG	1
Steering Knuckle, Upper and Lower	CG	1
Wheel Bearings (remove) (Note 6)	WB	5
Tie Rod	CG	1
Drag Link	CG	1
Spring Shackle	CG	1
Drag Link	CG	1
Steering Gear (Seasonal grade)	GO	1
Pedal Shaft	CG	1
Clutch Relay Shaft	CG	1
Brake Master Cylinder (Refill to ¾" below hole)	HB	1
Brake Vacuum Cyl. (plug) (sparingly)	VO	5
Clutch Cross Shaft	CG	1
Disc Brake	CG	1

Interval ● Lubricant

5	GO	Front Axle Diff. (See Table) (Note 5)

Serviced From Under Hood

1	WB	Generator (grease cups) (Refill cup, turn 1 full turn)
1	CG	Front Engine Support
2		*Oil Filter* (Note 10)
1	GO	Universal Joint (SAE 140) (Reached from under vehicle) (Note 8)
1	EO	Crankcase (See Table) Drain, flush, refill. (Note 2) Check level daily
1	WB	Distributor (grease cup) (Refill cup, turn 1 full turn)
2	EO	Wick under rotor (Note 9)
1	WB	Tachometer Drive (Refill cup, turn 1 full turn)
1	EO	Starter (oilers) (sparingly) (Some models 2 oilers) (Note 11)
	CG	Reduction Gear Case (plug) (Note 12)
1	GO	Universal Slip Joint (SAE 140) (Note 8)
1	GO	Universal Joint (SAE 140) (Note 8)
1	WB	Clutch Release Brg. (fitting) (Remove bottom plate of clutch housing)
5	GO	Trans. and Transfer Case (See Table) (Note 5)
1	GO	Universal Slip Joint (SAE 140) (Note 8)
1	GO	Universal Joint (SAE 140) (Note 8)
5	GO	Rear Axle Diff. (See Table) (Note 5)
1	CG	Idler Support Brgs.

— KEY —

Lubricants

EO—Engine Oil
    Crankcase grade
GO—Gear Oil
CG—Chassis Grease
    No. 0 (below 32° F.)
    No. 1 (above 32° F.)
WB—Wheel Bearing Grease
    No. 2
PO—Penetrating Oil
SA—Shock Absorber Fluid, Heavy.
HB—Hydraulic Brake Fluid
VO—Vacuum Cylinder Oil

Intervals

1—1,000 miles
2—2,000 miles
5—5,000 miles

Check Daily

Crankcase
and
Air Cleaners

This lubrication chart for a U.S. Army half-track shows the chassis layout, which is a modified heavy-duty truck chassis with the half-track assemblies replacing the rear wheels.

U.S. Army M2 series half-tracks in use as 57mm Antitank Guns M1 prime movers on Omaha Beach in northern France about D-Day. The U.S. Army also used half-tracks as prime movers for the 105mm Howitzer M2.

RA PD 4568

U.S. Army Half-Track Car M2 with cover.

MODELS: Half-Track Cars M2 and M2A1

WEIGHTS: Fighting: M2: 19,800 lbs.; M2A1: 19,600 lbs.

DIMENSIONS: Length: with roller 19 ft., 6-3/4 in., with winch: 20 ft., 1-5/8 in. Height: M2: 7 ft., 5 in., M2A1: 8 ft., 10 in.; Width: 7 ft., 2-1/2 in.

ARMAMENT: M2: 1-cal. .50 Browning Machine Gun M2-HB and 2-cal. .30 Browning Machine Guns M1919A4 on skate mounts around vehicle body interior; M2A1: 1-cal. .50 Browning Machine Gun M2-HB in ring mount M49 above co-driver's seat and 1-cal. .30 Browning Machine Gun M1919A4 with pintle sockets on both sides and rear of body.

ARMOR: 1/4 in. with 1/2 in. for windshield.

CHASSIS: White Motor Company, front wheels and tracks driven. Motor: White model 160 AX gasoline, 386 cu. in. rated 127 hp at 2,800 rpm. Transmission: 4 speeds forward and reverse. Winch capacity: 10,000 lbs. max. pull.

NORMAL SPEED: 45 mph. max.

CREW: Driver and 9 passengers.

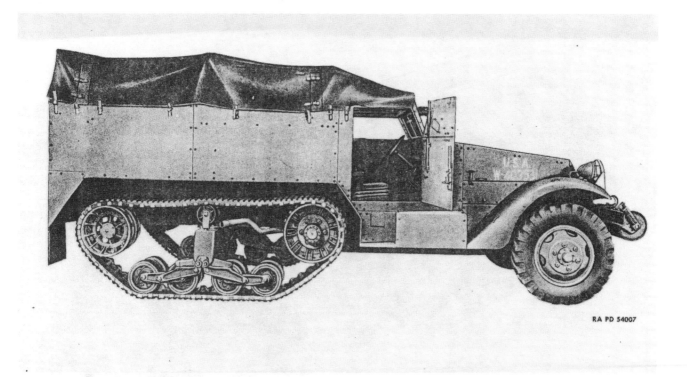

U.S. Army Half-Track Personnel Carrier M3 with cover.

MODELS: Half-Track Personnel Carriers M3, M3A1, M3A2, and M3A3

WEIGHTS: Fighting: M3: 20,000 lbs.; M3A1: 20,500 lbs., M3A3: 21,200 lbs.

DIMENSIONS: Length: with roller: 19 ft., 6-3/4 in., with winch: 20 ft., 3-1/2 in. Height: M3: 7 ft., 5 in.; M3A1 & M3A2: 8 ft., 10 in. Width: 7 ft., 2-1/2 in.

ARMAMENT: M3: 1-cal. .50 Browning Machine Gun M2-HB or 1-cal. .30 Browning Machine Gun M1919A4 on pedestal (post) mount. M3A1 and M3A2: 1-cal. .50 Browning Machine Gun M2-HB in ring mount above co-driver's seat.

ARMOR: 1/4 in. with 1/2 in. for windshield.

CHASSIS: White Motor Co., front wheels and tracks driven. Motor: White model 160 AX gasoline, 386 cu. in. rated 128 hp at 2,000 rpm. Transmission: 4 speeds forward and reverse. Winch capacity: 10,000 lbs. max. pull.

NORMAL SPEED: 45 mph. max.

CREW: M3A1 and M3A2: Driver and 12 passengers. M3A3: Driver and 5 to 11 passengers depending on stowage provisions.

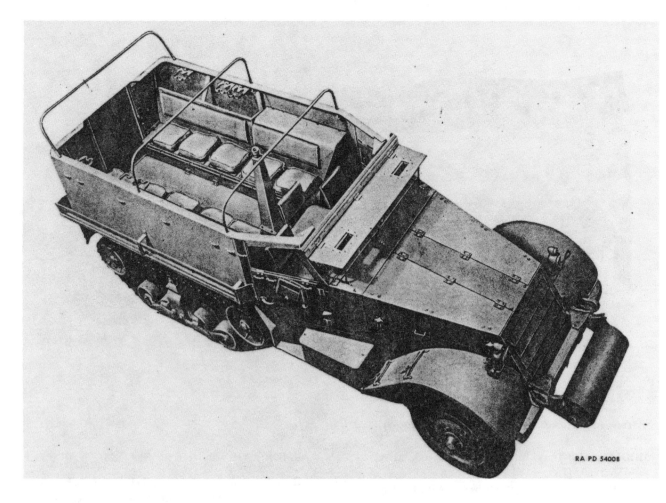

U.S. Army Half-Track Car M5A1.

MODELS: Half-Track Cars M5, M5A1 and M5A2

WEIGHTS: Fighting: M5: 20,500 lbs.; M5A1: 21,500 lbs.; M5A2: 22,500 lbs.

DIMENSIONS: Length: with roller: 20 ft., 2-3/16 in.; with winch: 20 ft., 9-1/16 in. Height: M5: 7 ft., 7 in.; M5A1 & M5A2: 9 ft., 0 in., Width 7 ft., 3 in.

ARMAMENT: M5: 1-cal. .50 Browning Machine Gun M2-HB on pedestal (post) mount and 1-cal. .30 Browning Machine Gun M1919A4 with pintle sockets on both sides and rear; M5A1 and M5A2: 1-cal. .50 Browning Machine Gun M2-HB in ring mount above co-driver's seat and 1-cal. .30 Browning Machine Gun M1919A4 with pintle sockets on both sides and rear

ARMOR: 5/16 in. with 5/8 in. for windshield.

CHASSIS: International Harvester Company, front wheels and tracks driven. Motor: International Harvester model Red Seal 4508, gasoline, 451 cu. in. rated 143 hp at 2,700 rpm. Transmission: 4 speeds forward and reverse. Winch capacity: 10,000 lbs. max. pull.

NORMAL ROAD SPEED: 45 mph max.

CREW: M5 and M5A1: Driver and 12 passengers. M5A2: Driver and 5 to 10 passengers depending on stowage provisions.

U.S. Army Half-Track Car M9A1.

MODELS: Half-Track Cars M9 and M9A1

WEIGHTS: Fighting: M9: 19,000 lbs.; M9A1: 21,200 lbs.

DIMENSIONS: Length: with roller: 20 ft., 2-3/16 in., with winch: 20 ft., 9-1/16 in. Height: M9: 7 ft., 7 in.; M9A1: 9 ft., 0 in. Width: 7 ft., 3 in.

ARMAMENT: M9: 1-cal. .50 Browning Machine Gun M2-HB on M25 pedestal (post) mount M25 and 1-cal. .30 Browning Machine Gun M1919A4 with pintle sockets on both sides and rear; M9A1: 1-cal. .50 Browning Machine Gun M2-HB in ring mount M49 above co-driver's seat and 1-cal. .30 Browning Machine Gun M1919A4 with pintle sockets on both sides and rear.

ARMOR: 5/16 in. with 5/8 in. for windshield.

CHASSIS: International Harvester Company, front wheels and tracks driven Motor: International Harvester model Red Seal 4508, gasoline, 451 cu. in. rated 143 hp at 2,700 rpm. Transmission: 4 speeds forward and reverse. Winch capacity: 10,000 lbs. max.

NORMAL ROAD SPEED: 45 mph. max.

CREW: Driver and 9 passengers.

Chapter 7
Tracked Landing Vehicles

The development of the unique American tracked landing vehicle, LVT, was a pre-World War II U.S. Marine Corps project. By the end of World War II, these "amtracks," amphibious tractors, had become a key element of U.S. Army and U.S. Marine Corps amphibious operations.

The LVT was invented by a private citizen as a solution to a serious problem: hurricane rescues. After many people died because they could not be rescued in Florida's disastrous 1935 Labor Day hurricane, John A. Roebling's wealthy grandfather suggested he develop some sort of hurricane rescue vehicle. In 1937, the 26-year-old Roebling had built a working prototype of what would become the LVT.

The U.S. Marine Corps, always on the lookout for anything which would make their mission of landing on beaches safer and simpler, saw the publicity on Roebling's amphibious rescue vehicle and became interested in the military possibilities of the machine. In 1939, Roebling built an aluminum-hulled prototype of his tracked amphibian for the U.S. Marine Corps to test, and it was an unqualified success.

In 1940, Roebling was given a contract to develop a new version of his amphibian built to U.S. Navy and U.S. Marine Corps

U.S. Marine Corps Landing Vehicles Tracked LVT-1 operating at sea in the late 1941.

U.S. Marine Corps Landing Vehicles Tracked LVT-1 landing on Guadalcanal, the first place where they were used in combat, in late 1942.

requirements. One of these requirements was that the machine be built of steel because aluminum, which was used to build the earlier prototypes, was already becoming scarce and would not be available for such use under wartime conditions.

Roebling did not have facilities to build improved versions of his "Alligator," as the machine was now called in honor of that famous Florida amphibian. He arranged for the Dunedin, Florida division of Food Machinery & Chemical Corp. to come into the program with their engineering and manufacturing facilities.

The first completely redesigned military version of the Alligator rolled out of the Dunedin plant in July 1941. It was immediately adopted as the Landing Vehicle Tracked Mark I, and later redesignated the LVT-1. Two hundred were ordered, and it was immediately put in production.

The LVT-1 was a steel barge with tracks, which propelled it in water, on land and about anything in between. The simply made track, Roebling's invention, was a pair of industrial roller chains, like bicycle chains, with connecting cross-bar paddle assemblies running between them. This track ran on integral ball bearing wheels, like roller skate wheels, in an unsprung channel fixed to the amphibian's hull. People familiar with tracked vehicle design recognized this unsprung track was absurd, but it worked reasonably well both in the water and on sand or soft ground. It did not

U.S. Marine Corps Landing Vehicles Tracked LVT-1 negotiating difficult jungle terrain on Guadalcanal in early 1943.

U.S. Marine Corps Landing Vehicles Tracked LVT-1 being carried as deck cargo on an attack transport in 1943. The ship's cranes were used to lower them into the water. Note their well decks. This was a typical manner of transporting LVTs for an amphibious operation.

U.S. Marine Corps Landing Vehicle Tracked LVT-1 crossing a river in the Pacific Theater of Operations in 1943.

work well on hard ground or paved roads, and its life was very short.

The power train of the LVT-1 was composed of commercial motor truck assemblies, and it was powered by a liquid-cooled automobile engine. Since the LVT-1 used many "off-the-shelf" parts and assemblies, it was very easily put in production. By the end of 1941, enough LVT-1s were available for the U.S. Marine Corps to form their first LVT units. It was first used in combat by the U.S. Marine Corps in the Guadalcanal Landings in August 1942, and proved very successful.

This picture of a U.S. Marine Corps Landing Vehicle Tracked LVT-1 shows the major defect of the LVT-1 and LVT-2: the necessity to disembark "over the side" under fire. (Guam 1944)

Although LVT-1s were still in service at the end of World War II, it was not employed in combat after the U.S. Marine Corps Tarawa amphibious operation in November 1943 proved it was far too vulnerable to enemy fire. Of the 1,225 LVT-Is built from 1941 to 1943, some 485 went to the U.S. Army, 540 to the U.S. Marine Corps, and 200 to the British as Lend-Lease. The U.S. Marines were the only people to use the LVT-1 in combat, and it was declared obsolete at the end of World War II.

In early 1942, the improved Landing Vehicle Tracked Mark II, soon redesignated the LVT-2, was introduced. It was designed and built at Food Machinery and Chemical Corp.'s Riverside, California plant so it would not interfere with the production of the LVT-1. This version brought the U.S. Army Ordnance Department's Tank Engineering Division into the project.

The biggest improvement in the LVT-2 was a new suspension with eleven bogie wheels per track, which were sprung on Torsi-lastic rubber springs, improving both track life and the amphibian's speed and maneuverability on land. The LVT-2's power train was an adapted version of that of the standard U.S. Army M3 light tank's power train powered by the Wright air-cooled radial engine.

The LVT-2's hull was about five feet longer than the LVT-1's, which improved its performance in water. The LVT-2 was also equipped with machine gun mounts, which had not been provided on the LVT-1s in manufacture.

The LVT-2 was first used by the U.S. Marine Corps in the Tarawa landings in November 1943, and it remained in use for the rest of the war. It was primarily used as an amphibious cargo carrier because of a lack of armor, but field improvised armor was added to some.

This U.S. Army Landing Vehicle Tracked LVT-4 in use in the Philippines in 1944 shows the rear loading ramp in the down position for loading.

This mix of U.S. Marine Corps Landing Vehicles Tracked LVT-1 and LVT-2 are landing on Emirau Island in the Pacific in March 1944.

On the left is a column of U.S. Marine Corps Landing Vehicles Tracked LVT-2 landing on Tinian Island in the Pacific in 1944. An LVT-2 moves into the water on the right.

U.S. Marine Corps Landing Vehicles Tracked in a Pacific Theater of Operations amphibious operation in 1943. In the fore-ground below these LVT-2s is a U.S. Army Cargo Carrier M29C (Amphibian), an unarmored vehicle that saw limited service with the U.S. Marine Corps.

A total of some 2,963 LVT-2s were built; 1,507 went to the U.S. Army, 1,456 to the U.S. Marine Corps, and 100 to the British under Lend-Lease. Both the U.S. Marine Corps and U.S. Army made extensive use of them in the Pacific Theater of Operations, and the U.S. Army used them in the European Theater of Operations. The LVT-2 became obsolete at the end of World War II.

The obvious requirement for an armored LVT was first met when a number of otherwise standard LVT-2s were built with light steel armor hulls for the U.S. Army. These were designated as Landing Vehicle Tracked (Armored) LVT(A)-2. A total of 450 were built in 1943-1944 with 250 going to the U.S. Marine Corps and 200 to the U.S. Army. It is difficult, if not impossible, to visually distinguish an LVT(A)-2 from an unarmored LVT-2. They were used interchangeably until they became obsolete at the end of World War II.

At the same time, there was a requirement for an LVT armed and armored for offensive combat as an amphibious tank. A number of amphibious tanks had been built and tested in the 1920s and 1930s, but none had been very successful or practical. Then one was built by adding an armor top to the LVT(A)-2, which mounted the 37mm gun turret from a standard U.S. Army M3A1 light tank, and the first really successful amphibious tank was created. It was quickly adopted as the LVT(A)-1. The U.S. Marine Corps first used the LVT(A)-1 in 1943 operations, and it proved an invaluable asset. Of the 509 built for the U.S. Marine Corps, some 328 were trans-ferred to the U.S. Army, and they were still in service at the end of World War II.

The Landing Vehicle Tracked LVT-3 was an unarmored model developed for cargo carrying, incorporating a new loading ramp in its stern to eliminate the necessity of loading and unloading it "over-the-side" required by the earlier models. A total of 2,962 LVT-3s were built for the U.S. Marine Corps, but production prob-lems delayed their combat introduction until the April 1945 Oki-nawa operation. This successful model was used by the U.S. Marine Corps long after World War II.

Of all the World War II models, the Landing Vehicle Tracked LVT-4 was the one built and used in the largest numbers. Mechan-ically, the LVT-4 was identical to the LVT-2 except for the location of its Wright air-cooled radial engine. The engine was moved from the rear to the front to accommodate the loading ramp incorporated in the LVT-4, and this was a major improvement. During its pro-duction, an armored cab was phased into the LVT-4, and a number of them built without it were modified to add cab armor.

The LVT-4 first saw action in the Pacific Theater of Operations in 1943, but it was also used in the European Theater of Opera-tions. In all, some 8,343 LVT-4s were built from 1943 until the war ended in 1945. A total of 6,083 were made for the Army, but most of these were transferred to the U.S. Marine Corps after the war; 1,760 went to the U.S. Marine Corps; and 500 went to the British under Lend-Lease. The LVT-4 remained in service long after World War II.

To improve combat effectiveness, a few of the 37mm gun turret-equipped LVT(A)-1s had their original turrets replaced with the interchangeable turrets from the standard U.S. Army 75mm Howit-zer Motor Carriage M8, and this proved very successful. This modi-fication was put in production as the LVT(A)-4 because the LVT-4 hull without the rear loading ramp was used, and some 1,890 were built in 1944-1945. It was used in combat by the U.S. Army and

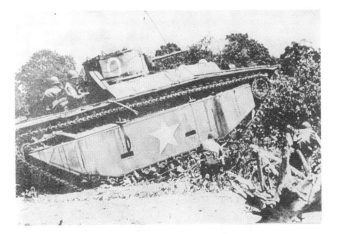

This U.S. Army Landing Vehicle Tracked LVT(A)-2 is in use in a training operation in 1943.

U.S. Marine Corps primarily in the Pacific Theater of Operations. This model remained in service with the U.S. Marine Corps long after World War II.

By the end of the war, an improved model of the LVT(A)-4 had been put in production. This Landing Vehicle Tracked LVT(A)-5 used an improved 75mm howitzer turret with gyrostabilizers to improve its effectiveness when fired from water or on land. Some

259 of these were built, and, although they were built too late to see use in World War II, the U.S. Marine Corps used them long after World War II ended.

While the U.S. Army used LVTs pretty much "as issued" in World War II, the nature of U.S. Marine Corps operations led them to make many modifications, rendering them more effective combat vehicles. They fired their standard 60mm and 81mm infantry mortars from them, and, after reinforcing the well deck, even fired their 4.2-in. chemical mortars from them. In at least one case, the U.S. Marine Corps modified an LVT-4 well deck so they could fire, with reduced charges, a standard 105mm Howitzer M2 from it.

To help overcome the difficulty with tenacious dug-in Japanese troops, the U.S. Marine Corps often armed LVTs with flame throwers. In the field, they modified both the 37mm gun-armed LVT(A)-l and 75mm howitzer armed LVT(A)-4 with heavy flame throwers in place of the turret cannon.

The U.S. Marine Corps also used LVTs equipped with various multiple rocket launchers. Some LVTs had their hulls filled with them, while LVT(A)-1s and LVT(A)-4s had automatic multiple rocket launchers mounted on their hull top armor (see chapter on rocket artillery).

Post-World War II evaluations rated the unique LVTs as very useful and effective combat vehicles for not only amphibious operations, but in operations in swampy terrain and river crossing operations. Although the LVT is most famous for its service with the U.S. Marine Corps in World War II, U.S. Army records indicate they used them as much or more than the U.S. Marine Corps.

A U.S. Army Landing Vehicle Tracked in operation in northern Europe in the winter of 1944-1945. It is either an LVT-2 or an LVT-4.

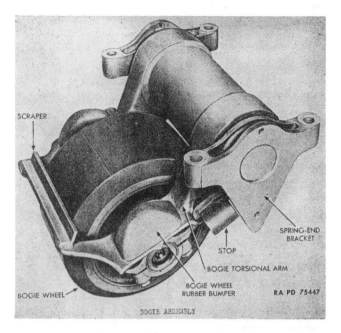

U.S. Marine Corps Landing Vehicles Tracked LVT(A)-4 firing as infantry support artillery in the Pacific Theater of Operations in late 1944.

This is the basic torsion type track bogie assembly used in all LVT-2s, LVT-3s and LVT-4s.

A U.S. Army Landing Vehicle Tracked LVT-4 preparing to ford a 57mm Antitank Gun M1 and a Jeep across a river in northern Europe in the spring of 1945.

This group of Landing Vehicles Tracked LVT(A)-4s (left) and an LVT(A)-2 (right) shows the wake of the LVTs on water.

A Landing Vehicle Tracked LVT-1.

MODEL: Landing Vehicle Tracked LVT-1

WEIGHT: Fighting: 32,500 lbs.

DIMENSIONS: Length: 21 ft., 6 in. Height: 8 ft., 1-1/2 in. Width: 9 ft., 10 in.

ARMAMENT: None as issued; cal. .50 Browning Machine Gun M2-HB and cal. .30 Browning Machine Guns M1917 (water-cooled) and M1919A4 (air-cooled) fitted in field.

ARMOR: None

ENGINE: Hercules model WXLC-3, 6-cylinder, water-cooled, 404 cu. in. rated 146 hp at 2,900 rpm.

TRANSMISSION: Manual type.

NORMAL ROAD SPEED: 12 mph max. Water speed: 6.1 mph max.

CREW: 3

PAYLOAD: 4,500 lbs.

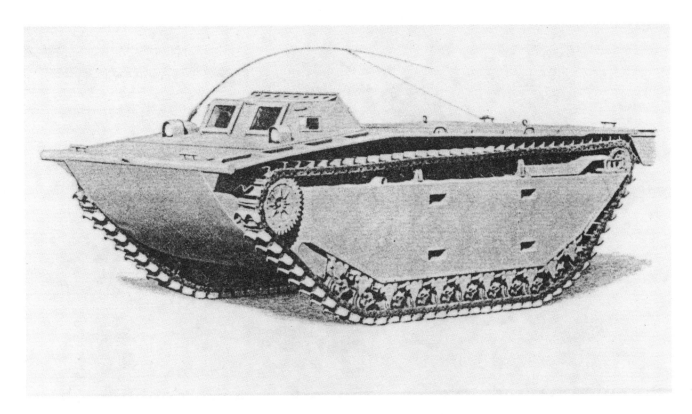

Landing Vehicle Tracked LVT-2.

MODELS: Landing Vehicles Tracked LVT-2 and LVT(A)-2

WEIGHT: Fighting: 30,000 lbs.

DIMENSIONS: Length: 26 ft., 11 in. Height: 8 ft., 1 in. Width: 10 ft., 8 in.

ARMAMENT: 1-cal. .50 Browning Machine Gun M2-HB and 1 to 3 cal. .30 Browning Machine Guns M1919A4, all on rail mount around entire hull well.

ARMOR: LVT-2: none; LVT(A)2: 1/2 in., on cab, 1/4 in. on hull.

ENGINE: Wright 7-cylinder air-cooled radial model W670, 667 cu. in. rated 250 hp at 2,400 rpm

TRANSMISSION: Manual derived from light tank M3.

NORMAL ROAD SPEED: 20 mph max. Water: 7.5 mph max

CREW: 3.

PAYLOAD: LVT-2: 6,500 lbs.; LVT(A)2: 5,500 lbs.

Landing Vehicle Tracked LVT(A)-2.

Landing Vehicles Tracked LVT(A)-2. Back end of LVT-2 identical.

Landing Vehicle Tracked LVT(A)-1.

MODEL: Landing Vehicle Tracked LVT(A)-1

WEIGHT: Fighting: 30,000 lbs.

DIMENSIONS: Length: 26 ft., 1 in. Height: 10 ft., 1 in. Width: 10 ft., 8 in.

ARMAMENT: 1-37mm Tank Gun M6 in coaxial mount with 1-cal. .30 Browning Machine Gun M1919A4 in turret from light tank M3; 2-cal. .30 Browning Machine Guns M1919A4 on external pintle mounts aft of turret.

ARMOR: Cab and turret sides: 1/2 in.; Hull: 1/4 in.

ENGINE: Wright 7-cylinder air-cooled radial model W670, 667 cu. in. rated 250 hp at 2,400 rpm.

TRANSMISSION: Manual derived from light tank M3.

NORMAL ROAD SPEED: 20 mph max. Water: 7.5 mph max.

CREW: 6.

Landing Vehicle tracked LVT-3.

MODEL: Landing Vehicle Tracked LVT-3

WEIGHT: Fighting: 38,600 lbs.

DIMENSIONS: Length: 24 ft., 6 in. Height: 9 ft., 11 in. Width: 11 ft., 2 in.

ARMAMENT: Pintle mounts for cal. .50 and cal. .30 machine guns provided on top of cab and sides of hull.

ARMOR: None (kits to armor cab provided)

ENGINE: Common output twin Cadillac V-8 Model 42, 346 cu. in. rated 110 hp at 4,000 rpm each with common power output.

TRANSMISSION: Hydramatic (automatic) type

NORMAL ROAD SPEED: 17 mph max. Water: 6 mph max.

CREW: 3.

PAYLOAD: 9,000 lbs.

NOTE: Loads over retractable stern ramp.

Landing Vehicle Tracked LVT-4.

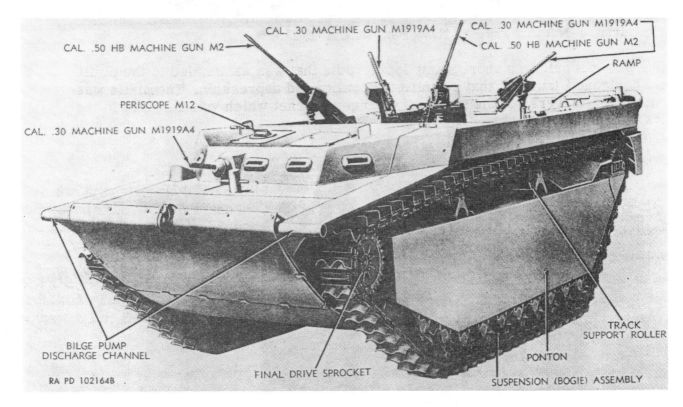

Landing Vehicle Tracked LVT-4 with armored cab.

MODEL: Landing Vehicle Tracked LVT-4

WEIGHT: Fighting: 36,400 lbs.

DIMENSIONS: Length: 26 ft., 1 in. Height: 8 ft., 1 in. Width: 10 ft., 8 in.

ARMAMENT: Pintle mounts for cal. .50 and cal. .30 machine guns provided on top of cab and sides of hull.

ARMOR: None (Kits to add 1/4 in. to cab provided)

ENGINE: Wright 7-cylinder air-cooled radial model W670,667 cu. in. rated 250 hp at 2,400 rpm.

TRANSMISSION: Manual derived from Light Tank M3.

NORMAL ROAD SPEED: 20 mph max. Water: 7.5 mph max.

CREW: 3

PAYLOAD: 8,600 lbs.

NOTE: Loads over retractable stern ramp.

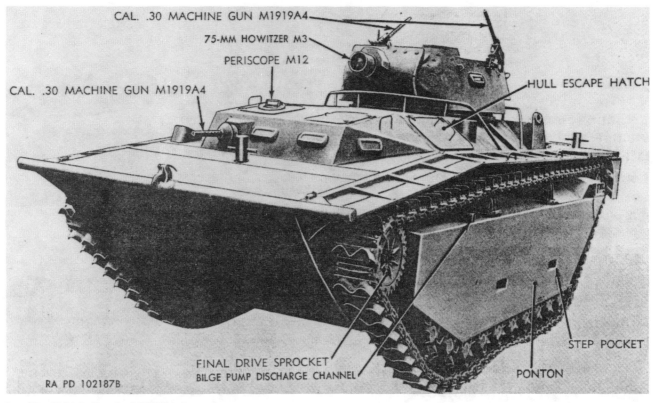

CAL. .30 MACHINE GUN M1919A4
75-MM HOWITZER M3
PERISCOPE M12
CAL. .30 MACHINE GUN M1919A4
HULL ESCAPE HATCH
STEP POCKET
PONTON
FINAL DRIVE SPROCKET
BILGE PUMP DISCHARGE CHANNEL
RA PD 102187B

Landing Vehicle Tracked LVT(A)-4.

MODEL: Landing Vehicle Tracked LVT(A)-4

WEIGHT: Fighting: 39,460 lbs.

DIMENSIONS: Length: 26 ft., 2 in. Height: 10 ft., 2-1/2 in. Width: 10 ft., 8 in.

ARMAMENT: 1-75mm Howitzer M3 in turret from 75mm Howitzer Motor Carriage M8; 1-cal. .50 Browning Machine Gun M2-HB in ring mount on turret top; 1-cal. .30 Browning Machine Gun M1919A4 in ball mount left side of "windshield."

ARMOR: Cab and turret sides: 1/2 in; Hull: 1/2-1/4 in.

ENGINE: Wright 7-cylinder air-cooled radial model W670, 667 cu. in. rated 250 hp at 2,400 rpm.

TRANSMISSION: Manual derived from light tank M3.

NORMAL ROAD SPEED: 20 mph max. Water: 7.5 mph max.

CREW: 6

Chapter 8
Armored Cars

The World War II era U.S. Army requirement for armored cars was very ambivalent. Armored cars were used in substantial numbers by every other army in the war, and the U.S. Army used them, but it never seemed quite sure of what to do with them. This was in no small part because the U.S. Army had all the tanks it wanted, and a tank could do anything an armored car could, and do it better.

The U.S. Army actually began experimenting with armored cars before World War I, and continued experimenting with them all through the 1920s and 1930s. A type of armored car which met the U.S. Army's concept and requirement was adopted before World War II. In June 1939, after five years of development, the U.S. Army adopted the Scout Car M3 and put it in production. The M3 armored scout car was a simple and unique answer to a requirement for them for use with armored and horse cavalry. The M3 armored scout car was based on a heavy-duty short wheelbase 4x4 truck built by White Motor Company. It had an open top body and engine cover of light armor plate. A rail ran all around the top of the body to movable pintle mounts for cal. .30 or cal. .50 machine guns. More than one gun could be mounted, and they could easily be moved any place on the track. The windshields were "bullet proof" glass with armor covers. A canvas "top" cover was provided, but it was seldom used in the field.

This simple Armored Scout Car M3 quickly proved useful, and, although it was designated as a "scout car," it became an armored utility vehicle. The Scout Car M3 was the basis of the famous U.S. Army World War II armored half-track when its rear wheels were replaced by a half-track adapter.

The Scout Car M3 was in wide service in the U.S. Army when it entered World War II. A few saw action in the defense of the Philippines in 1941-1942. During the rest of World War II, it went practically every place the U.S. Army did, but it was never a spectacular combat vehicle. It could be found doing rear area road patrol and truck convoy escort, and occasionally it was used to scout roads at the head of advancing units. Although it was an old-fashioned vehicle in some mechanical respects, it was rugged, reliable and easy to maintain. A total of 20,918 M3 armored scout cars were built between 1939 and 1944. It went out of service several years after World War II.

U.S. Army Scout Cars M3A1 leading a column on a road in North Africa in 1942.

A fully loaded and armed U.S. Army Scout Car M3A1 in a demonstration in 1941. Note the pioneer tools on the vehicle's rear end.

U.S. Army Scout Cars M3A1 operating with horse-mounted cavalry on maneuvers in 1941.

In July 1941, after observing British operations in North Africa, the U.S. Army adopted a requirement for a cannon-armed armored car. The first was the Ford 6x6 Armored Car T17 adopted in September 1941. A total of 205 were built on a limited-production program for test, but the U.S. Army rejected them. They were then offered to the British under Lend-Lease, but they also rejected them.

The trouble with the T17 was that it was as big and heavy as a light tank, and, despite a 37mm gun armed turret, it was much less effective and useful than a light tank. After limited use by the U.S. Army Military Police as road patrol vehicles in the United States, they were scrapped long before the end of World War II.

A second armored car built under the July 1941 requirement was the T17E1. It was a Chevrolet 4x4 design, built along the lines of existing British armored cars, and also was armed with a turret mounted 37mm gun. It was also almost as big and heavy as a light tank. The U.S. Army tested and rejected it, however, the British tested it and requested it be built for them under Lend-Lease. A total of 1,500 T17E1s armed with 37mm guns and another 1,000 armed with a twin cal. .50 Browning Machine Gun M2-HB-armed antiaircraft turret were built for the British as Lend-Lease in 1942-1943.

However, the U.S. Army requirement for an armored car would not go away, and a new requirement for a light armored car was issued in 1942.

In late 1942, Ford produced a 6x6 design with a 37mm armed gun turret, which was adopted as the Light Armored Car M8. Some 8,523 M8 armored cars were built in 1942-1943. They saw service, particularly in the European Theater of Operations for the rest of the war, performing unspectacular road patrol, escort and scouting missions. With their light armor and 37mm gun, they were completely inadequate for combat missions.

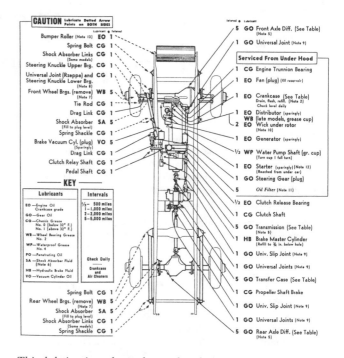

This lubrication chart shows the chassis layout of the U.S. Army Scout Car M3A1.

This 1942 photo shows the Ford prototype of the U.S. Army Light Armored Car M8 (6x6). Note its gun is a dummy. (Ford Motor Co. photo)

A U.S. Army Light Armored Car M8 in a liberated town in northern France in late 1944.

A U.S. Army Armored Utility Car M20 in action in northern Europe in 1945.

A U.S. Army Light Armored Car M8 in action in Italy in 1944.

A U.S. Army of Occupation Light Armored Car M8 on guard at a municipal building in Tokyo, Japan in late 1945.

This led to the suggestion that the 37mm gun turret could be removed from the M8 armored car to make it lighter and still allow it to perform the missions it was suitable for. In April 1943, the U.S. Army adopted the Armored Utility Car M20, which was an M8 armored car with the turret removed and replaced with an armor box surmounted by a ring mounted cal. .50 Browning Machine Gun M2-HB. Some 3,791 M20s were built in 1943 and 1944.

This rear view of a U.S. Army Scout Car M3A1 also shows its skate rail machine gun mount with the cal. .30 and cal. .50 machine guns with which it was normally armed during the war.

Although both the M8 and M20 saw wide use in the European Theater of War in 1944 and 1945, their most important use came after it was over. Both were used extensively as patrol vehicles by the Armies of Occupation in Germany and Japan. They were rugged, reliable and easily maintained vehicles excellent for this work.

Post-World War II reports, however, usually said very little about armored cars except to speculate why so much effort had been expended designing and building such combat-unworthy vehicles.

A U.S. Army Armored Utility Car M20 on a training exercise in 1942.

U.S. Army Scout Car M3A1 with standard armament.

MODEL: Scout Car M3A1 (4x4)

WEIGHT: Fighting: 12,400 lbs.

DIMENSIONS: Length: 18 ft., 5-1/2 in. Height: 6 ft., 6-1/2 in. Width: 6 ft., 8 in.

ARMAMENT: 1-cal. .50 Browning Machine Gun M2-HB and 1-cal. .30 Browning Machine Gun M1919A4 on mounts on skate rail, which encircles interior of body.

ARMOR: 1/4 in. with 1/2 in. for windshield.

ENGINE: Hercules JXD; 320 cu. in. rated at 87 hp at 2400 rpm.

TRANSMISSION: 4 speeds and reverse.

NORMAL ROAD SPEED: 50 mph max.

CREW: 8.

RA PD 347076

U.S. Army Scout Car M3A1 with cover.

U.S. Army Armored Car T17.

MODEL: Armored Car T17 (6x6)

WEIGHT: Fighting: 32,000 lbs.

DIMENSIONS: Length: 18 ft., 2 in. Height: 7 ft., 7 in. Width: 8 ft., 6 in.

CANNON: 37mm Gun M6. Mount includes co-axial cal. .30 Browning Machine Gun M1919A4. Range: 12,850 yards max., 500 yards antitank. Ammunition: fixed HE, AP, APC and canister, M3 tank — AT gun series only. Projectile Weight: 1.5 to 2 lbs.

TRAVERSE: 360 degrees. Elevation: +45 degrees, -10 degrees.

ADDITIONAL ARMAMENT: 2-cal. .30 Browning Machine Guns M1919A4, one in bow mount and one in pintle mount on turret.

ENGINE: 2-Hercules JXD, 320 cu. in. each, rated at 110 hp. at 3,000 rpm. each with common power output.

TRANSMISSION: 8 forward speeds and 2 reverse speeds.

NORMAL ROAD SPEED: 60 mph. max.

CREW: 5.

RA PD 45963

U.S. Army Armored Car T17E1.

MODEL: Armored Car T17E1 (4x4)

WEIGHT: Fighting: 30,705 lbs.

DIMENSIONS: Length: 18 ft., 0 in. Height 7 ft., 9 in. Width: 8 ft., 10 in.

CANNON: 37mm Gun M6. Mount includes co-axial cal. .30 Browning Machine Gun M1919A4. Range: 12,850 yards max, 500 yards antitank. Ammunition: fixed HE, AP, APC and cannister, M3 tank-AT gun series only. Projectile Weight: 1.5 to 2 lbs.

TRAVERSE: 360 degrees. Elevation: 40 degrees, -7 degrees.

ADDITIONAL ARMAMENT: 2-cal. .30 Browning Machine Guns M1919A4, one in bow mount, one in pintle mount on turret.

ENGINE: 2-GMC model 270, 270.5 cu. in. rated 97 hp at 3,000 rpm each with common power output.

TRANSMISSION: 4 speeds forward and reverse, 2-speed transfer case.

NORMAL ROAD SPEED: 55 mph max.

CREW: 5.

U.S. Army Light Armored Car M8.

MODEL: Light Armored Car M8 (6x6)

WEIGHT: Fighting: 17,400 lbs.

DIMENSIONS: Length: 16 ft., 5 in. Height: 7 ft., 4-1/2 in. Width: 8 ft., 4 in.

CANNON: 37mm Gun M6. Mount includes co-axial cal. .30 Browning Machine Gun M1919A4. Range: 12,850 yards max., 500 yards antitank. Ammunition: Fixed HE, AP, APC and canister, M3 tank-AT gun series only. Projectile Weight: 1.5 to 2 lbs.

TRAVERSE: 360 degrees. Elevation: +20 degrees, -10 degrees.

ADDITIONAL ARMAMENT: 1-cal. .50 Browning Machine Gun M2-HB in pintle mount on turret.

ENGINE: Hercules Model JXD, 320 cu. in. rated 110 hp at 3,000 rpm.

TRANSMISSION: 4 speeds forward and reverse with 2-speed transfer case.

NORMAL ROAD SPEED: 55 mph max.

CREW: 4.

U.S. Army Armored Utility Car M20.

MODEL: Armored Utility Car M20 (6x6)

WEIGHT: Fighting: 17,500 lbs. max.

DIMENSIONS: Length: 16 ft., 5 in. Height: 7 ft., 7 in. Width: 8 ft., 4 in.

ARMAMENT: 1-cal. .50 Browning Machine Gun M2-HB on ring mount above hull open top.

ARMOR: 5/8 in. max, 1/4 in. min.

ENGINE: Hercules Model JXD, 320 cu. in. rated 110 hp at 3,000 rpm.

TRANSMISSION: 4 speeds forward and reverse with 2-speed transfer case.

NORMAL ROAD SPEED: 55 mph max.

CREW: 2 to 6, depending on use.

Chapter 9
The Field Artillery System

It is acknowledged that the U.S. Army's field artillery made a tremendous contribution to the Allied victory in World War II. Its weapons, ammunition, fire control and direction and communications network were all superior, and the most advanced of their time. One key element of the U.S. Army's World War II field artillery was the "field artillery system," a family of towed field artillery cannon able to perform all fire missions.

The U.S. Army World War II field artillery system included light, medium, heavy and super heavy cannon. Each of these included a long barreled gun and a short barreled howitzer mounted on the same basic carriage in each class. Development of this U.S. Army field artillery system began right after the end of World War I. In 1919, the U.S. Army "Westervelt Board Report" on artillery armament, calibers, types of materiel, etc. projected the field artillery the U.S. Army would need in a future war. It also stabilized the classification of cannon into light, medium, heavy and super heavy types as a "field artillery system." Guns and howitzers in each of these classes were used by the U.S. Army Field Artillery in World War II.

A number of basic features for all the towed field guns in this system were established in the very early 1920s. They were all to have split trail carriages to give them wide fields of fire. All were to have their barrels trunioned near their breeches and counterbalanced by "equilibrator" springs; however, this system was not used on the super heavy cannon. This allowed them to fire at high elevations without the need of excavating pits for their barrels to recoil

A U.S. Army 3-in. Gun M5 being towed by a U.S. Army half-track in northern France in late 1944. The 3-in. gun was a much-used effective antitank gun, and it was also an effective field gun.

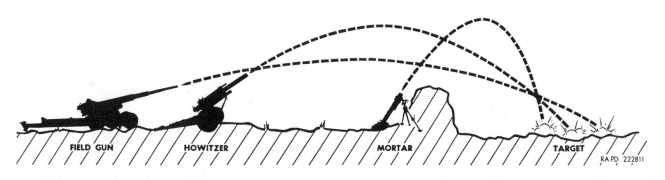

FIELD GUN   HOWITZER   MORTAR   TARGET   RA PD 222811

U.S. Army field artillery definitions:

GUN: *A long barrel cannon which normally fires with a flat trajectory, can fire with a high trajectory, and has a longer range than either a howitzer or mortar of the same caliber.*

HOWITZER: *A cannon with a medium-length barrel which normally fires with a high trajectory, can fire with a flat trajectory, and has a shorter range than a gun and longer range than a mortar of the same caliber.*

MORTAR: *A cannon with a short barrel which can only fire with a high trajectory and has a shorter range than either a gun or howitzer of the same caliber.*

In U.S. Army World War II era publications, it was standard procedure to list field artillery weapons, guns, howitzers and mortars of the same caliber with guns first, howitzers second and mortars last.

On the left is a U.S. Army 37mm Antitank Gun M3; on the right is a U.S. Army 3-in. Gun M5. This picture, taken in 1942, shows the 37mm AT gun with a muzzle brake, which the U.S. Army did not adopt. The 3-in. gun could fire as an antitank gun as well as a field gun.

into. They were all to use very efficient hydraulic energy-absorber pneumatic spring recoil systems of the type the U.S. Army had adopted with the French field artillery weapons it used in World War I.

Development of the light gun and howitzer of the system began about 1919. The gun was to be a 75mm caliber, firing better ammunition than the French 75mm Gun M1897 the U.S. Army had adopted as standard in World War I. The howitzer was to be a 105mm, adopted as a result of the observation and testing of the German Army's excellent World War I howitzers in this caliber. Several models in these calibers, which mounted on a common

carriage, were being tested by 1920. By the late 1920s, the prototype of the carriage, which would be used for 75mm guns and 105mm howitzers, had been perfected, but several budgetary limitations and other higher priority needs allowed only a handful of prototypes to be produced. This 1920s design was to be horse-drawn.

Although the U.S. Army Field Artillery was still armed with either horse-drawn World War I French 75 or modernized versions of this gun with pneumatic rubber-tired wheels for motor truck towing, by the late 1930s the U.S. Army began preparing to pro-

A U.S. Army 105mm Howitzer M2 in action in North Africa in late 1942.

A U.S. Army 155mm Howitzer M1 in action in northern France in late 1944.

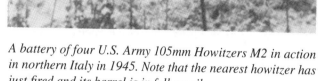
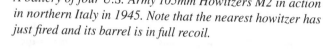

A U.S. Army 155mm Howitzers M1 being fired by the U.S. Marine Corps in the Pacific Theater of War in 1945. The howitzer's barrel is in full recoil.

A battery of four U.S. Army 105mm Howitzers M2 in action in northern Italy in 1945. Note that the nearest howitzer has just fired and its barrel is in full recoil.

U.S. Army 105mm Howitzers M2 in action in the Philippines in 1944.

A U.S. Army 155mm Gun M1 on the march in Italy in 1944. These and other U.S. Army heavy and super heavy field artillery weapons had great difficulty negotiating the confined town streets in Europe and in the Pacific Theater of Operations.

A U.S. Army 4.5-in. Gun M1 in action in Belgium in January 1945.

duce the new 75mm gun and 105mm howitzer. However, their common carriage was to be equipped with pneumatic rubber-tired wheels for motor truck towing.

The new 105mm howitzer would fire newly developed 105mm howitzer ammunition, however, the U.S. Army Field Artillery Board was reluctant to adopt the new 75mm ammunition for the gun. However, the new 3-in. antiaircraft gun ammunition had the ballistic qualities desired for the light gun, and the U.S. Army Ordnance Department suggested the new light field gun could be made

to fire it. The U.S. Army Field Artillery Board immediately adopted this suggestion.

The new light 3-in. Gun M5 and 105mm Howitzer M2 were adopted by the U.S. Army in 1939. They shared a common carriage, and both were put into production in 1940. Both the M5 3-in. gun and M2 105mm howitzer were first used in combat by the U.S. Army in North Africa in 1942. Both proved to be excellent light field artillery weapons. The 105mm Howitzer M2 was the most used U.S. Army field artillery weapon in World War II.

A U.S. Army 155mm Gun M1 in action in the Philippines in 1944.

A U.S. Army 155mm Gun M1 emplaced in northern Europe in the winter of 1944-1945 with its barrel at its maximum angle of elevation.

A U.S. Army 105mm Howitzer M2 on the march behind its most common prime mover, the GMC U.S. Army truck: 2-1/2-ton 6x6 "Gimmy Duce-and-a-Half." The howitzer is covered with its canvas gun cover.

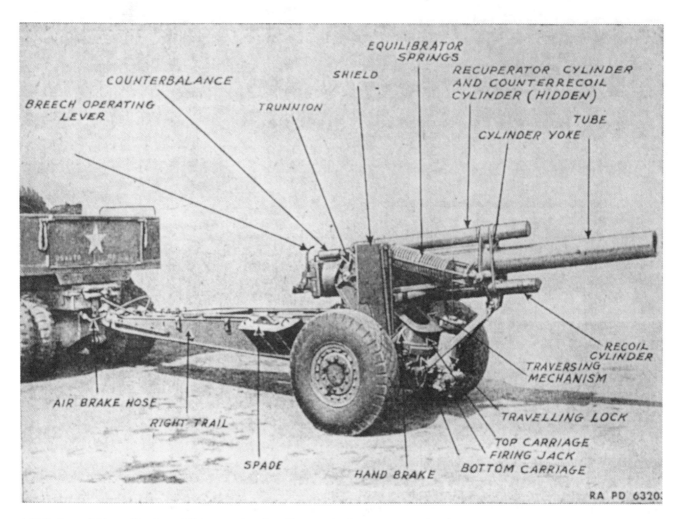

A U.S. Army 155mm Howitzer M1 in march order. The standard prime mover for this howitzer was the Diamond T U.S. Army truck, four-ton, 6x6.

A crew loading a U.S. Army 240mm Howitzer M1. The heavy projectiles of all U.S. Army separate loading ammunition field artillery weapons required the use of such a tray as seen here to protect their breech from damage.

The 3-in. Gun M5 proved a somewhat redundant field artillery piece; however, it could fire armor-piercing ammunition. It was the best antitank gun the U.S. Army had in North Africa, and many were used in this role there and for the rest of World War II. The 3-in. Gun M5 was modified with a new shield more suitable for antitank use in 1943. Although it was frequently used as an antitank gun for the rest of World War II and was often called the "3-in. antitank gun," it was officially a light field gun and was often used as one. The U.S. Army dropped the 3-in. Gun M5 at the end of World War II, and later rebarreled many of them as 105mm howitzers.

The 105mm Howitzer M2 was one of the outstanding field artillery weapons of World War II, remaining in service long after that war.

The development of a medium gun and howitzer began in the very early 1920s with experimental 4.7-in. guns and 155mm howitzers mounted on a common carriage. Budgetary limitations and the large stock of French 155mm Schneider howitzers used to fill the medium field gun role caused this project to proceed very slowly. However, by the late 1930s, it became important when the U.S. Army's project requirements for medium field artillery weapons for a future war called for new models to be produced.

In 1939, development of new medium weapons, a 4.7-in. gun and a 155mm howitzer, were given a high priority. In 1941, the new 155mm Howitzer M1 was going into production, and a new 4.7-in. gun was ready for production, but its introduction had to be delayed because the ammunition for it required new production facilities, which had yet to be built.

To overcome the 4.7-in. gun ammunition problem, the U.S. Army Ordnance Department was instructed to change the caliber of the gun to fire the newly adopted British 4.5-in. gun ammunition, which was being produced under Lend-Lease. This was quickly and easily done, and the new medium field artillery weapon was adopted as the 4.5-in. Gun M1.

While the 155mm Howitzer M1 proved to be one of the best field artillery weapons of its class in World War II, the 4.5-in. Gun M1 was marginal and redundant. The trouble was that the British-designed 4.5-in. gun ammunition it fired was never brought up to the standard of range or accuracy the U.S. Army desired. The U.S. Army stopped using the 4.5-in. Gun M1 at the end of World War II, and eventually rebarreled many of them as 155mm howitzers. The 155mm Howitzer M1 was retained long after World War II.

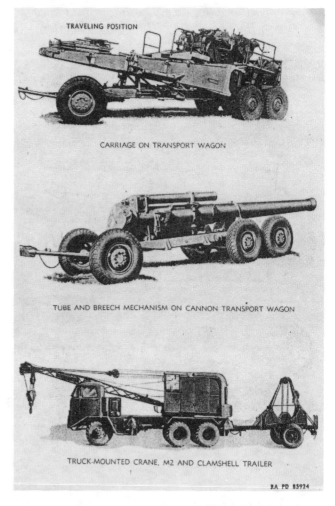

A U.S. Army 240mm Howitzer M1 loaded on its transport wagons in march order with the U.S. Army twenty-ton Truck Crane M2 required to emplace the howitzer. The transport wagons and crane for the 8-in. Gun M1 are practically identical.

A U.S. Army 155mm Howitzer M1 in action in Italy in 1944. Note the muddy ground has made the howitzer's firing jack useless, and its wheels have sunk in the mud until the bottom of its carriage is resting on the ground.

The first U.S. Army 8-in. Howitzer M1 at its roll-out at the U.S. Army Rock Island Arsenal in 1928.

Mobile heavy artillery was introduced in World War I when the use of crawler tractors made it practical. The U.S. Army used two heavy artillery weapons in World War I: the French 155mm GPF model 1917 gun and the British 8-in. Vickers howitzer also introduced in 1917, and both were made mobile with Caterpillar tractors for prime movers. The French 155mm GPF gun was a modern weapon with a then novel split trail carriage, and, in modernized forms, it was used in World War II. The British 8-in. Vickers howitzer was considered inadequate by the U.S. Army because of its lack of range, accuracy and other limitations.

By the early 1920s, the U.S. Army was experimenting with new carriages that could mount either a 155mm gun or 8-in. howitzer. Since there was a requirement for an 8-in. howitzer, its development was pushed, and in 1928 the U.S. Army adopted the new 8-in. Howitzer M1. It was a very advanced design for its time, being mounted on a pneumatic rubber-tired carriage only suitable for towing by motor vehicles. This was the 8-in. howitzer the U.S. Army used in World War II, and by any standards it was a superior weapon.

Although some experimenting was done, development of the 155mm gun, which would share the 8-in. Howitzer M1's carriage, was not adopted until 1938 because the available stock of the still excellent World War I French 155mm GPF guns were adequate when modernized with pneumatic rubber tires for motorized towing.

The 155mm gun M1, which shared the carriage of the 8-in. Howitzer M1, was also a superior field artillery weapon noted for its excellent long-range accuracy. It was the only U.S. Army World War II towed artillery weapon with a commonly used nickname: "The Long Tom."

Both the 155mm Gun M1 and the 8-in. Howitzer M1 first saw action in North Africa in 1942-1943, and they both rendered outstanding service any place the U.S. Army fought for the rest of World War II. Both were retained by the U.S. Army after World War II, and their top carriage equilibrator and recoil basic designs are incorporated in U.S. Army artillery weapon's designs in service fifty years later.

Although most of the super heavy artillery used in World War I was in the railway gun class, the U.S. Army adopted two mobile super heavy artillery weapons in World War I. One was the French-designed 240mm howitzer of 1917; the other was the U.S. Navy 7-in. Gun designed in 1918. Both of these powerful weapons were made mobile by the use of Caterpillar tractors, however, neither of them was ready for action in time for use in World War I. The 1919 evaluation of the Westervelt Board stated improved artillery weapons in both their calibers would be required for a future war, but that these would be adequate for the foreseeable future.

Preliminary development work of new super heavy field artillery weapons and their ammunition was done in the 1920s and 1930s, but none were built. The U.S. Army was planning for its

An emplaced U.S. Army 240mm Howitzer M1 in northern Italy in mid-1944.

On the left is a captured German 17-cm (7-in) heavy field gun; on the right the more powerful, longer range U.S. Army 8-in. Gun M1.

The barrel and recoil of a U.S. Army 8-in. Gun M1 on the march in northern Europe in late 1944. The prime mover is a U.S. Army Full Track Prime Mover M35 converted from a 3-in. Gun Motor Carriage M10.

A U.S. Army 8-in. Gun M1 firing at German fortifications in northern France in the fall of 1944.

A U.S. Army 8-in. Gun M1 being emplaced with its U.S. Army twenty-ton Truck Crane M2 lowering the barrel and recoil assembly on to the carriage.

A U.S. Army 8-in. Howitzer M1 firing with its barrel in full recoil.

forces to be made highly mobile by the use of motorization, and there were serious doubts that super heavy artillery could be made mobile enough for such forces because there were no high speed tractors powerful enough to tow them.

In 1940, with the encouragement of the U.S. Army Field Artillery Board, the U.S. Army Ordnance Department completed designs for new super artillery cannon. However, this was not a priority project, and the new designs were not officially adopted until 1942 as the 8-in. gun M1 and 240mm Howitzer M1. Limited production of both was begun immediately.

Both the 8-in. Gun M1 and 240mm Howitzer were huge weapons by any field artillery standard. The 8-in. gun fired the same projectile as U.S. Army's late model 8-in. coast artillery and railway gun, which had been built to fire the same projectile as the latest U.S. Navy 8-in. cruiser gun — a unique bit of Army-Navy cooperation. The 240mm howitzer fired new ammunition developed from that for the World War I howitzers.

U.S. Army artillerymen emplacing a U.S. Army 8-in. Howitzer M1 in Germany in 1945.

A U.S. Army 155mm Gun M1 in action in the Philippines in 1944. The gun has just fired and its barrel is in full recoil.

Both the 8-in. Gun M1 and 240mm Howitzer M1 were transported in two loads: one the barrel and recoil, the other the carriage, on special trailers. A crane was required to emplace and assemble them, and a special high-speed tractor was being developed to pull them. The U.S. Army Ground Forces Command still had great doubts about the mobility of the huge guns in the field.

The U.S. Army did not deploy any super heavy artillery in North Africa in 1942-1943, but it encountered a handful of German weapons in this class. Their effectiveness caused the U.S. Army to establish a new, and urgent, requirement for super heavy field artillery.

Although the weapons existed, organizing, training and fully equipping super heavy field artillery units was something that could not be done in a hurry. Production of the 8-in. Gun M1 and 240mm Howitzer M1 were pushed and given new priority.

Some forgotten genius then solved the problem of the heavy-duty high-speed tractors needed for the guns. A new heavy high-speed artillery tractor had been developed, but there were problems getting it into production due to other projects with much higher priority. Then it was suggested that it would be possible to refit obsolescent M3 Grant medium tanks, or some of the 3-in. Gun Motor Carriages M10 in depot storage, to suitable prime movers for the super heavy artillery. This was easily and quickly tested, and both conversions worked and both were adopted and used. This solved the problem of the required tractors for the guns for the rest of World War II.

The first super heavy artillery in action was a battery of 240mm Howitzers at the Anzio Beachhead in Italy in September 1943. They quickly went into action and proved an instant success, par-

ticularly in firing "counterbattery" against German guns in their class with precision long range accuracy.

The first 8-in. guns M1 went into action at the Anzio Beachhead in April 1944, and they also proved an instant success. Combined super heavy artillery and air attacks not only put enemy artillery out of action, but destroyed targets as small as German heavy tanks. They played a role in putting the German railway gun, "Anzio Annie," now displayed in the Ordnance Museum at Aberdeen Proving Grounds, Maryland, out of action.

Both the 8-in. Gun M1 and 240mm Howitzer proved very valuable against difficult targets such as heavy concrete fortifications. They saw considerable action in the war in Europe until its end in 1945. Super heavy artillery was also deployed in the Philippines in 1944 and on Okinawa in 1945, but few targets really justified the need for them. Both weapons were retained by the U.S. Army at the end of World War II.

By the end of World War II, the requirements for many of the weapons in the U.S. Army's field artillery system were disappearing. Future warfare would be mobile, and without the heavy concrete fortifications that were the most suitable targets for super heavy artillery, the 8-in. Gun M1 and 240mm Howitzer were never employed again. Improvement in the ammunition for the 105mm howitzer and 155mm howitzer made the 3-in. gun and 4.5-in. gun redundant, and they were retired.

There was also a vast improvement in air-to-ground attack by airplanes armed with rockets, bombs and guns, which were able to do some old support missions better than field artillery weapons. Although in its infancy, field artillery rockets were showing promise, and so were the first very primitive field artillery guided missiles. (See chapter on artillery rockets).

However, the U.S. Army's World War II field artillery system of weapons was undoubtedly the best of it kind. Not only did the U.S. Army field these weapons in great numbers, but the weapons' fire was very effective. The quality of all the weapons was superior. They played a major role in the Allied victory.

A U.S. Army 155mm Gun M1 in service with the U.S. Marine Corps on New Georgia Island in 1944. Moving the large U.S. Army field artillery weapons over jungle roads and trails was very difficult, requiring crawler tractors such as the one being used here.

A U.S. Army 8-in. Howitzer M1 crossing a Bailey bridge in northern France in late 1944. The gun has its canvas cover in place, and its prime mover is a full-track U.S. Army eighteen-ton High Speed Tractor M4.

A U.S. Army 8-in. Howitzer M1 on the march in northern Europe in the winter of 1944-1945, with a full-track U.S. Army eighteen-ton High Speed Tractor M4 as its prime mover. Movement of this and all other World War II military vehicles and artillery over snow and ice required very careful driving.

U.S. Army 155mm Howitzers M1 on the march in Germany in 1945 with full-track U.S. Army thirteen-ton High Speed Tractors M5 series as prime movers.

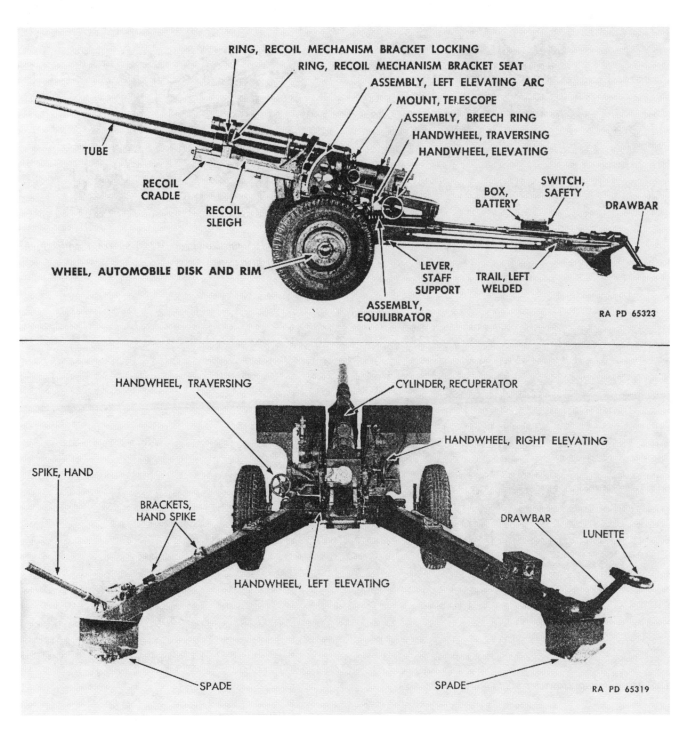

RING, RECOIL MECHANISM BRACKET LOCKING
RING, RECOIL MECHANISM BRACKET SEAT
ASSEMBLY, LEFT ELEVATING ARC
MOUNT, TELESCOPE
ASSEMBLY, BREECH RING
HANDWHEEL, TRAVERSING
HANDWHEEL, ELEVATING

TUBE

RECOIL
CRADLE

RECOIL
SLEIGH

BOX,
BATTERY

SWITCH,
SAFETY

DRAWBAR

WHEEL, AUTOMOBILE DISK AND RIM

LEVER,
STAFF
SUPPORT

TRAIL, LEFT
WELDED

ASSEMBLY,
EQUILIBRATOR

RA PD 65323

HANDWHEEL, TRAVERSING

CYLINDER, RECUPERATOR

HANDWHEEL, RIGHT ELEVATING

SPIKE, HAND

BRACKETS,
HAND SPIKE

DRAWBAR

LUNETTE

HANDWHEEL, LEFT ELEVATING

SPADE

SPADE

RA PD 65319

Above: the U.S. Army 3-in. Gun M5 in march order. Below: the gun with its trails deployed for emplacement.

MODEL: 3 in. Gun M5

WEIGHT: 4,875 lbs.

DIMENSIONS: Length: 23 ft., 2 in. Height: 5 ft., 0 in. Width: 5 ft., 10 in.

RANGE: 16,100 yards max., 1,000 yards antitank.

RATE OF FIRE: Rounds per minute in bursts: 10; in prolonged fire: 2.

AMMUNITION: Fixed HE, AP, APC, Heat and chem. smoke. Projectile Weight: 13 to 15.5 lbs.

CARRIAGE: Type: 2-wheel split trail. Traverse: 22.5 degree R&L Elevation: +30 degrees, -5 degrees. Fires from wheels. Min. time to emplace: 3 min.

NORMAL TOWING SPEED: 35 mph max.

MODIFICATIONS: Improved gun shield for antitank use issued in 1944-1945.

NOTE: Built on same carriage and recoil as 105mm Howitzer M2.

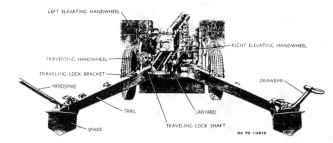

U.S. Army 105mm Howitzer M2 with trails spread for emplacement.

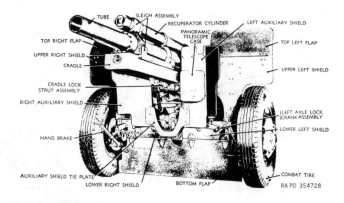

U.S. Army 105mm Howitzer M2 from front with shield deployed for firing.

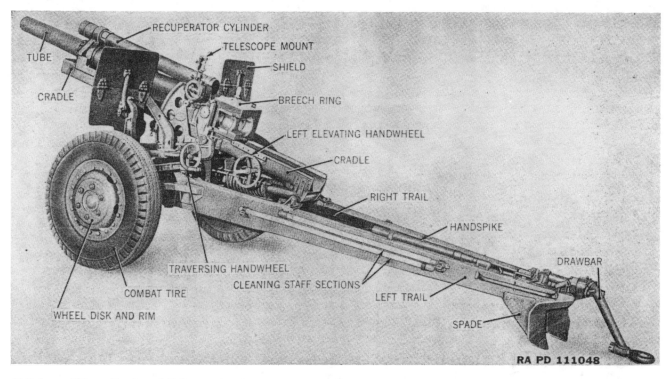

U.S. Army 105mm Howitzer M2 in march order.

MODEL: 105mm Howitzer M2

WEIGHT: 4,980 lbs.

DIMENSIONS: Length: 19 ft., 8 in. Height: 5 ft., 5 in. Width: 6 ft., 8 in.

RANGE: 12,200 yards max.

RATE OF FIRE: Rounds per minute in bursts: 4; in prolonged fire: 2.

AMMUNITION: Semifixed HE, Heat, WP and chem. smoke, M2 Howitzer series only. Projectile Weight: 28 to 33 lbs.

CARRIAGE: Type: 2-wheel split trail. Traverse: 22.5 degree R&L Elevation: +64 degrees, -0 degrees. Fires from wheels. Min. time to emplace: 3 min.

NORMAL TOWING SPEED: 35 mph max.

NOTE: Built on same carriage and recoil as 3-in. gun M5.

U.S. Army 4.5-in. Gun M1 emplaced for firing.

MODEL: 4.5 in. Gun M1

WEIGHT: 13,400 lbs.

DIMENSIONS: Length: 26 ft., 6 in. Height: 6 ft., 11-1/2 in. Width: 7 ft., 11-1/2 in.

RANGE: 16,600 yards normal; 21,125 yards with super-charge

RATE OF FIRE: Rounds per minute in bursts: 4; in prolonged fire: 1.

AMMUNITION: Separate loading. HE, WP and chemical smoke. Projectile Weight: 55 lbs.

CARRIAGE: Type: 2-wheel split trail. Traverse: 26-1/2 degrees R&L Elevation: +60 degrees, -2 degrees. Fires from wheels or firing jack. Min. time to emplace: 5 min.

NORMAL TOWING SPEED: 35 mph max.

NOTE: Built on same carriage and recoil as 155mm Howitzer M1.

U.S. Army 155mm Howitzer M1 emplaced for firing.

MODEL: 155mm Howitzer M1
WEIGHT: 12,800 lbs.
DIMENSIONS: Length: 24 ft., 0 in. Height: 6 ft., 9-1/2 in. Width: 7 ft., 11-1/2 in.
RANGE: 16,355 yards max.
RATE OF FIRE: Rounds per minute in bursts: 4; in prolonged fire: 1.
AMMUNITION: Separate loading HE, WP and chem. smoke; M1 Howitzer series only. Projectile Weight: 95 lbs.
CARRIAGE: Type: 2-wheel split trail. Traverse: 26-1/2 degrees R&L Elevation: +63 degrees, -2 degrees. Fires from wheels or firing jack. Min. time to emplace: 5 min.
NORMAL TOWING SPEED: 35 mph. max.
NOTE: Built on same carriage and recoil as 4.5-in. gun M1

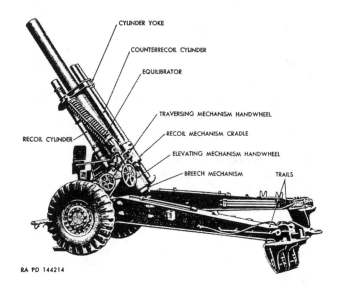

U.S. Army 155mm Howitzer M1 with barrel at a maximum elevation.

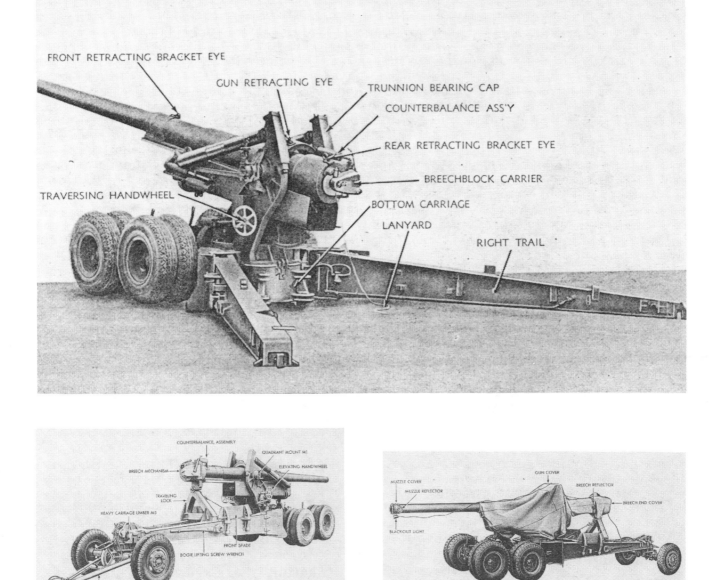

Top: U.S. 155mm Gun M1 emplaced for firing. Lower left: U.S. Army 155mm Gun M1 in march order. Lower right: U.S. Army 155mm Gun M1 in march order with canvas gun cover in place.

MODEL: 155mm Gun M1

WEIGHT: 30,600 lbs.

DIMENSIONS: Length: 33 ft., 6 in.

WEIGHT: 8 ft., 6-1/4 in. Width: 8 ft., 2-1/2 in., in traveling configuration.

RANGE: 25,395 yards max. with supercharge.

RATE OF FIRE: Rounds per minute in bursts: 1; in prolonged fire: 1/2.

AMMUNITION: Separate loading HE and APC for M1 gun only. Projectile Weight: 95 to 100 lbs.

CARRIAGE: Type: Split trail with detachable wheels. Traverse: 30 degree R&L Elevation: +63 degrees, -1 degree. Fires from ground with wheels detached. Min. time to emplace: 30 min.; 6 hrs. max.

NORMAL TOWING SPEED: 25 mph max.

NOTE: Built on same carriage and recoil as 8-in. Howitzer M1.

RA PD 45866   FIRING POSITION

TRAVELING POSITION   RA PD 45865

U.S. Army 8-in. Howitzer M1 emplaced and in traveling positions.

MODEL: 8 in. Howitzer M1

WEIGHT: 30,000 lbs.

DIMENSIONS: Length: 40 ft., Height: 8 ft., 6-1/4 in. Width: 8 ft., 2-1/2 in. in traveling configuration.

RANGE: 18,510 yards max.

RATE OF FIRE: Rounds per minute in bursts: 1; in prolonged fire: 1/2.

AMMUNITION: Separate loading HE for M1 Howitzer only. Projectile Weight: 200 lbs.

CARRIAGE: Type: Split trail with detachable bogie wheels and limber. Traverse: 30 degrees R&L Elevation: +65 degrees, -2 degrees. Fires from ground with wheels detached. Min. time to emplace: 30 min; 6 hrs. max.

NORMAL TOWING SPEED: 25 mph. max.

NOTE: Built on same carriage and recoil as 155mm gun M1.

U.S. Army 8-in. Gun M1 emplaced.

MODEL: 8 in. Gun M1

WEIGHTS: 69,500 lbs. emplaced; 103,720 lbs. with its two transport wagons.

DIMENSIONS: Length: Barrel on wagon: 41 ft., 2 in.; carriage on wagon: 35 ft., 6 in.

RANGE: Normal: 30,315 yards; 35,653 yards with supercharge.

RATE OF FIRE: Rounds per minute in bursts: 2; in prolonged fire: 1/2.

AMMUNITION: Separate loading HE (US Army or U.S. Navy projectiles). Projectile Weight: 200 to 240 lbs.

CARRIAGE: Type: Split trail with 2 transport wagons. Traverse: 20 degrees R&L. Elevation: +10 degrees to +50 degrees. Fires emplaced only. Min. time to Emplace: 1 to 2 hours: requires mobile crane for excavation and lifting.

NORMAL TOWING SPEED: 25 mph. max.

NOTE: Built on same carriage and recoil as 24mm Howitzer M1.

U.S. Army 240mm Howitzer M1 emplaced.

MODEL: 240mm Howitzer M1

WEIGHT: 64,700 lbs. emplaced; 98,820 lbs with its two transport wagons.

DIMENSIONS: Length: Barrel on wagon: 36 ft., 6 in.; carriage on wagon: 35 ft., 6 in.

RANGE: 25,225 yards max.

RATE OF FIRE: Rounds per minute in bursts: 2; in prolonged fire: 1/2.

AMMUNITION: Separate loading HE, M1 Howitzer series only. Projectile Weight: 360 lbs.

CARRIAGE: Type: Split trail with two transport wagons. Traverse: 22-1/2 degrees R&L Elevation: +15 degrees to +65 degrees. Fires emplaced only. Min. time to emplace: 1 to 2 hours. Requires mobile crane for excavation and lifting.

NORMAL TOWING SPEED: 25 mph. max.

NOTE: Built on same carriage and recoil as 8-in. Gun M1.

Chapter 10
Field Artillery Fire Control and Direction

One reason the U.S. Army's Field Artillery was such a great success was because of its superior fire control and direction system. This system was very flexible and easily expanded to include tank guns and antiaircraft guns when they were being fired as field artillery.

The U.S. Army World War II artillery weapons were excellent, and their accuracy was ensured by their excellent fire control instruments. These are the part of the cannon used to set the point at which the cannon is aimed and give its barrel the necessary elevation for the range to the target. They did this with a high degree of precision.

Artillery weapons set their point of aim — azimuth — with an optical panoramic sight. The elevation angle was set with a clinometer often incorporated into the cannon's panoramic sight mount. All tank and tank destroyer guns had provisions for measuring the azimuth of their turret traverse, and for measuring their gun's angle of elevation so they could fire as field artillery. Antiaircraft guns often had provisions to use regular field artillery aiming instruments, and they could also be set for azimuth and elevation with their antiaircraft fire control and direction system.

Artillery weapons used their fire control instruments to aim for "indirect fire" in which the cannon are unable to directly observe their targets. In World War II, the vast majority of all field artillery fire missions involved indirect fire. To provide the critical firing data for azimuth and elevation of a cannon, the U.S. Army used Fire Direction Centers, also known as FDCs.

The U.S. Army FDC had its origins in World War I, and the system used in World War II was perfected just as the U.S. Army entered the war. It was a unique U.S. Army system, and it employed elements invented and developed by the U.S. Army Field Artillery. The FDC system gave the U.S. Army Field Artillery the most effective and flexible fire control and direction of any army in World War II.

In World War II, the basic U.S. Army Field Artillery unit was the battalion consisting of several batteries of weapons and a headquarters unit which included an FDC. Each FDC used the U.S. Army graphical firing chart and graphical firing table system for making firing data calculations. It had both air and ground firing observers to direct and correct fire. Telephone and radio communications were used to connect the observers to the FDC, and the FDC to the firing batteries.

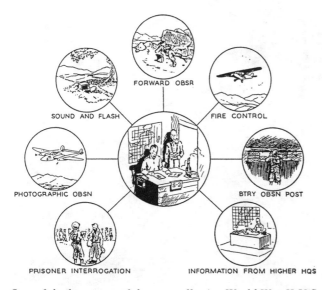

One of the key parts of the very effective World War II U.S. Army field artillery fire was its rapid response to requests for artillery fire. This manual illustration shows the principal sources of target acquisition used, all filtered through a fire control and direction system.

A U.S. Army field artillery forward observer in the Philippines in 1944 using a twenty-power Observation Telescope.

116

In the World War II U.S. Army organization, each combat division had three or more field artillery battalions and a field artillery section in its divisional headquarters. Each corps — two or more divisions — could have additional artillery battalions and had a field artillery section in its headquarters. Each army — two or more corps — could also have additional artillery battalions and had a field artillery section in its headquarters. All these units' FDCs and field artillery sections were linked in a communications network, and this made the U.S. Army field artillery fire the best coordinated and directed of World War II.

The simplified U.S. Army Field Artillery graphical firing chart and graphical firing table system was used to make the gunnery calculations to provide the firing data used to aim cannon. In World War I, field artillery gunnery calculations had to be made by a highly skilled mathematician, and by the end of the war the U.S. Army was having trouble filling their requirements for them. In the 1920s and 1930s, the U.S. Army Field Artillery created the graphical firing chart system for preparing firing data, but it still required skilled mathematicians to prepare the range components of the firing data.

In 1940, a U.S. Army National Guard officer, Capt. Abbot H. Burns, was called to active duty, and as a skilled mathematician he became a Field Artillery officer making gunnery calculations. He hated making complex, repetitive calculations, so, using an element commonly used by civilian mathematicians, in just a couple

A U.S. Army field artillery forward observer in the Philippines in 1944 using a twenty-power Observation Telescope.

of hours he invented a simple device for making them! Capt. Burns' invention was the Graphical Firing Table — GFT — an adaptation of the civilian slide rule hand calculator widely used before electronic calculators were invented. The GFT made the difficult range calculations without the need of either complex mathematical calculations or the cumbersome range table manuals packed with tables of range calculation data.

A U.S. Army Jeep mounted field artillery forward observer section. Note the FM communications radio mounted in the Jeep.

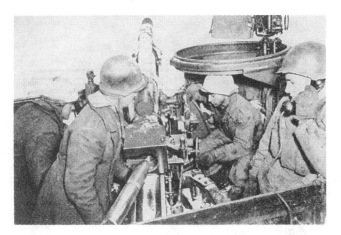

A U.S. Army 105mm Gun Motor Carriage M7 Priest in action in Italy in 1944 with the man on the left receiving firing data via telephone.

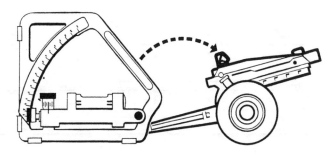

The U.S. Army Field Artillery clinometer used to measure cannon barrel angles of elevation.

The Piper Aircraft U.S. Army L4 Cub or "Grasshopper" used by U.S. Army Field Artillery Air OPs (Air Observation Posts) in World War II. All U.S. Army Field Artillery battalions were provided with two of these aircraft.

The L4 was a military adaptation of the commercial Piper J-3 Cub Tandem Trainer developed in the late 1930s. It was powered by a 65-horsepower engine which ran on the same gasoline as standard U.S. Army motor vehicles. It operational speed was from about 40 to 80 miles per hour with a cruising range of 250 miles and a maximum operational altitude of 10,000 feet.

It was a fabric-covered aircraft with a metal tube fuselage frame and wood wing frames. It was unarmed, but its field artillery fire control and direction observations made it a devastating weapon much feared by the enemy.

The U.S. Army procured about 6,830 L4 aircraft in World War II.

A typical U.S. Army World War II Graphical Firing Table slide rule used in making firing data calculations.

Using GFT range data and azimuth data from the graphical firing chart to prepare firing data was so simple that anybody with good mathematical skills could be taught to use it. It eliminated the U.S. Army Field Artillery's huge requirement for skilled mathematicians. It also made firing data calculations twenty times faster than the old system, and considerably more accurate.

Special GFTs were designed for each cannon-ammunition system and were in general use in the U.S. Army field Artillery by 1942. Their inventor, Capt. Burns, "made" general by the end of World War II.

The use of observers to correct and direct field artillery fire was another World War I practice. In the U.S. Army Field Artillery, the ground observers were in the front lines, and they were called "forward observers." In World War II they were linked to their FDCs by either telephone or radio communications. They directed and corrected field artillery fire, and, when the situation required, requested fire at "targets of opportunity" they observed. This was a very efficient and effective system, but in World War II the U.S. Army Field Artillery complemented it with another observer system which was, if anything, better. In 1942, the U.S. Army Field Artillery adopted the Air Observation Post, Air 0P, which used observers in light aircraft. This light aircraft, the "lightplane," had been perfected in the United States in the 1930s, and by 1939 it was being built and flown in large numbers.

Beginning in 1939, the U.S. Army began testing lightplanes as a replacement for U.S. Army Air Corps observation aircraft, which were too big, clumsy and expensive to perform many missions, including aerial observation for the Field Artillery. Regular Field Artillery ground forward observers went up in lightplanes with a radio for communications with the ground, and their reports were found to be more useful and accurate than those of regular ground forward observers.

One man in the crew of every U.S. Army Field Artillery in World War II was, like this one, detailed to receive firing data via telephone or radio.

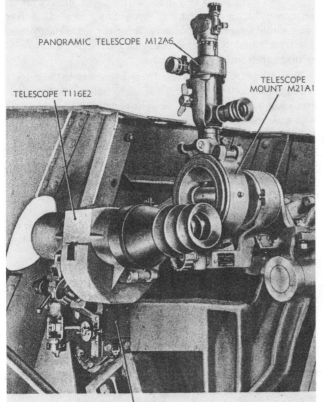

PANORAMIC TELESCOPE M12A6

TELESCOPE T116E2

TELESCOPE MOUNT M21A1

TELESCOPE MOUNT T89

This combination of a direct fire telescopic sight and an indirect fire panoramic telescope sight was typical of what was used on U.S. Army antitank guns and antiaircraft guns with dual purpose antitank and field artillery fire capabilities.

In late 1941, the U.S. Army Field Artillery began using a military version of the Piper Cub lightplane, designated the L4 liaison aircraft, to fly its air observers. The L4 Piper Cubs soon earned the nickname "Grasshoppers" because that's just what the little olive drab planes looked like bouncing on and off primitive forward area airstrips. In early 1942, the U.S. Army added an Air 0P section, with two L4 Grasshoppers, to the organization of each field artillery battalion FDC.

U.S. Army Field Artillery Air 0P sections with L4 Grasshoppers were first used in combat in North Africa in the November 1942 landings. Although the U.S. Army Air Force had predicted the tiny, low performance Grasshoppers would only fly "suicide missions" in combat areas, the Air 0P casualty rate proved to be lower than the forward observers'. In fact, the Grasshopper Air 0Ps proved extremely able to perform their mission, and they were an integral part of the U.S. Army Field Artillery for the rest of World War II.

From the first, the enemy recognized the danger which was imminent when an Air 0P Grasshopper appeared. Because anything that moved could be fired at very quickly, the enemy not only hid from Grasshoppers, but they were reluctant to shoot at them. The unarmed Grasshoppers frightened them more than many high-performance military aircraft.

The Air 0P Grasshoppers remained an integral part of the U.S. Army Field Artillery long after World War II. A key element of their outstanding success was the radio communications system the U.S. Army used in World War II.

In the late 1930s, FM commercial radio broadcasting began for the first time any place in the world. FM radio had the advantages of being free of most of the static and other interference of the older AM radio system. Through the World War II era, the United States was the only country in the world with an electronics industry large enough to produce FM radio equipment in vast quantities for military use.

The U.S. Army Signal Corps began development of military FM radio equipment in 1939. By 1942, FM radio communications equipment had been adopted by the U.S. Army and was in mass production. There were versions with special frequencies for use by the Field Artillery, Armored Force and Infantry. FM radio equipment was used by all U.S. Army Field Artillery battalion FDCs in World War II, and practically all U.S. Army tanks and other armored fighting vehicles were equipped with it. The FM radio was an essential part of the Field Artillery Air 0P to provide the communications link between the Grasshopper and its FDC.

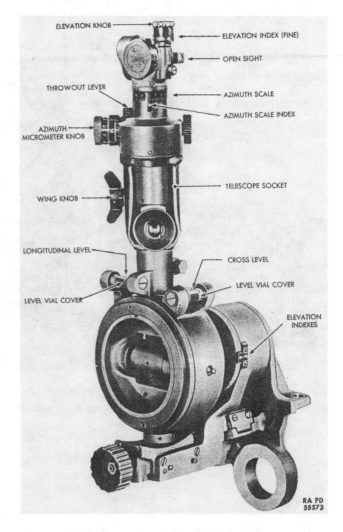

ELEVATION KNOB

ELEVATION INDEX (FINE)

OPEN SIGHT

THROWOUT LEVER

AZIMUTH SCALE

AZIMUTH SCALE INDEX

AZIMUTH MICROMETER KNOB

TELESCOPE SOCKET

WING KNOB

LONGITUDINAL LEVEL

CROSS LEVEL

LEVEL VIAL COVER

LEVEL VIAL COVER

ELEVATION INDEXES

RA PD 55573

A typical U.S. Army panoramic telescopic sight on a mount with elevation correction provisions as used on U.S. Army World War II field artillery weapons.

The U.S. Army was the only one to use FM radio in World War II, except for the British and French armies, to which it lent a few. This had a secondary advantage: The enemy did not have sets to intercept or transmit FM unless they had captured them.

While smaller artillery units, such as antitank batteries, infantry regimental cannon companies and pack artillery batteries, could be hooked into an FDC system, they did not need to. They all had integral fire control and direction detachment including forward observers.

Using the FDCs, headquarters field artillery sections, and their communications network allowed some very special World War II U.S. Army artillery tactics. One of the most effective was the Time-on-Target — TOT — fire mission. In this mission, a large number of field artillery batteries fired at an area target with their fire timed so it all simultaneously arrived at the target. The effect of TOT fire was devastating on such targets as tank concentrations, infantry assembly areas and artillery positions.

Another tactic was a very quick response with artillery fire on any enemy "target of opportunity" spotted by a forward observer or an Air 0P Grasshopper observer. This tactic made enemy tank, infantry and artillery movement difficult, and could be used to neutralize targets such as antitank guns.

While the FDC system worked very effectively on the indirect fire targets it was intended for, it was not suitable for direct fire targets when the gunners could see their targets. This was the case with tank and antitank guns, so these all had optical telescopic sights for aiming at targets they could see. Direct fire telescopic sights were also applied to many forward area antiaircraft guns so they could fire as antitank guns, making them triple purpose weapons: antiaircraft, antitank and field artillery weapons.

The U.S. Army Field Artillery fire control and direction system based on the FDC was the best used in World War II. Even though it was used long after World War II, it was improved soon after the war ended.

The array of sighting equipment on the U.S. Army 8-in. Howitzer Motor Carriage M43 built in late World War II. It has both telescopic sights for direct fire and a panoramic telescope for indirect fire.

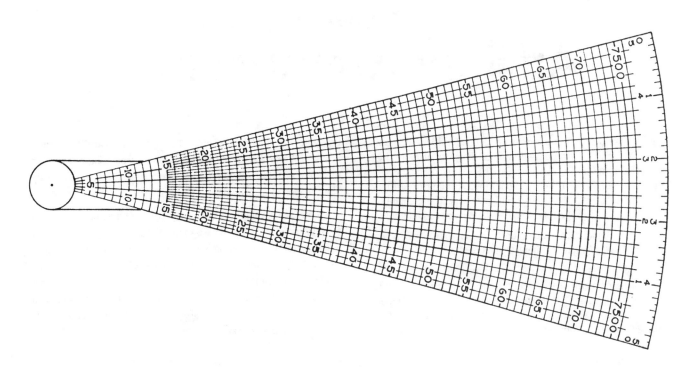

The U.S. Army Field Artillery Deflection Fan used in making graphical fire control data calculation on a map or similar target plot.

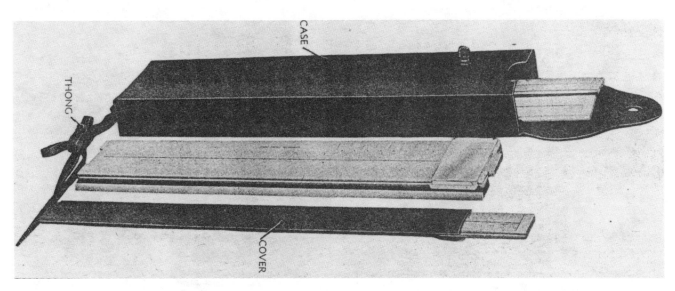

A World War II U.S. Army Graphical Firing Table slide rule with its carrying case and extra slides for several types of ammunition in the caliber with which it is used.

Chapter 11
Artillery Ammunition

During World War II, the U.S. Army defined artillery ammunition as any fired in a weapon with a bore diameter of more than .60-in. (15.2mm). During the war, the U.S. Army procured over 900 million rounds of artillery ammunition. A round of artillery ammunition comprises the components necessary to fire a cannon once: a projectile, a propelling charge and the primer to ignite it.

Complete rounds of ammunition came in four basic types: fixed, semifixed, separate loading and separated.

Fixed ammunition is that in which the projectile, propellant and primer are permanently assembled in a metallic cartridge case as they are in rifle and pistol ammunition. When the projectile requires a point fuse to detonate it, it will come with the fuse assembled to do it, however, the fuse may be removed and replaced with another if required. U.S. Army fixed artillery ammunition in World War II was fired in weapons from 37mm caliber up to 105mm caliber, the latter being the heaviest that can be easily hand-loaded into a cannon.

Semifixed ammunition has a projectile that may be removed from its metallic cartridge case so that the propelling charge can be adjusted for various firing ranges. Like fixed ammunition, it is loaded into the cannon in one piece. In World War II, U.S. Army 75mm and 105mm howitzers were the only artillery weapons that fired semifixed ammunition; however, mortar ammunition that did not use a cartridge case was also considered semifixed since its propellant charge was also adjustable.

The U.S. Army field artillerymen on the left are preparing ammunition for the gunners on the right to load and fire in a U.S. Army 105mm Howitzer M2 in Germany in 1945.

U.S. Army tankers loading 75mm gun ammunition into their Medium Tank M3 in North Africa in early 1943.

U.S. Army Chemical Warfare Service mortarmen with the ammunition for their U.S. Army 4.2-in. Chemical Mortar in northern Europe in 1944.

Separate loading ammunition consists of a separate projectile, a separate propellant charge packaged in "powder bags" and delivered in airtight containers, and a separate primer. The projectile's fuse is usually shipped separately and is installed in the projectile when it is being prepared to fire. The primer is a special blank cartridge. In most separate loading ammunition, the propellant charge is made up in several parts so it can be adjusted for range. In World War II, separate loading ammunition was fired in all guns of 4.5-in. caliber and larger, and in all howitzers of 155mm caliber and larger.

Separated ammunition has the propelling charge loaded in a sealed metallic cartridge case, which also has its primer; the projectile is separately provided. The only U.S. Army World War II artillery weapon using separated loading ammunition was the 120mm antiaircraft gun.

Obviously, the projectile fired will determine the effect artillery fire will have on a target. During World War II, the U.S. Army had available and/or developed a large number of sizes and types of artillery projectiles, however, only a small number of these were used in appreciable quantities.

During World War II, the U.S. Army fired much more high-explosive shell (HE) projectiles than any other type. HE was fired in all field artillery guns and howitzers, tank guns, antiaircraft guns and mortars. HE was suitable for practically any target from enemy personnel and materiel on the ground to enemy aircraft when fired from antiaircraft guns.

The importance of HE in the U.S. Army is shown in the amount issued based on the standard "units of fire" tables, which indicate the percentage of ammunition issued to all artillery weapons. The ubiquitous U.S. Army 105mm howitzer's normal issue of HE was 75% to 80%, and the equally important 155mm howitzer fired 80% or more HE. A 155mm gun normally fired 90% or more HE, while the 8-in. howitzer, 8-in. gun and 240mm howitzer fired practically nothing but HE. Tank and antitank guns fire anywhere from 25% to 50% HE, and antiaircraft guns only fire HE at hostile aircraft. The manufacture of HE shells was one of the largest U.S. Army Ordnance Department projects of World War II.

A variation of the HE shell the U.S. Army used in World War II was the high explosive antitank (HEAT) type. These utilized a shaped charge for antitank effect, and they also had the same effect of a regular HE shell. The HEAT projectile was only used in the 75mm, 105mm and 155mm howitzers to blow holes in tanks, pill boxes and similar hard targets. Although there was a lot of U.S. Army publicity given the HEAT shell during World War II, it was mostly propaganda since in combat it proved to be less effective than regular HE for most uses. Although as much as 5% HEAT was offered to howitzer batteries, many did not fire it.

While the U.S. Army used NO toxic chemical ammunition of any type in World War II, chemical smoke artillery ammunition was extensively and effectively used. Three basic type of smoke shells were used: FM, HC and WP.

FM smoke shell was filled with liquid titanium tetrachloride, a chemical that produces dense clouds of smoke when exposed to the air. FM smoke shell was developed for use in artillery fired smoke screen barrages, and it was also used in World War II when single rounds were fired to designate targets. Because of its limited use, few batteries carried more than a few rounds of FM smoke.

U.S. Army field artillerymen cleaning projectiles so they can be fired in their U.S. Army 155mm Gun M1. The photo was taken in the Philippines in 1944, and they are ankle deep in rain water.

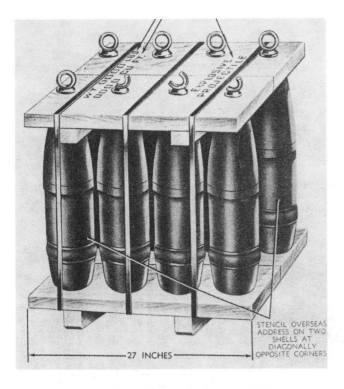

For shipping, the U.S. Army palletized separate and separated loading artillery projectiles in this manner.

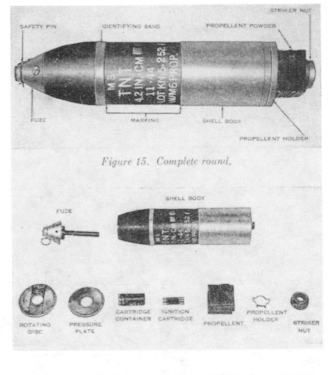

Figure 15. Complete round.

This U.S. Army 4.2-in chemical mortar high explosive (HE) semifixed round.

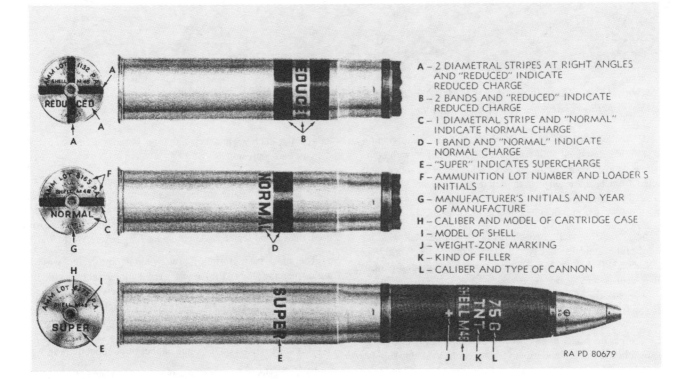

A – 2 DIAMETRAL STRIPES AT RIGHT ANGLES AND "REDUCED" INDICATE REDUCED CHARGE
B – 2 BANDS AND "REDUCED" INDICATE REDUCED CHARGE
C – 1 DIAMETRAL STRIPE AND "NORMAL" INDICATE NORMAL CHARGE
D – 1 BAND AND "NORMAL" INDICATE NORMAL CHARGE
E – "SUPER" INDICATES SUPERCHARGE
F – AMMUNITION LOT NUMBER AND LOADER'S INITIALS
G – MANUFACTURER'S INITIALS AND YEAR OF MANUFACTURE
H – CALIBER AND MODEL OF CARTRIDGE CASE
I – MODEL OF SHELL
J – WEIGHT-ZONE MARKING
K – KIND OF FILLER
L – CALIBER AND TYPE OF CANNON

RA PD 80679

Three types of fixed ammunition were used in U.S. Army 75mm guns. They are, top to bottom: reduced or low velocity, normal or standard velocity, and super or high velocity. In combat, only normal and super types were used.

U.S. Army 155mm Gun Motor Carriages M12 in action in Germany in 1944. The artilleryman in the right foreground is carrying the propelling charge for one of these 155mm gun's separate loading ammunition.

HC smoke shell was a type developed for target designation use, and that was about all it was used for. It was filled with combustible smoke composition pellets, which were ignited and ejected from its base when it impacted on its target. Since HC smoke shell had a limited use, batteries carried few rounds, however, it was very useful in aiding field artillery observers.

The U.S. Army white phosphorus (WP) smoke shell was the most useful chemical smoke type the U.S. Army had in World War II. When a WP shell detonates on its target, its white phosphorus filling shatters and ignites on exposure to the air, producing not only a great deal of smoke, but a number of burning fragments. Burning fragments of white phosphorus are a very effective incendiary. In World War II, the United States was the only country with the resources necessary to produce WP ammunition in large quantities. Although the demand usually exceeded the available supply, as much as 5% to 10% WP was sometimes issued to artillery batteries armed with guns and howitzers up to and including 155mm caliber. Throughout World War II, U.S. Army intelligence sources reported that incoming WP shell, usually mixed in with HE shell,

caused the enemy great consternation because it inflicted both damage and confusion.

Armor-piercing projectiles were used often in tank and antitank guns, and occasionally in heavy and super heavy field artillery when it was fired at enemy fortifications. Most of the armor-piercing projectiles were developed from basic designs developed for use by naval and sea coast defense guns long before World War II.

The most basic form of armor-piercing projectile was the armor-piercing shot (AP). AP was a solid alloy steel projectile that punched a hole the size of its diameter in targets and then demolished everything in its path as it went through the target. U.S. Army tank and antitank AP was usually fitted with a tracer element to assist in aim correction. AP was supplied for U.S. Army World War II guns from 37mm to 90mm caliber throughout the war.

A more effective form of armor-piercing projectile often used by the U.S. Army in World War II was the capped armor-piercing shot (APC). The APC was an armor-piercing shot tipped with a soft steel element, to improve its armor penetration, and a ballistic "windshield" to improve its ballistic qualities. APC was fired in tank and antitank guns from 37mm to 90mm calibers, and it was usually equipped with a tracer element for aim correction.

Many types of AP and APC projectile had cavities in their bases to reduce their weights to the weights required, and these cavities could be filled with high explosive detonated by a base fuse. In World War II, the Army used this type of AP shell in limited quantities for tank and antitank guns of 75mm, 76mm and 90mm caliber, and it was usually fitted with a tracer element for aim correction. Base fused AP shell was also used in 155mm and 8-in. guns to fire at enemy fortifications, and for this use the tracer element was not employed.

The third type of armor-piercing projectile used by the U.S. Army in World War II was the high-velocity armor piercing shot (HVAP), pronounced "hi-vap," developed in 1942-1943. This lightweight projectile consisted of a high-density tungsten alloy shot in an aluminum alloy jacket, and it was fired at velocities well over 3,000 fps. Although HVAP was developed for guns from 37mm to 155mm caliber, it was only manufactured for use in 76mm tank guns and 3-in. and 90mm tank and antitank guns.

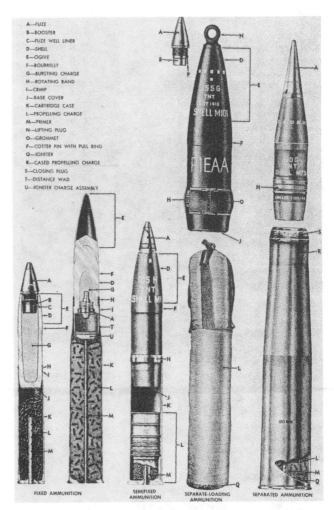

A—FUZE
B—BOOSTER
C—FUZE WELL LINER
D—SHELL
E—OGIVE
F—BOURRELET
G—BURSTING CHARGE
H—ROTATING BAND
I—CRIMP
J—BASE COVER
K—CARTRIDGE CASE
L—PROPELLING CHARGE
M—PRIMER
N—LIFTING PLUG
O—GROMMET
P—COTTER PIN WITH PULL RING
Q—IGNITER
R—CASED PROPELLING CHARGE
S—CLOSING PLUG
T—DISTANCE WAD
U—IGNITER CHARGE ASSEMBLY

FIXED AMMUNITION   SEMIFIXED AMMUNITION   SEPARATE-LOADING AMMUNITION   SEPARATED AMMUNITION

Complete rounds of U.S. Army World War II artillery ammunition, left to right: 75mm gun fixed high-explosive shell, 90mm gun fixed capped armor-piercing shell, 105mm M2 series howitzer semi-fixed high-explosive shell, 155mm M1 series gun separate loading high-explosive shell and 4.5-in gun separate loading high-explosive shell.

Typical U.S. Army World War II artillery ammunition packaging. On the far left is the fiber type; on the far right is the much less used metal "tank" type. The example shown is 105mm M2 series howitzer ammunition.

HVAP ammunition had to be carefully conserved and only fired at appropriate targets, such as heavily armored enemy tanks, because it was always in short supply. The shortages were caused by the limited amount of tungsten available for making the cores, as well as the difficulty of manufacturing the projectile. In combat, HVAP could, would and did punch devastating holes in the best enemy armor it was fired at.

According to the ammunition allotment tables used by the U.S. Army in World War II, tanks usually carried as much as 50% armor-piercing ammunition of whatever type or types were available. The rest of their ammunition was mostly HE with a few FM smoke and cannister rounds in case they needed them. Antitank guns were issued as much as 75% armor-piercing ammunition, and the rest of their supply was HE for fire at appropriate targets. Anti-aircraft guns in combat zone forward areas usually carried 5% to 10% armor-piercing ammunition so they could fire as antitank guns when and if necessary.

A stack of 155mm howitzer projectiles in a U.S. Army field ammunition dump in Italy during the winter of 1943-1944.

This U.S. Army World War II CP (Concrete Piercing) point fuse for artillery projectiles allowed them to penetrate "hard" targets before detonating. Invented in World War II, the fuse's body was made of hard, tough steel alloy.

U.S. Army Aberdeen Proving Grounds test crew preparing to fire an acceptance test of long-range projectiles in a U.S. Army 8-in. Gun M1 in late 1944.

When World War II began, the shrapnel projectile was a standard type still available in large quantity for use in such artillery weapons as 75mm guns, 3-in. antiaircraft guns and 155mm howitzers. A shrapnel projectile is a type of shell filled with steel balls in a matrix with a charge to project them out in its base and a point time fuse to detonate it at the desired point in its trajectory. Improved high-explosive shells with time fuses made shrapnel

The type of metallic container or "tank" used for U.S. Army World War II separate loading artillery ammunition propellant. This was little used in World War II. This example is for the 155mm M1 series howitzer.

In World War II, the U.S. Army revived the old-time cannister artillery projectile it had not used since black powder cannon days. The cannister projectile is a lightweight metal case or can filled with 1/2-in. to 1-in. steel balls packed in wood flour or some similar soft matrix so they will not rattle. When a cannister is fired, it converts the cannon into a giant shotgun, and the scattering steel balls can have a devastating effect on targets ranging from charging enemy soldiers to houses or other light structures. In World War II, the U.S. Army provided cannister ammunition for guns from 37mm to 90mm caliber, but its use was always very limited because of the limited targets on which it could be used. One frightening use of the cannister projectile was when enemy troops would swarm on a friendly tank, and another friendly tank would fire a round of cannister to "dust them off."

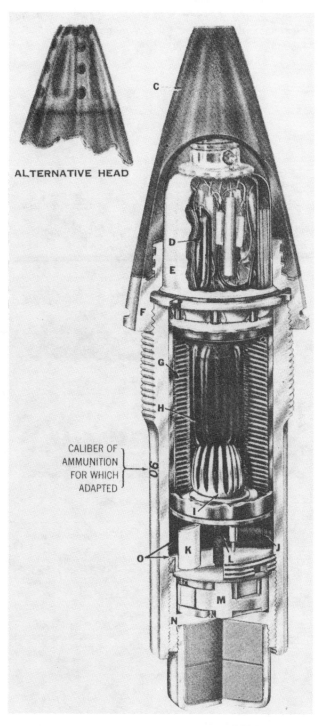

This U.S. Army VT (Variable Time) or "proximity" radar-actuated fuse for artillery ammunition was one of the most important and effective World War II inventions.

The U.S. Army World War II HVAP (High Velocity Armor Piercing) projectile. These were made for 76mm, 3-in. and 90mm guns only, and were effective against any World War II era tank.

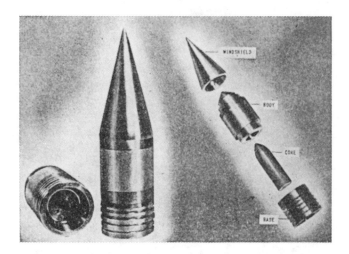

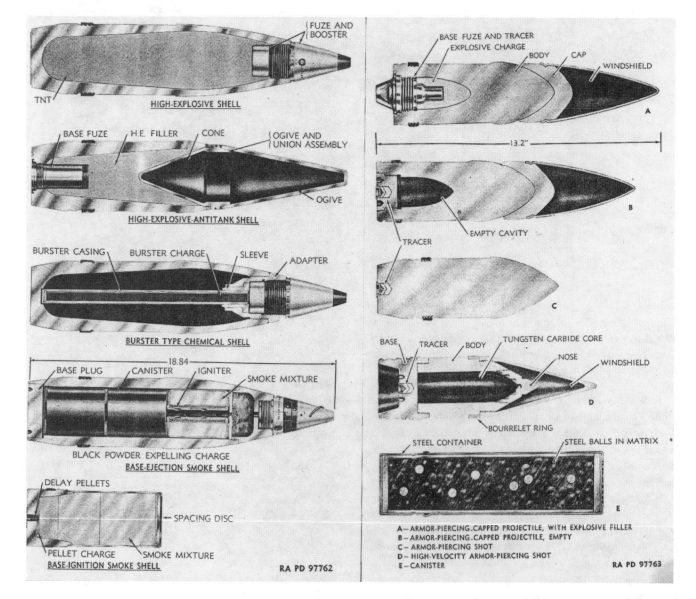

Typical U.S. Army World War II artillery projectiles.

obsolete by World War II, and the only combat use it saw in the war was in antiaircraft guns in the war's opening months. Since shrapnel time fuses could also function on impact, the U.S. Army expended its stock of shrapnel in World War II as training ammunition.

The fuse of an exploding artillery projectile is the element which causes the projectile to detonate where, when and under the circumstances desired. It is a critical element of the shell's effect, and U.S. Army World War II fuses were excellent. The fuse most used on U.S. Army World War II artillery shells was the "point fuse," which screws into the nose of the projectile. These function in a number of ways, they come in a number of types, and some combine more than one way of functioning and are set to the desired function.

One fuse type was the time fuse, which was set for time-of-flight so it detonated the projectile before it reached the target. The two timing mechanisms used in them were a powder train "fuse" and a mechanical clockwork. All time fuses had a feature that would detonate the shell when and if it struck a target. Another point fuse type was the impact fuse, and these came in several sub-types. One sub-type, which would detonate the shell the instant it hit the target, was called the "superquick" fuse. A second type, called the "nondelay," would detonate as it penetrated the target. A third type, called the "delay," would detonate the shell a small fraction of a second after it hit the target so it would detonate the shell inside the target. The most-used U.S. Army World War II impact fuse was a combination type, which could be set to either function as a superquick or as a delay.

The "concrete piercing" (CP) fuse was an important variation of the point impact fuse used by the U.S. Army in World War II. It was made with an alloy steel body, which would not crush on impact with a hard target such as a concrete fortification, and it was a delay type so it would explode after penetrating its target.

The "variable time" or "proximity" point fuse was an entirely new type invented in the United States during World War II and only used by U.S. Forces in the war. This "VT" fuse used a miniature radar set to detonate the shell as it approached its target or as it passed close to it. The VT fuse was used for antiaircraft fire and to

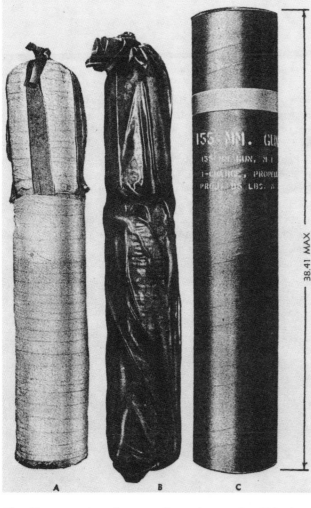

The fiber container for propellant charges for U.S. Army World War II artillery ammunition. This is for the 155mm gun M1 series. "A" is the actual propellant charge, "B" is the waterproof plastic sack, and "C" is the fiber container.

Typical primers used with World War II U.S. Army separate loading artillery ammunition. The primers used in fixed and semifixed rounds are similar to the three at the top of this illustration.

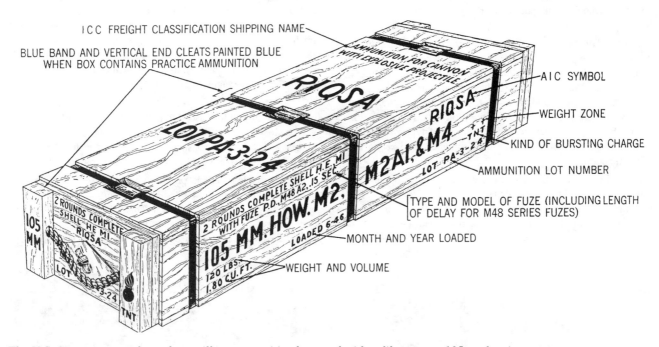

ICC FREIGHT CLASSIFICATION SHIPPING NAME

BLUE BAND AND VERTICAL END CLEATS PAINTED BLUE
WHEN BOX CONTAINS PRACTICE AMMUNITION

AMMUNITION FOR CANNON
WITH EXPLOSIVE PROJECTILE

RIQSA

LOT PA-3-24

AIC SYMBOL

WEIGHT ZONE

KIND OF BURSTING CHARGE

AMMUNITION LOT NUMBER

TYPE AND MODEL OF FUZE (INCLUDING LENGTH
OF DELAY FOR M48 SERIES FUZES)

MONTH AND YEAR LOADED

WEIGHT AND VOLUME

RIQSA
M2AI, & M4
TNT
LOT PA-3-24

2 ROUNDS COMPLETE SHELL H.E. MI
WITH FUZE P.D., M48 A2, .15 SEC.
105 MM. HOW. M2,
LOADED 6-46
120 LBS.
1.80 CU. FT.

105
MM

2 ROUNDS COMPLETE
SHELL H E MI
RIQSA
LOT
3-24
TNT

The U.S. Army two-round wooden artillery ammunition box used with calibers up to 105mm howitzers.

detonate shells above ground targets. It proved very effective for both these uses.

The VT fuse was introduced in late 1943 for antiaircraft use, and those used for this purpose incorporated an impact element to detonate the shell when it hit a target and a time element so they would not fall back to the ground and detonate if they totally missed any target. Those VT fuses fired at ground targets incorporated an impact element that would detonate the shell in the event the radar element did not function properly.

Base fuses were used by the U.S. Army in World War II tank and antitank explosive projectiles as mentioned above. These came in both non-delay and delay types, and many of them had a tracer element for aim correction. Base fuses were also used in heavy and super heavy field artillery shells; these were usually of the delay type since target penetration was desirable, and they did not have tracer elements.

Post-World War II studies of U.S. Army artillery ammunition show it was not only the most effective of the war, but also the safest. Serious accidents caused by either the propellant detonating or the projectile detonating in or near the cannon were very unusual due to the care in both loading and firing it. In addition, all the fuses the U.S. Army used in World War II incorporated "bore safe" elements, which prevented them from functioning while the projectile was in the cannon barrel or to close to the gun.

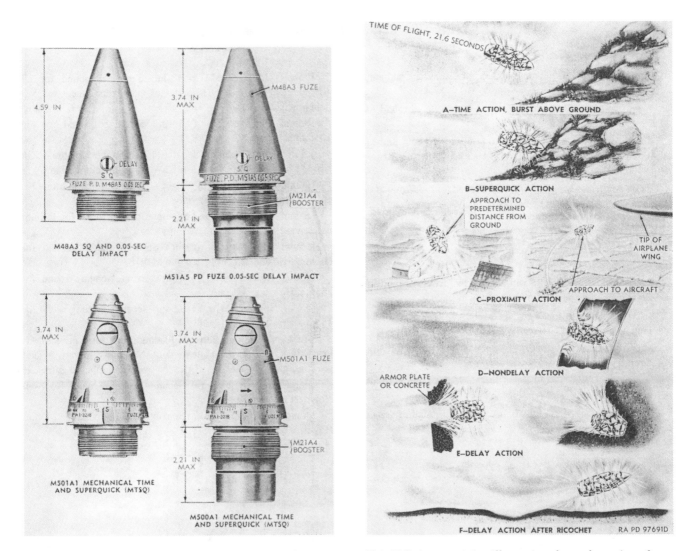

Typical World War II U.S. Army artillery projectile point fuses.

This U.S. Army training illustration shows the action of various types of artillery projectile fuses.

U.S. Army World War II Artillery Ammunition

37mm Gun: (1.46-in.) Fixed round for all 37mm tank and anti-tank guns.

37mm Automatic Antiaircraft Gun. (1.46-in.) Fixed round for all 37mm automatic antiaircraft guns.

40mm Automatic Antiaircraft Gun. (1.57-in.) Fixed round for all 40mm automatic antiaircraft guns. Also known by the British name 40mm Bofors gun.

57mm Antitank Gun. (2.24-in.) Fixed round for the 57mm anti-tank gun only. Also known by the British name 6-pounder antitank gun.

75mm Gun. (2.95-in.) For all 75mm field, tank and self-propelled guns. Also known as French 75mm M1897 gun ammunition.

75mm Pack Howitzer. (2.95-in.) Semifixed or fixed round for all 75mm pack, field and self-propelled howitzers.

3-in. Gun. (76mm) Fixed round for all 3-in. antiaircraft, tank and field guns.

3-in. Antiaircraft Gun M1918. (76mm) Fixed round for 3-in. Antiaircraft gun M1918 only.

76mm Gun. (3-in.) Fixed round for all 76mm tank and tank destroyer guns.

4.2-in. Chemical Mortar. (107mm) Semifixed round of 4.2-in. chemical mortar only.

105mm Howitzer M2. (4.13-in.) Semifixed round for all 105mm field, self-propelled and tank howitzers except the M3 field howitzer.

105mm Howitzer M3. (4.13-in.) Semifixed round for the 105mm Howitzer M3 only.

4.5-in. Gun. (114.5mm) Separate loading round for the 4.5-in gun M1 only. Also known as British 4.5-in. gun ammunition.

120mm Antiaircraft Gun. (4.7-in.) Separated loading round for 120mm Antiaircraft Gun M1 only.

155mm Gun M1. (6.1-in.) Separate loading round for 155mm field and self-propelled gun M1 only.

155mm Gun M1918. (6.1-in.) Separate loading round for 155mm field and self-propelled gun M1918 only.

155mm Howitzer M1. (6.1-in.) Separate loading round for 155mm Howitzer M1 only.

155mm Howitzer M1918. (6.1-in.) Separate loading round for 155mm Howitzer M1918 only.

8-in. Gun. (203mm) Separate loading round for 8-in. gun M1. Projectile same as fired in late model U.S. Army 8-in. railway and sea coast guns and late model U.S. Navy 8-in. shipboard guns.

8-in. Howitzer. (203mm.) Separate loading round for 8-in. Howitzer M1 only.

240mm Howitzer. (9.45-in.) Separate loading round for 240mm Howitzer M1 only.

Chapter 12
Modernized World War I Artillery

World War I U.S. Army 75mm Guns M1897, French 75s, in a horse-drawn field artillery exercise in the mid-1930s. The U.S. Army Field Artillery motorized its last horse-drawn field artillery batteries in 1943.

Like every other combatant in World War I, the U.S. Army had used an assortment of modern, obsolescent and obsolete artillery weapons. Unlike other armies, the U.S. Army retired the obsolete artillery weapons immediately after the war, and got rid of the obsolescent and impractical by the early 1930s. The artillery weapons the U.S. Army used in the 1930s were the best it had in World War I, and several of them were used in World War II in different ways.

During World War I, the U.S. Army had an American-built version of the standard British light field gun, their eighteen-pounder, known as the 75mm Gun M1917. About 1,000 of these weapons, which fired the standard U.S. Army French 75mm gun ammunition, were built, but none were ever used in combat in World War I.

In the 1930s, a kit was developed to modernize them by replacing their wooden wheels with pneumatic rubber-tired steel wheels. A number of these modernized 75mm Gun M1917 (British) were issued to train the Philippine Army in the late 1930s, and these were used in the defense of the Philippines in 1941-1942. The rest were given to the British, Canadian, Australian and other British Empire forces under Lend-Lease, and a few batteries of them saw action in North Africa and other places early in the war.

A U.S. Army 75mm Gun M1897A2 (High Speed) with a modified Ford commercial truck prime mover in the late 1930s. The last of these guns were not withdrawn from training service until early 1943, and none were used in combat in World War II.

U.S. Army field artillerymen training with a U.S. Army 240mm Howitzer M1918 in 1941. This howitzer was only used as a training weapon in World War II.

A U.S. Army 75mm Gun M1897A2 (High Speed), French 75, showing how the carriage was modified for truck draft in the mid-1930s. A second axle for the new pneumatic rubber-tired wheels with new brakes was installed under the axle housing for the original wooden wheels. Note the unique rotary breech mechanism of the gun.

U.S. Army field artillerymen familiarizing themselves with a modernized 75mm Gun M2 series, French 75, about 1938. Only the gun barrel, breech and recoil mechanism come from the original French 75, and they are considerably modified.

The U.S. Army also had designed and built several hundred 75mm Guns M1916 during World War I, and had developed a kit to modernize them by replacing their wooden wheels with pneumatic rubber-tired steel wheels. These guns never saw action in World War I and were only used as training weapons in 1939-1942. During World War I, the U.S. Army had built some 225 British 8-in. Vickers Howitzers to the U.S. Army's requirements for an 8-in. howitzer. Although a handful of them had gotten into action before the end of World War I, they were replaced by the 8-in. Howitzer M1 in 1928. The remaining stock were given to the British under Lend-Lease in 1940-1941.

At nearly the end of World War I, the U.S. Army adopted the French-designed 240mm Schneider M1918. Some fifty of these were built, mostly in the months just after World War I ended. While the 240mm Schneider was a very modern piece of mobile

A U.S. Army 75mm Gun M2 series, a modernized French 75, on maneuvers in late 1941 with an M2 armored half-track prime mover crossing a pontoon bridge. While the M2 series French 75 was very much used as a training weapon into 1943 very few of them saw combat in World War II.

artillery in 1918, it was obsolescent by 1938. While it was used to train men operating super heavy artillery, and a few were modernized with pneumatic rubber-tired wheels, none were used in combat in World War II.

The most used and successful World War I U.S. Army artillery weapon was the French-designed 75mm Field Gun Model of 1897, the legendary French 75. This remained the standard U.S. Army Field Artillery light gun until horse-drawn artillery was retired in 1943. The U.S. Army procured over 2,000 of these in 1917-1919. About 1930, the U.S. Army began modernizing some French 75s by replacing their wooden wheels with pneumatic rubber-tired steel wheels. Although this modernized French 75 was used to train artillerymen until 1942, it was never used in combat in World War II.

In the mid-1930s, the U.S. Army began extensively modernizing the French 75 by rebuilding them with a new carriage and an extensively rebuilt gun and recoil system. The new carriage was a split trail type with pneumatic rubber-tired steel wheels; building it and rebuilding the gun and recoil system was both easier and less expensive than building new guns would have been. The several variations of this modernized French 75 were collectively known as the 75mm Gun M2.

A few batteries of the modernized French 75 M2s were used in the defense of the Philippines in 1941-1942, but their chief use in World War II was as either a training gun or as a self-propelled field gun. The self-propelled version was the 75mm gun Motor Carriage M3 built on the U.S. Army's armored half-track, which saw combat service until the end of World War II. At the end of the war, all versions of the French 75 were declared obsolete and retired.

A modernized World War I U.S. Army 155mm Howitzer M1918A3 in action in North Africa in late 1942. The U.S. Army Field Artillery used this howitzer in North Africa, Sicily, Italy and the Pacific Theater of Operations throughout World War II, and a number were given to the Free French Army under Lend-Lease.

A modernized U.S. Army 75mm Gun M1917A1, the British 75, in use in the Philippines in 1941. The vast majority of the U.S. Army's stock of these guns was given to the British under Lend-Lease.

A World War I U.S. Army 155mm Gun M1918A1, the 155mm French GPF, in use as a coast defense gun by the U.S. Army Coast Artillery in Hawaii in late 1941. None of these 155mm GPF guns were used in combat until after they had been modernized.

At the end of World War I, the U.S. Army had some 2,900 French-designed 155mm Schneider Howitzers of both French and American manufacture. This was a proven weapon, and one of the best medium field howitzers of World War I.

In the 1930s, the U.S. Army began modernizing the 155mm Schneider Howitzers by replacing their wooden artillery wheels with pneumatic rubber-tired steel wheels and converting the French-built version to U.S. Army standards. Although the French-built howitzers were officially M1917s and the American-built were M1918s, the World War II U.S. Army referred to them as 155mm Howitzers M1918.

The modernized 155mm M1918 howitzer was an excellent weapon, and standard in the U.S. Army when World War II began. Practically all those on hand were modernized by 1942, and this made it possible for the U.S. Army to delay production of its replacement, the 155mm Howitzer M1, in favor of more urgent projects. Once the new 155mm Howitzer M1 was introduced, it and the 155mm Howitzer M1918 were co-standard until 1945.

The 155mm M1918 howitzer saw very heavy use in North Africa, Sicily, Italy and throughout the Pacific Theater, and it was considered accurate and effective. However, by the end of World War II, the elderly World War I howitzers were practically worn out. The 155mm Howitzers were declared obsolete in 1945, and retired.

Another French-designed artillery piece that served very effectively in World Wax II was the 155mm GPF, Grande Puissance Filloux or High Power Filloux, gun. The U.S. Army procured some 975 of these guns with the French-built version as the M1917 and the American-built version the M1918. The French-built guns were converted to U.S. Army standards in the 1920s, and they all became the U.S. Army 155mm GPF Gun M1918A1. A number of these were use to train heavy field artillerymen until about 1942, and a number were also used to supplement U.S. Army coastal defenses until about 1944.

In the late 1930s, the U.S. Army modernized a number of 155mm GPF guns M1918A1 by replacing their old hard rubber-tired cast steel whells with pneumatic rubber-tired steel wheels, and this model was known to the World War II U.S. Army as the 155mm Gun M3. This version was first used by the U.S. Army in the Pacific Theater of War when a battery of them was sent to support the U.S. Marine Corps operations on Guadalcanal in late 1942. The 155mm Gun M3 saw service in the Pacific Theater for the rest of the war.

Part of the U.S. Army's stock of World War I British 8-in. Vickers Howitzers in storage at Aberdeen Proving Grounds in 1920. These British-designed and American- and British-built howitzers were not used by the U.S. Army in World War II, so the available stocks of them were given to the British under Lend-Lease in 1941.

A modernized U.S. Army 75mm Gun M1917A1, the British 75, under test at Aberdeen Proving Grounds in 1936. This gun was the British World War I eighteen-pounder field gun converted to fire U.S. Army French 75 ammunition and manufactured in the United States in World War I.

A U.S. Army 155mm Gun M3, a modernized World War I French 155mm GPF Gun, in action supporting the U.S. Marine Corps on Guadalcanal in late 1942 and manned by U.S. Army artillerymen. The M3 155mm gun was used in the Pacific Theater of Operations into 1944, and a number of them were given to the Free French Army under Lend-Lease.

One of the most important uses of the 155mm GPF Gun M1918A1 was as a self-propelled heavy field gun. This was accomplished by mounting the gun, recoil and top carriage on a much modified M3 Grant medium tank chassis, and, thus, was known as the 155mm Gun Motor Carriage M12. This version of the gun played a very important role in the U.S. Army's campaigns in northern Europe in 1944-1945. By the end of World War II, the U.S. Army considered any and all versions of the 155mm GPF Gun M1918A1 obsolete, and they were retired.

A modernized World War II U.S. Army 155mm Howitzer M1918A3 in training exercise about 1938.

U.S. Marine Corps artillerymen manning a modernized U.S. Army 155mm Howitzer M1918A3 in combat in 1943. The Marines made much use of this howitzer in the Pacific Theater of Operations in World War II, and they, like all U.S. Marine Corps field artillery weapons and associated equipment, were provided by the U.S. Army.

U.S. Army 75mm Gun M2 series (modernized).

MODEL: 75mm Gun M2 Series (modernized), (Modernized 75mm Gun M1897)

WEIGHT: 3,400 lbs.

DIMENSIONS: Length: 17 ft., 3 in. Height: 4 ft., 8 in. Width: 6 ft., 8 in.

RANGE: 13,600 yards max, 1,000 yards antitank.

RATE OF FIRE: Rounds per minute in bursts: 10; in prolonged fire: 3.

AMMUNITION: Fixed HE, AP, APC and chem. smoke. Projective weight: 13 to 15 lbs.

CARRIAGE: Type: 2-wheel split trail. Traverse: 30 degrees R&L. Elevation: +49.5 degrees, -9 degrees. Fires from wheels or carriage firing support. Min. time to emplace: 3 min.

NORMAL TOWING SPEED: 30 mph max.

MODIFICATIONS: M2A1 and M2A2 with firing jack. M2A3: Trails shortened 1 ft., 7 in. and has wheel segment firing supports on axle.

U.S. Army 155mm Gun M3 (modernized).

MODEL: 155mm Gun M3 (modernized), (Modernized 155mm Guns M1918A1)

WEIGHT: 25,905 lbs.

DIMENSIONS: Length: 31 ft., 10 in. Height: 6 ft., 2-3/8 in. Width: 8 ft., 10 in.

RANGE: 20,000 yards max.

RATE OF FIRE: Rounds per minute in bursts: 1; in prolonged fire: 1/2.

AMMUNITION: Separate loading HE, AP, WP and chem. smoke for M1918 gun only. Projectile Weight: 95 to 100 lbs.

CARRIAGE: Type: 2-wheel split trail with limber. Traverse: 30 degrees R&L. Elevation: +35 degrees, -0 degrees. Fires from wheel. Min. time to emplace: 1 hr or 6 hrs if recoil pit is dug for high elevation fire.

NORMAL TOWING SPEED: 20 mph max.

MODIFICATIONS: M3 modernized French manufacture M1917 or U.S. manufacture M1918 guns.

U.S. Army 155mm Howitzer M1918A3 (modernized).

MODEL: 155mm Howitzer M1918A3 (modernized), (Modernized 155mm Howitzers M1917 and 1918)

WEIGHT: 9,000 lbs.

DIMENSIONS: Length: 21 ft., 5 in. Height: 6 ft., 10 in. Width: 7 ft., 10 in.

RANGE: 12,775 yards

RATE OF FIRE: Rounds per minute in bursts: 5; in prolonged fire: 2.

AMMUNITION: Separate loading HE, WP and chem. smoke; M1918 Howitzer series only. Projectile Weight: 95 lbs.

CARRIAGE: Type: 2-wheel open box trail. Traverse: 3 degrees R&L Elevation: +42 degrees, -0 degrees. Fires on wheels. Min. time to emplace: 5 min.

NORMAL TOWING SPEED: 25 mph max.

MODIFICATIONS: M1917A3: French manufacture modernized. M1918A3: U.S. manufacture modernized.

U.S. Army 240mm Howitzer M1918 (modernized)

MODEL: 240mm Howitzer M1918 (modernized)

WEIGHT: 55,000 lbs. including 2 transport wagons

DIMENSIONS: Length barrel on wagon: 30 ft., 5 in., carriage on wagon: 27 ft.,

RANGE: 16,400 yards

RATE OF FIRE: Rounds per minute in bursts: 2; in prolonged fire: 1.

AMMUNITION: Separate loading HE, M1918 Howitzer series only. Projectile Weight: 345 lbs.

CARRIAGE: Type: Emplaced with two transport wagons. Traverse: 10 degrees R&L Elevation: +60 degrees, -10 degrees. Fire emplaced. Min. time to emplace: 3 to 12 hours. Requires mobile crane for excavation and lift.

NORMAL TOWING SPEED: 20 mph max.

NOTE: Employed as training weapon only.

Chapter 13
Antitank Guns

As soon as the first tanks lumbered onto World War I's battlefields, the need for antitank weapons came to be. The U.S. Army never had to fight German tanks in World War I because the Germans did not have the industrial capacity to build them. However, during World War I, the U.S. Army considered that its field artillery and antiaircraft artillery weapons could fight tanks should the need arise.

The need for a special class of artillery weapons known as antitank guns was one of the future artillery weapons requirements included in the U.S. Army's 1919 Westervelt Board Report on the status and future of U.S. Army artillery. In the 1920s, the U.S. Army experimented with a very small cannon called an "infantry accompanying gun," and antitank fire was one of its purposes. However, this little gun could never be a very effective antitank gun, and U.S. Army doctrine continued to list field artillery guns and antiaircraft guns as antitank weapons.

After the U.S. Army's armored force experiments around 1930, the requirement for an antitank gun caused development work to begin. Several experimental guns were built in calibers from 37mm to 57mm, and experimental antitank ammunition was tested. All these guns had muzzle velocities around 2,000 to 2,400 fps, somewhat inadequate for antitank use.

At the same time the U.S. Army was studying foreign antitank gun development. Around 1933-1935, the U.S. Army procured

A U.S. Army 37mm Antitank Gun M3 in training in 1942.

and tested several foreign antitank guns including the French 25mm Hotchkiss and others up to 47mm caliber. Of these, the most interesting was the German 37mm Rhinemetall, a small gun with ammunition rated at 2,600 fps. This little gun used a pneumatic rubber-tired split trail carriage, and it was light enough to be

In 1940-1941, this photo of a prototype Bantam BRC-40 "Jeep" jumping with a 37mm Antitank Gun M3 was widely circulated as an example of the latest U.S. Army modern materiel.

U.S. Marine Corps gunners firing a U.S. Army 37mm Antitank Gun M3 with its trails in traveling position at a Japanese emplacement on Guam in 1944.

pulled by a one-ton motor vehicle and easily manhandled by its crew.

While testing and design work proceeded, no new antitank guns were built, however, considerable ammunition research and development work was carried on.

In September 1937, World War II was considered a serious possibility, and the U.S. Army Chief of Staff issued a requirement for the development of a new U.S. Army antitank gun as soon as possible. The money for the project was provided in the U.S. Army's budget, and work immediately began.

In a very short time, the U.S. Army Ordnance Department had built and tested the 37mm Antitank Gun T3. The requirement was for a weapon weighing no more than 1,000 pounds, and the T3 weighed just over 900 pounds. Much of its general design was copied from the German 37mm Rhinemetall gun, but many of its details were of U.S. Army Ordnance Department origin. While the

original experimental prototype used a rotary breech derived from the U.S. Army's French 75mm field gun, this design was quickly replaced with a dropping block breech, which was not only simpler to manufacture, but faster and easier to load.

The ammunition for the 37mm T3 antitank gun was a very important consideration. The first rounds developed fired at 2,600 fps, and this was improved to 2,900 fps by the time the little gun went into combat. In addition to antitank ammunition, a 3.13-pound high-explosive shell was provided for the little gun for use on unarmored targets. This 37mm gun was also the basis for the nearly identical 37mm gun used in U.S. Army World War II tanks.

In 1939, the little gun was adopted by the U.S. Army as the 37mm Antitank Gun M3, and its production began at once. By the time the U.S. Army entered World War II on Dec. 7, 1941, the new 37mm AT gun had been widely issued in the rapidly expanding U.S. Army. Production continued until 1943, and by the time it stopped, some 20,000 of the little guns had been built. This far exceeded the U.S. Army requirement for them.

The 37mm Antitank Gun M3 was first used in combat in North Africa in late 1942, and there it was found to be too light a caliber for the tanks encountered. The 37mm AT gun was, however, marginally effective against any and all Japanese tanks encountered in World War II. By the end of 1943, it had been relegated to use as a training weapon for antitank gunners. But another use had been found for it. The 37mm gun was very accurate, and it could regularly hit point targets at ranges up to 1,500 yards or more using its telescopic sight. The U.S. Marine Corps began using it as a long-range sniper weapon firing its high-explosive shell, and this practice spread to the U.S. Army in the Pacific. It was effectively used there until the end of World War II.

The second antitank gun used by the U.S. Army was the British-developed 57mm Antitank Gun M1. The British began work

A U.S. Army 57mm Antitank Gun M1 firing and in full recoil. This gun "bucked" viciously when fired, as is shown by this gun's wheels being off the ground.

U.S. Army Airborne Command troops load a U.S. Army 37mm Antitank Gun M3 in a Douglas C47 cargo plane in training in early 1942.

U.S. Army troops in Australia in late 1942 with Jeep-drawn U.S. Army 37mm Antitank Guns M3.

U.S. Army antitank gunners manhandling a U.S. Army 37mm Antitank Gun M3 in training in 1940.

U.S. Army gunners unhooking a U.S. Army 57mm Antitank Gun M1 from its armored half-track prime mover to go into action in northern Europe in early 1945.

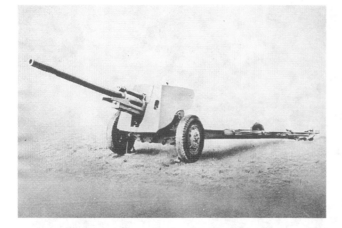

This is the prototype of the limited production U.S. Army 90mm antitank Gun T8 developed in 1943-1944. This gun used the barrel of the 90mm antiaircraft gun in a modified M2 series 105mm howitzer recoil with front gun slide extensions and the modified carriage of the M2 series 105mm howitzer with lengthened trails.

on this design in early 1938 as a replacement for their two-pounder equivalent of the U.S. Army's 37mm Antitank Gun M3. They adopted the 57mm gun in 1940, calling it a "six-pounder" under their artillery naming system. Interestingly, the cartridge and caliber of the six-pounder were adopted from a French Hotchkiss Company gun developed before 1900! The British ordered the new six-pounder antitank gun into production in 1940, however, their beleaguered industries had great difficulties in manufacturing them. The first of the new six-pounders were issued to the British Army in 1941, and they first saw action in North Africa late that year.

To meet their urgent need for the six-pounder, the British asked the United States to supply them under Lend-Lease, and this was authorized in February 1941. The U.S. Army Ordnance Department had the design reworked to incorporate American manufacturing practices and standards, and the gun was ordered into production in May 1941 as the U.S. Army 57mm Antitank Gun M1. The British and American versions of the gun were practically interchangeable.

Although the 57mm antitank gun was in production in 1942, the first used by the U.S. Army in North Africa were reverse Lend-Lease guns received from the British. The U.S. Army first used the U.S.-made 57mm gun in North Africa in 1942.

The 57mm Antitank Gun M1 was a 2,700-pound weapon with a muzzle velocity of about 2,800 fps with armor-piercing ammunition. It used a split trail carriage, and the U.S. Army usually used an armored half-track to pull it. In addition to armor-piercing ammunition, high-explosive shell was also provided for firing at appropriate targets. The 57mm gun had a horrendous recoil compared to U.S. Army-designed guns, and U.S. Army troops did not like the gun because of this.

Over 16,000 57mm Antitank Guns were built in America between 1942 and early 1944 when its production was halted. It was very widely used by the U.S. Army in the European Theater of Operations, but few, if any, of the guns were used in the Pacific. At the time its production ceased, the 57mm gun was already proving inadequate against late model German armor despite improved

U.S. Army airborne troops loading a 57mm Antitank Gun M1 into a Waco CG4A glider in training in early 1944.

A U.S. Army 57mm Antitank Gun M1 ready for action in northern Europe in late 1944.

antitank ammunition being made for it. The 57mm Antitank Gun M1 was considered obsolescent by the end of World War II, and the U.S. Army did not use it after World War II.

Another antitank weapon the U.S. Army used first in North Africa was the 3-in. Gun M5. This gun was not designed as an antitank gun when it was adopted in December 1941, but as a light field gun to replace the French 75mm M2. The 3-in. gun M5 used the same carriage as the standard U.S. Army 105mm Howitzer M2 to mount a barrel firing the same ammunition as the standard U.S. Army 3-in. antiaircraft gun; only a very limited number were produced in 1942.

The 3-in. gun M5 was a 5,000-pound weapon with an antitank muzzle velocity over 2,600 fps. Use in North Africa in 1943 proved this light field gun was also an excellent antitank gun, and more were requested with improvements to better adapt it for the antitank role. Although its production was still limited, in 1943 the improved version was adopted with a new gun shield better adapted to its antitank use, and the existing guns had this shield installed to replace the original one.

Production of the 3-in. Gun M5 was halted in early 1944 because other weapons were filling its role, and it was no longer required for its original light field gun use. However, the 3-in. M5 was widely and effectively used in the European Theater of War from 1943 until the end of the war in 1945. It was seldom, if ever, used in the Pacific Theater of War as there was no requirement for its use there. The 3-in. Gun M5, along with all other weapons firing the same 3-in. gun ammunition, was declared obsolete in the U.S. Army in 1945, and none were used after World War II. (See field artillery system chapter.)

Another type of antitank weapon in the World War II U.S. Army was the antiaircraft gun. When the war began, both the standard 3-in. and 90mm antiaircraft guns were considered usable as

U.S. Marine Corps gunners firing a U.S. Army 37mm Antitank Gun M3 with a new shield at Japanese fortifications on Iwo Jima in 1945.

U.S. Army gunners manhandle a U.S. Army 57mm Antitank Gun M1 into position in Germany in late 1944.

antitank guns, but neither had yet been equipped with sights suited to the role. This was done beginning in 1942, and in May 1943, the U.S. Army adopted the 90mm Antiaircraft Gun M2 meeting the requirement that antiaircraft guns must be able to fire as antitank guns and field artillery guns. It is a matter of record that the 90mm gun, also used in the M36 tank destroyer and the M26 Pershing heavy tank, could devastate any German armored vehicle. This was proven in the campaigns in northern Europe in 1944-1945.

As a result of the success of the 90mm gun on German armor, the U.S. Army ordered the design of a 90mm antitank gun in 1944. The result was a much redesigned 3-in. Gun M5 known as the 90mm antitank Gun T8. This was a limited production weapon.

The 200 or so built were not ready for use until after they were needed for World War II.

The clumsy 6,800-pound 90mm T8 was tested in competition with other antitank weapons and found rather unsatisfactory. It saw no combat use in World War II, and the U.S. Army made little, if any, use of it after the war.

Post-war evaluations of World War II U.S. Army antitank guns all stressed that, as the 3-in. Gun M5 was, they all had to be usable as either field artillery or antitank guns. They further stated that the best antitank weapon was either a light one such as the legendary 2.95-in. Bazooka infantry hand-held antitank rocket launcher or another tank armed with a gun powerful enough to defeat enemy armor.

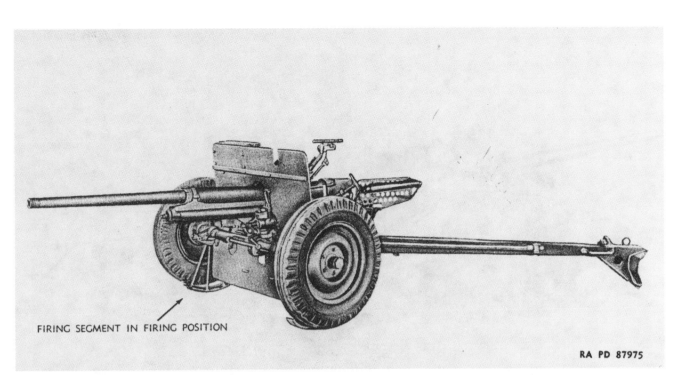

FIRING SEGMENT IN FIRING POSITION

RA PD 87975

The U.S. Army 37mm Antitank Gun M3.

MODEL: 37mm Antitank Gun M3

WEIGHT: 912 lbs.

DIMENSIONS: Length: 10 ft., 10-1/2 in. Height: 3 ft., 1-7/8 in. Width: 5 ft., 3-1/2 in.

RANGE: 12,850 yards max.; 500 yards antitank.

RATE OF FIRE: Rounds per minute in bursts: 20; in prolonged fire: 5.

AMMUNITION: Fixed HE, AP, APC and Cannister, M3 Tank-AT gun series only. Projectile Weight: 1.5 to 2 lbs.

CARRIAGE: Type: 2-wheel split trail. Traverse: 30 degrees R&L Elevation: +15 degrees, -10 degrees. Fires from wheels or axle pivoted firing segments. Min. time to emplace: 1-1/2 min.

NORMAL TOWING SPEED: 35 mph max.

NOTES: 1. Employed for direct fire at visible targets only. 2. In 1943-1945, the U.S. Marine Corps provided new gun shields to afford improved crew protection against small arms fire and shell fragments.

TYPE OF CASTER WHEEL

RA PD 87973

The U.S. Army 57mm Antitank Gun M1.

MODEL: 57mm Antitank Gun M1

WEIGHT: 2,700 lbs.

DIMENSIONS: Length: 16 ft., 8-1/2 in. Height: 4 ft., 2 in. Width: 6 ft., 3 in.

RANGE: 10,860 max., 1,000 yds. antitank.

RATE OF FIRE: Rounds per minute in bursts: 10; in prolonged fire: 5.

AMMUNITION: Fixed HE, AP and APC

PROJECTILE WEIGHT: 6.3 to 7.3 lbs.

CARRIAGE: Type: 2-wheel split trail. Traverse: 45 degrees R&L. Elevation: +15 degrees, -5 degrees. Fires from wheels or axle pivoted firing segments. Min. time to emplace: 1-1/2 mins.

NORMAL TOWING SPEED: 35 mph max.

NOTE: Employed for direct fire at visible targets only.

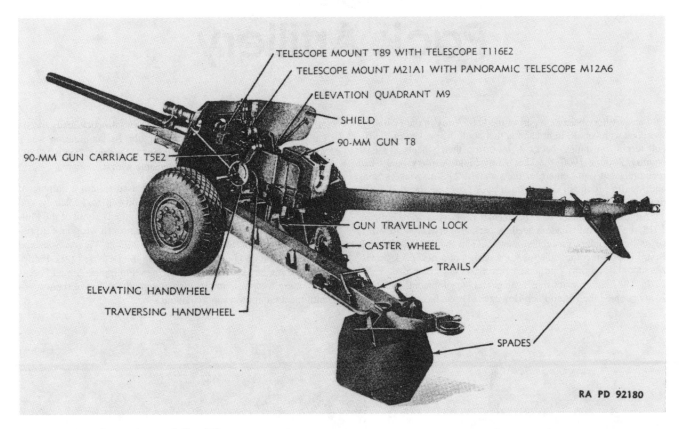

TELESCOPE MOUNT T89 WITH TELESCOPE T116E2
TELESCOPE MOUNT M21A1 WITH PANORAMIC TELESCOPE M12A6
ELEVATION QUADRANT M9
SHIELD
90-MM GUN T8
90-MM GUN CARRIAGE T5E2
GUN TRAVELING LOCK
CASTER WHEEL
TRAILS
ELEVATING HANDWHEEL
TRAVERSING HANDWHEEL
SPADES
RA PD 92180

The U.S. Army 90mm Antitank Gun T8.

MODEL: 90mm Antitank Gun T8

WEIGHT: 6,800 lbs.

DIMENSIONS: Length: 26 ft., 6 in. Height: 5 ft., 9 in. Width: 8 ft., 0 in.

RANGE: 21,400 yards max., 1,000 yards antitank.

RATE OF FIRE: Rounds per minute in bursts: 10; in prolonged fire: 2.

AMMUNITION: Fixed HE, APC, HVAP and chem. smoke.

PROJECTILE WEIGHT: HE: 23.4 lbs, HVAP: 16.8 lbs.

CARRIAGE: Type: 2-wheel split trail. Traverse: 31-1/2 degrees R&L Elevation: +22-1/2 degrees, -11 degrees. Fires from wheel. Min. time to emplace: 1/2 min.

NORMAL TOWING SPEED: 35 mph max.

NOTE: Employed for direct fire at visible targets or for indirect fire at targets which cannot be observed.

Chapter 14
Pack Artillery

Pack artillery became a part of the U.S. Army in the 1830s. Its weapons were small, light cannon that could be packed into difficult terrain on mules' backs or towed on their wheels in easier country. Around 1900, the U.S. Army Field Artillery board had recommended replacement of the standard 2.95-in. Vickers Sons and Maxim Mountain Gun, a small pack howitzer standard at the time.

Although a number of experimental prototypes were built by 1915, the U.S. Army had no need for pack artillery in World War I, so its development proceeded slowly. Then the 1919 Westervelt Board Report recommended that the design of a new pack howitzer should be a priority project, and work on one proceeded.

In 1927, after extensive testing and development, the U.S. Army adopted the 75mm Pack Howitzer M1, the basic model used in World War II. It could be broken down into pack loads for six mules or be towed behind a single mule. Its ammunition was a semifixed modification of the standard U.S. Army 75mm M1897 gun ammunition, but not interchangeable with it.

The 75mm Pack Howitzer M1 was used to arm a number of "pack batteries" in the 1930s, and it proved to be handy and acceptably accurate. It first saw combat in the Defense of the Philippines in 1941-1942, where it became a proven weapon. Surprisingly, several batteries of the venerable 2.95-in. Vickers Sons and Maxim Mountain Guns also saw use in the Defense of the Philippines. These had been issued to the new Philippine Armed Forces as training weapons, and they gave a good account of themselves until the ammunition supply ran out.

The U.S. Army 2.95-in. Vickers Sons and Maxim Mountain Gun procured about 1900 and used in the Defense of the Philippines in 1941-1942. This little howitzer was about the same size as the U.S. Army Pack Howitzer M1 and was mule packed the same way.

U.S Army field artillerymen drilling with a U.S. Army 75mm Pack Howitzer M1 in the 1930s.

In the mid-1930s, the U.S. Cavalry developed a requirement for a light horse artillery piece to accompany horse-drawn cavalry units, and a modification of the 75mm Pack Howitzer M1 was developed for this need. A new split trail, pneumatic rubber-tired carriage was developed for the pack howitzer and its recoil mechanism. In 1937, it was adopted as the 75mm Pack Howitzer M3, and it was rated equally suitable for horse or motor draft.

The 75mm pack howitzer was the last horse-drawn artillery piece adopted by the U.S. Army, however, it never saw service as one since no U.S. Army horse cavalry saw action in World War II. It did remain in use with the U.S. Army Armored Cavalry as a motor-drawn gun, and a self-propelled version of it mounted on a U.S. Army armored half-track was used in combat in the war.

U.S Army field artillerymen setting up a mule packed U.S. Army 75mm Pack Howitzer M1. A well-trained crew could take the howitzer from mule back to firing position in about two minutes. The U.S. Army used mule packed howitzers in the Pacific Theater of Operations, China-Burma-India, and Italy in World War II.

When the U.S. Army began modernizing in the late 1930s, parachute troops were added to its organization, and this caused a requirement for Airborne Field Artillery. Initially, this requirement was met by using the standard 75mm Pack Howitzer M1. Then the M1 pack howitzer was modified by equipping it with pneumatic rubber-tired wheels to replace the original wooden wheels so it could be towed by a light motor vehicle. This modification was designated the 75mm Pack Howitzer M8 (Airborne).

When first adopted, the 75mm Pack Howitzer M8 (Airborne) was supposed to be carried into action in cargo planes or gliders. It was in combat in World War II. On the ground, a Jeep was its prime mover. In 1943, a system of seven "paracrates" was adopted so the little gun could be dropped with paratroops. This paracrate system was used in a number of World War II airborne operations, including those in southern France in late 1944.

In 1942, the U.S. Army added the Regimental Cannon Company to its infantry organization. Initially, these cannon companies were equipped with 75mm Pack Howitzers M3 and M8 simply because they were available. Units with the M3 pack howitzer were used in combat in North Africa in late 1942 and 1943, and a number of cannon companies in the Pacific Theater of Operations used the M8. In addition, mule packed batteries with the original 75mm Pack Howitzer M1 saw service in World War II in a number of places in the Pacific Theater, in China-Burma-India, and in Italy. While these were all effective artillery units, the U.S. Army Ground Forces Command developed a requirement for a more powerful weapon for the cannon companies in 1942.

To meet the requirement for a more powerful weapon the size and weight of the 75mm Pack Howitzer M3, they simply mounted a new short 105mm barrel on it! The ammunition it fired was a modification of the standard U.S. Army 105mm M2 howitzer's,

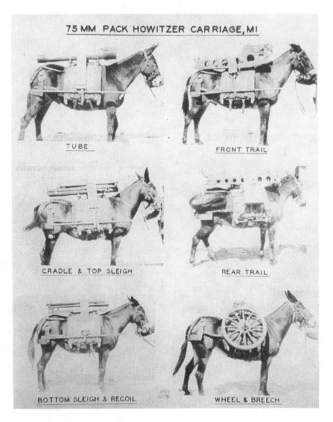

The six mule pack loads for the U.S. Army 75mm Pack Howitzer M1.

A U.S. Army 75mm Pack Howitzer M8 (Airborne) with its barrel and recoil assembly shifted to its towing trunnions being towed by a Jeep.

A U.S. Army 75mm Pack Howitzer M1 in action in the Pacific Theater of Operations in 1944.

but it was not interchangeable with it. This little cannon was adopted as the 105mm Howitzer M3 in 1942, and immediately was put in production.

Although the 105mm Howitzer M3 was widely used by the U.S. Army in 1944 and 1945, this little weapon was not a very successful design. Its barrel was too short to properly stabilize the 105mm projectile, and this caused it to lack the standard of accu-

racy the U.S. Army required. The 105mm Howitzer M3 was retired at the end of World War II.

The 75mm Pack Howitzer M3 was also retired at the end of World War II as its role was being filled with new infantry weapons: the 57mm and 75mm recoilless rifles.

The 75mm Pack Howitzers M1 and its pack artillery batteries remained in the U.S. Army long after World War II, as did the 75mm Pack Howitzer M8 (Airborne).

A U.S. Army 105mm Howitzer M3 in action in northern Europe in the winter of 1944-1945. The howitzer has just fired and its barrel is at full recoil.

U.S. Army field artillerymen man a U.S. Army 75mm Pack Howitzer M3 at a road block in training in 1943. Very few of this model pack howitzer saw combat use in World War II.

U.S. Army airborne troops loading a U.S. Army 75mm Pack Howitzer M8 (Airborne) into a Waco CG4A glider in training in 1943.

U.S. Marine Corps ground troops using a U.S. Army 75mm Pack Howitzer M8 (Airborne) on Guadalcanal in late 1942.

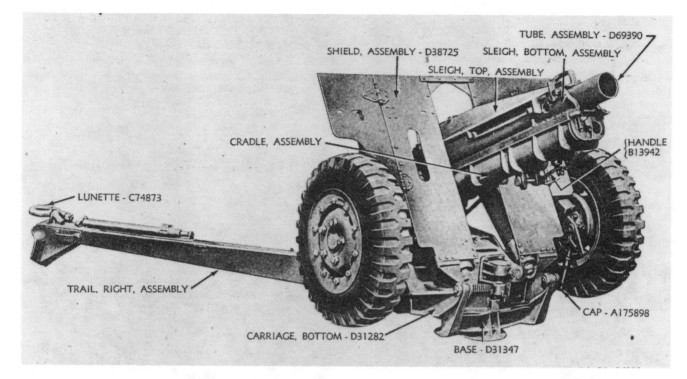

A U.S. Army 75mm Pack Howitzer M3 emplaced to fire. This example is equipped with the gun shield seldom, if ever, issued for this howitzer.

A U.S. Army 75mm Pack Howitzer M3 in service as a U.S. Army Cavalry horse artillery gun about 1938. The last of these cavalry horse artillery batteries were dismounted in 1943, and none ever saw combat in World War II.

A U.S. Army 105mm Howitzer M3 emplaced to fire with its
wheels elevated off the ground.

A U.S. Army 105mm Howitzer M3 in action in northern
Europe in the winter of 1944-1945. Note the howitzer is firing from its wheels and not from the carriage on the ground
with its wheels retracted.

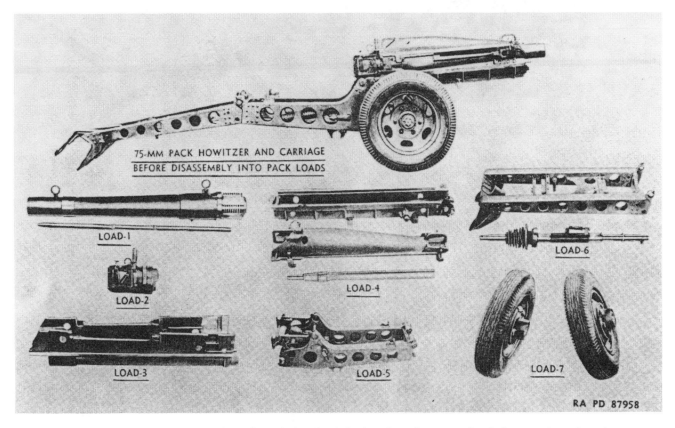

The U.S. Army 75mm Pack Howitzer M8 (Airborne) showing it broken down into seven loads for parachute dropping.

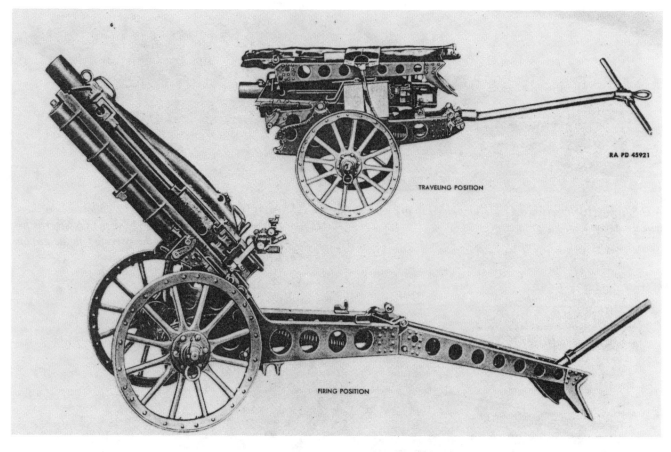

The U.S. Army 75mm Pack Howitzer M1 broken down for man or animal draft and in firing position.

MODEL: 75mm Pack Howitzer M1

WEIGHT: 1,269 lbs.

DIMENSIONS: Length: 12 ft., 0 in. Height: 2 ft., 10 in. Width: 3 ft., 11 in.

RANGE: 9,600 yards max.

RATE OF FIRE: Rounds per minute in bursts: 6; in prolonged fire: 3.

AMMUNITION: Semifixed or fixed HE, HEAT and chem. smoke. Projectile Weight: 13 to 15 lbs.

CARRIAGE: Type: 2-wheel box trail that could be disassembled. Traverse: 3 degrees R&L Elevation: +45 degrees, -5 degrees. Fires from wheel. Min. time to emplace: 1/2 min.; 3 min. when disassembled.

NORMAL TOWING SPEED: 5 mph max.

NOTE: Disassembles into six loads for pack mule transport, and trail may be folded for mule or light vehicle towing.

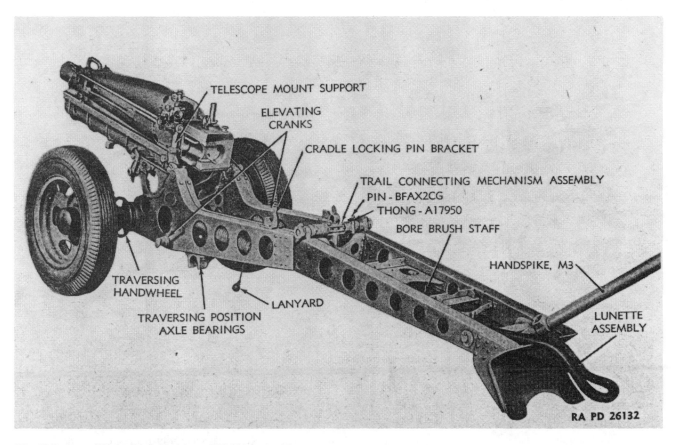

The U.S. Army 75mm Pack Howitzer M8 (Airborne).

MODEL: 75mm Pack Howitzer M8 (Airborne)

WEIGHT: 1,339 lbs.

DIMENSIONS: Length: 12 ft., 0 in. Height: 2 ft., 10 in. Width 3 ft., 11 in.

RANGE: 9,600 yards max.

RATE OF FIRE: Rounds per minute in bursts: 6; in prolonged fire: 3.

AMMUNITION: Semifixed or fixed HE, Heat and chem. smoke. Projectile Weight: 13 to 15 lbs.

CARRIAGE: Type: 2-wheel box trail that could be disassembled. Traverse: 3 degrees R&L Elevation: +45 degrees, - 5 degrees. Fires from wheels. Min. time to emplace: 1/2 min.; 3 min when disassembled.

NORMAL TOWING SPEED: 10 mph max.

NOTE: Disassembles into seven loads for parachute delivery.

The U.S. Army 75mm Pack Howitzer M3 in traveling position.

MODEL: 75mm Pack Howitzer M3

WEIGHT: 2,224 lbs.

DIMENSIONS: Length: 9 ft., 9 in. Height: 2 ft., 11 in. Width: 5 ft., 11 in.

RANGE: 9,600 yards max.

RATE OF FIRE: Rounds per minute in bursts: 6; in prolonged fire: 3.

AMMUNITION: Semifixed or fixed HE, Heat and chem. smoke. Projectile Weight: 13 to 15 lbs.

CARRIAGE: Type: 2-wheel split trail. Traverse: 22-1/2 degrees R&L Elevation: +49-1/2 degrees, -9 degrees. Fires from wheels or firing jack. Min. time to emplace: 1 min.

NORMAL TOWING SPEED: 25 mph max.

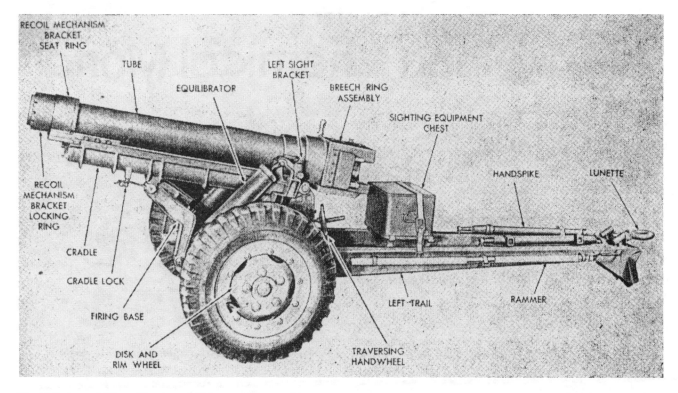

The U.S. Army 105mm Howitzer M3 in traveling position.

MODEL: 105mm Howitzer M3

WEIGHT: 2,673 lbs.

DIMENSIONS: Length: 12 ft., 11 in. Height: 4 ft., 1-3/4 in. Width: 5 ft., 7-3/16 in.

RANGE: 8,295 yards

RATE OF FIRE: Rounds per minute in bursts: 6; in prolonged fire: 2.

AMMUNITION: Semifixed HE and Heat, M3 series Howitzer only. Projectile Weight: 29 to 33 lbs.

CARRIAGE: Type: 2-wheel split trail. Traverse: 22-1/2 degrees L, 20-1/2 degrees R. Elevation: +65 degrees, -9 degrees. Fires on wheels or firing jack. Min. time to emplace: 1 min.

NORMAL TOWING SPEED: 25 mph max.

NOTE: Carriage and recoil adapted from 75mm Pack Howitzer M3.

Chapter 15
The 4.2-Inch Chemical Mortar

The 4.2-in. chemical mortar, known as the "Four Deuce" in World War II, was a unique weapon. It was designed, provided, and manned by the U.S. Army Chemical Warfare Service although its primary use was as a support weapon for infantry and armored troops. To provide its most effective use, it was integrated into the regular U.S. Army Field Artillery fire control and direction systems.

The 4.2 chemical mortar was evolved from the muzzle-loading World War I British-developed 4-in. Stokes Chemical Mortar Mark I. This mortar was developed in 1917 to provide the lightest model capable of firing a large enough projectile to carry an effective charge of toxic gas or chemical smoke. The U.S. Army adopted it in 1918 as a Chemical Warfare Service weapon.

Although the 4-in. Chemical Mortar Mark I was retained by the Chemical Warfare Service after World War I and was used as a training weapon in World War II, they set out to build an improved model to replace it in 1924. The new model was to have improved range and accuracy.

The World War I U.S. Army 4-in. Stokes Chemical Mortar, which saw limited use as a training mortar in World War II. This was a smooth bore mortar.

U.S. Army 4.2-in. Chemical Mortar M2 in action in the Pacific Theater of Operations. This is a rifled mortar.

The 4-in. Stokes was a smoothbore mortar, and the new one was to be a rifled mortar. While it would also be muzzle-loading "drop fired," it would have a much more stable mount than the Stokes. The improved rifled model was adopted in 1928 as the 4-in. Chemical Mortar M1. Its development had been aided by the U.S. Army Ordnance engineers from Aberdeen Proving Grounds, Maryland, which was literally next door to the Chemical Warfare Service's Edgewood Arsenal, where it was developed.

The 4-in. Chemical Mortar M1 had all the features of the later models and was practically identical in appearance. A dozen or so were built, and it was given extensive field testing. While it proved to be capable of doing what it was supposed to, there were no Chemical Warfare Service units regularly equipped with it as anything except one of their many weapons.

When the U.S. Army began planning for World War II in the mid-1930s, the Chemical Warfare Service made a number of minor improvements in the M1 chemical mortar, which had been suggested by their testing. The improved model was adopted as the 4-in. Chemical Mortar M1A1 about 1936, and then, at the suggestion of the U.S. Army Ordnance Department to prevent ammunition confusion, it was soon redesignated the 4.2-in. Chemical Mortar M1A1. The small number of M1s were modified into M1A1s. and the M1A1 was put in limited production. However,

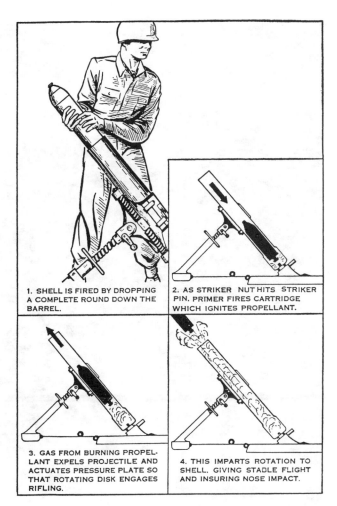

1. SHELL IS FIRED BY DROPPING A COMPLETE ROUND DOWN THE BARREL.

2. AS STRIKER NUT HITS STRIKER PIN. PRIMER FIRES CARTRIDGE WHICH IGNITES PROPELLANT.

3. GAS FROM BURNING PROPELLANT EXPELS PROJECTILE AND ACTUATES PRESSURE PLATE SO THAT ROTATING DISK ENGAGES RIFLING.

4. THIS IMPARTS ROTATION TO SHELL. GIVING STADLE FLIGHT AND INSURING NOSE IMPACT.

This U.S. Army training chart shows how the U.S. Army 4.2-in. Chemical Mortar functions when fired. The rotating disc for its rifling was derived from similar devices used on Civil War era U.S. Army rifled muzzle-loading field artillery guns.

the Chemical Warfare Service still did not form any units to be specifically armed with the chemical mortar.

Until World War II the 4.2-in. chemical mortar was provided with only chemical ammunition: chemical smoke shell, WP smoke shell, and, although it was not used in World War II, toxic gas shell. Although the 4.2-in. chemical mortar proved effective with this ammunition in its first combat use in North Africa in 1942, it was suggested it would be much more useful if it was provided with high-explosive shell, so in 1943 4.2-in. HE shell was authorized and put into manufacture to improve the mortar's capability. It did, and the demand for more and improved 4.2-in. chemical mortars came from all U.S. Army commands.

The improved 4.2-in. Chemical Mortar M2 was adopted in 1943. It had a stronger baseplate and barrel, allowing it to fire to longer ranges and to use heavier projectiles. A number of existing M1A1 4.2s were modified into M2s, and the latter model was used during and long after World War II.

The size and weight of the 4.2-in. chemical mortar and its ammunition made its transportation a problem. When it was designed, it was for a World War I style army and did not require the mobility of a motorized army. A simple hand cart drawn by

A U.S. Army Chemical Warfare Service mortarman aiming a U.S. Army 4.2-in. Chemical Mortar in Italy in 1944.

The U.S. Army Chemical Warfare Service crew of this well dug in 4.2-in. Chemical Mortar are firing a mission in northern France in the fall of 1944.

two soldiers was developed to move it, and this cart was used with it, particularly in the Pacific Theater of War, where moves were short and terrain difficult.

However, in the 1942-1943 North African Campaign, it, like everything else, had to be motorized. By this time the U.S. Army Chemical Warfare Service had established a 4.2-in. Chemical Mortar Battalion organization, which was a motorized unit with eighteen mortars. The standard transport vehicle for the mortar was either a Jeep with a half-ton trailer or a three-quarter-ton Dodge 4x4 Weapons Carrier. The twenty-six 4.2-in. Mortar Battalions and nine 4.2-in. Chemical Mortar Companies of the U.S. Army Chemical Warfare Service, plus a handful of U.S. Marine Corps 4.2-in. Chemical Mortar Companies, were the only units armed with the weapon in World War II.

Although several self-propelled versions of the 4.2-in. chemical mortar were tested, none were ever adopted. However, during the war it is known that U.S. Army Armored Force units occasion-

ally mounted them in armored half-tracks so they could be fired from the vehicles by placing a reinforced firing platform under them. The U.S. Marine Corps also fired them from tracked landing vehicles from reinforced platforms in their well decks.

Over 6,000 4.2-in. Chemical Mortars were built during World War II, and substantial numbers of them were supplied to the British, French and Chinese under Lend-Lease. At the end of the war, their use in the U.S. Army was rapidly expanding as they had proved to be as or more effective support weapons than the light 75mm or 105mm howitzers in the cannon companies.

Shortly after the end of World War II, the responsibility for the 4.2-in. chemical mortar was transferred from the Chemical Warfare Service to the Ordnance Department and became standard weapons of infantry and armored units. World War II evaluations rated the 4.2-in. chemical mortar as a very effective and useful weapon, and it remained in service for decades.

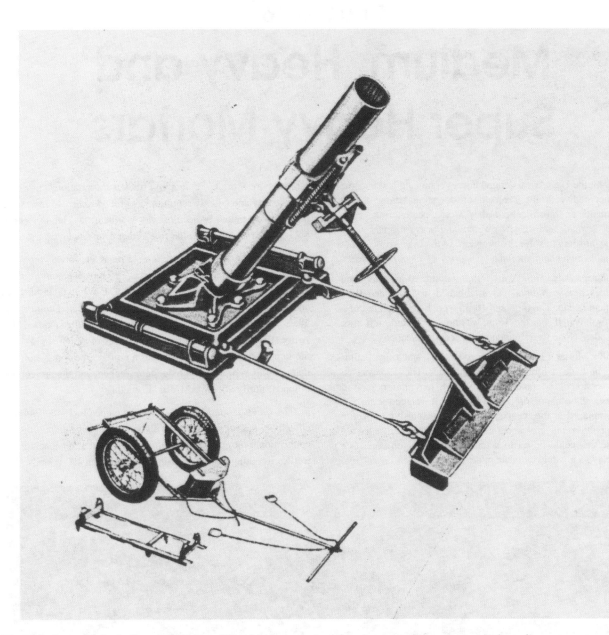

The U.S. Army 4.2-inch Chemical Mortar M2 with the man draft hand cart used to transport it short distances.

MODELS: 4.2 in. Chemical Mortar M1A1 and M2

WEIGHT: In firing order: M1A1: 283 lbs.; M2: 330 lbs.

RANGE: Min.: 600 yards; max. M1A1: 2400 yards, M2: 4,400 yards.

AMMUNITION: Semifixed chem. smoke, WP Smoke, high-explosive shell.

PROJECTILE WEIGHT: M1A1 chem. smoke and WP: 18 to 20 lbs., high-explosive: 22 lbs.; M2: chem. smoke and WP: 25 to 26 lbs, high-explosive: 24.5 lbs. and 32 lbs.

CARRIAGE: Dismountable mortar type; Traverse: 7 degrees R&L, Elevation: +45 degrees to +60 degrees.

RATE OF FIRE: Bursts: 20 rounds per minute; sustained: 1 round per minute max.

Chapter 16

Medium, Heavy and Super Heavy Mortars

By 1943, the U.S. Army Ground Forces command had become very concerned with the problem of defeating heavy enemy emplacements and fortifications they were encountering. They knew the Germans and Russians were using heavy mortars along with heavy artillery to solve this problem, so the U.S. Army set out to develop its own heavy mortars.

A requirement for U.S. Army 6-in. medium, 10-in. heavy and 36-in. super heavy mortars was established in 1943, and their development began. The 6-in. and 10-in. were both tested in combat in World War II, but the 36-in. was not completed until after the war ended. None were found to be successful weapons.

The 6-in. Mortar T25 was developed in 1944, and a small number were built on a limited production order. The T25 was an enlarged version of the standard U.S. Army 81mm infantry mortar, and it was a smoothbore, drop-fired weapon. It weighed some 571 pounds emplaced to fire its sixty-pound high-explosive projectile with a maximum range of about 2,000 yards. Its projectile used a point fuse that could be set to detonate it instantly on impact or with a delay so it would detonate in the target.

The 6-in. Mortar T25 required truck transportation; however, it was easily and quickly set up on the ground to fire. Muzzle loading the sixty-pound projectiles was a difficult and clumsy chore, but it had a rate of fire similar to all other drop-fired mortars.

The U.S. Army Ordnance Department engineers who had developed and tested the 6-in. Mortar T25 took a battery of them to the Philippines in 1945 for a combat test. While their accuracy and range proved adequate for the carefully selected combat fire missions, their effectiveness was not as good as the standard U.S. Army 105mm and 155mm howitzers, either of which could fire at the same high angles of elevation as a mortar. The conclusion was that the 6-in. mortar was a redundant weapon, and the project was dropped shortly after World War II ended.

The heavy 10-in. Mortar T6 was developed in 1943-1944 specifically to deliver plunging fire on concrete fortifications. It was a conventional muzzle-loading mortar fired by muzzle-loading projectiles weighing from 200 pounds to more than 400 pounds. Sev-

A U.S. Army Ordnance Department crew firing an experimental U.S. Army 6-in. Mortar T25 in the Philippines in late 1944.

The experimental U.S. Army 6-in. Mortar T25 with its standard sixty-pound projectile.

eral experimental models were built, one self-propelled model mounted in a much modified 105mm Howitzer Motor Carriage M7 "Priest."

One 10-in. mortar was taken to France in 1945 and was fired at the enemy in a combat test. It proved very difficult to load even though a crane was used to handle its heavy projectiles; it was deemed unsuitable for use by the U.S. Army. There were two other field artillery weapons, the 8-in. Howitzer M1 and 240mm Howitzer M1, which could deliver more effective plunging fire at longer ranges and with more accuracy than the 10-in. mortar. The 10-in. mortar project was dropped at the end of World War II.

Development of the super heavy 36-in. Mortar T1 was begun in late 1943 to provide the largest caliber mobile artillery weapon possible for defeating concrete fortifications of the Maginot and Siegfried line types with plunging fire. The result was the monster the U.S. Army called "Little David," a weapon which weighed 172,000 pounds — 86.5 tons — emplaced to fire. Its projectile weighed 3,650 pounds — over 1.75 tons — of which 1,585 pounds were high explosive. It had a maximum range of 9,000 yards — about five miles.

It took an immense effort to employ the huge 36-in. mortar. Its thirty-eight-foot barrel and eighteen-foot long carriage moved in separate loads on special trailers pulled by the twenty-five-ton Tractor Truck M26 also used to pull the standard tank transporter trailer. The crew was about 100 officers and men. The large number of vehicles required to support the huge weapon included a mobile crane, a standard U.S. Army ten-ton wrecking truck, and a number of ten-ton cargo trucks to carry the ammunition. A day or more was required to emplace the 36-in. mortar because a huge pit had to be excavated by its crane, and this had to be carefully aligned with the line-of-fire to its target.

Long before the 36-in. mortar was ready for use, the need for it had passed. Fortifications in the class with those of the Maginot and Siegfried lines had been encountered around Cherbourg, France in late 1944, and these were able to be reduced by the regular U.S. Army heavy and super heavy field artillery weapons. Testing of the 36-in. mortar continued after the end of World War II at the U.S. Army Aberdeen Proving Grounds in Maryland. It proved the monster weapon had fair accuracy and that it could fire about one round per hour. The detonation of the huge high-explosive shell caused people in a wide radius from the proving ground to flood telephone circuits with inquires about a local earthquake!

Although it was quickly agreed that the 36-in. mortar was an impractical weapon, its testing continued several years after the end of World War II. Then its barrel developed a small crack, and the weapon was transferred to the U.S. Army Ordnance Museum at Aberdeen Proving Ground where it is still on display.

On the left is an experimental U.S. Army 10-in. Mortar; in the middle a U.S. Army Ordnance Department crew is loading an experimental 6-in. Mortar T25; and on the right is a standard U.S. Army 4.2-in. Chemical Mortar M2.

A U.S. Army experimental 10-in. Mortar T6 under test at the U.S. Army Aberdeen Proving Grounds in Maryland in early 1944. A variation of this mortar mounted in place of the 105mm howitzer in a U.S. Army Gun Motor Carriage M7 "Priest" was test fired in combat in Germany in 1945.

The barrel of an experimental U.S. Army 36-in. Mortar T1 "Little David" towed by a U.S. Army forty-ton Truck Tractor M26 gives an idea of the size of this behemoth. This weapon was completed too late to see combat use in World War II.

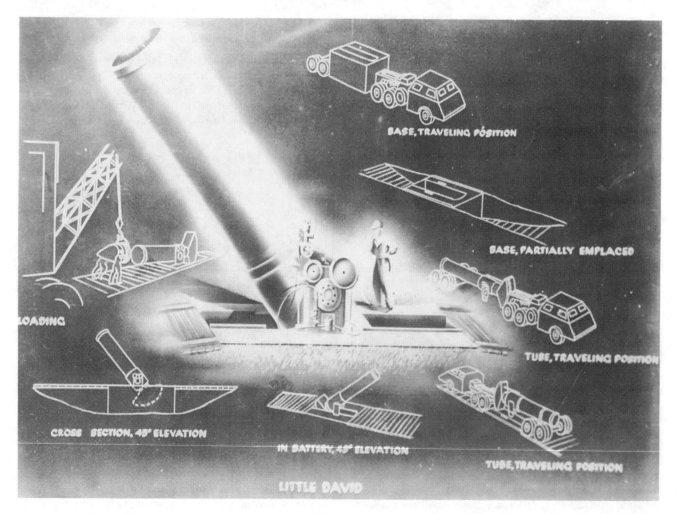

The U.S. Army Ordnance Department schematic instruction chart for the U.S. Army experimental 36-in. Mortar T1 "Little David."

"Little David"—New 36-inch Mortar

The 36-inch mortar's base assembly is hauled into a pit as the first step in erecting the Army's huge new weapon.

The tube assembly is now driven over the base on steel runways and is lowered into position by hydraulic jacks.

A ramp is built up to the 36-inch mortar's boxlike base assembly by the crane which also dug the emplacement.

The 3,650-pound mortar bomb is loaded into the rifled barrel with a davit loader. The tube is then elevated as shown below.

Earth is filled in around the base, and it is now ready for the installation of the 80,000-pound mortar tube assembly.

With the tube in firing position, "Little David" is now ready to hurl its deadly explosive charge to a range of 6 miles.

From Army Ordnance magazine for January-February 1946 with permission of the American Defense Preparedness Association.

Chapter 17
Half-Track Self-Propelled Artillery

The U.S. Army Ordnance Department began testing self-propelled artillery weapons during World War I, and a number of experimental models were built and tested in the 1920s and 1930s. After observing how the German Blitzkrieg overwhelmed the British and French armies in 1940, the U.S. Army developed an urgent requirement for self-propelled artillery weapons, and it was suggested that a quick, expedient way of filling it would be to mount cannon on the new, rugged U.S. Army armored half-track. This resulted in a series of armored half-track self-propelled artillery weapons.

The first was the 75mm Gun Motor Carriage M3. It mounted the gun, recoil and top carriage of the U.S. Army standard modernized French 75 M2 series gun on an M2 armored half-track with its frame reinforced to withstand the gun's recoil. The M3 half-track mounted 75 was standardized in November 1941 after early production units were already in the hands of the U.S. Army Armored Force. A handful of brand new half-track 75s reached the Philippines and were used there in 1941-1942. Although their use was very limited, due to a lack of spare parts, they proved very effective in combat.

When the U.S. Army landed in North Africa in November 1942, it had a substantial number of the half-track 75s. They saw use as tank destroyers, but they were only marginally effective

A U.S. Marine Corps U.S. Army 75mm Gun Motor Carriage M3 with winch landing in the Pacific Theater of Operations in 1943.

A U.S. Army 75mm Gun Motor Carriage M3 in North Africa in late 1942. Note the half-track's armor windshield is folded flat to allow the 75mm gun to depress.

because the old 75mm gun was not powerful enough for the role. However, they proved very useful as highly mobile self-propelled field artillery weapons.

M3 half-track 75s served well in Sicily, Italy and many places in the Pacific Theater of Operations for the rest of the war as self-propelled field guns. A number were issued to the U.S. Marine Corps for use in their Pacific Theater of Operations, and a number were issued to the British under Lend-Lease for use in Italy.

A total of some 2,200 75mm Gun Motor Carriages M3 had been built by early 1943, when their production was stopped when the supply of existing French 75s ran out. It was declared limited standard in March 1944 and obsolete in September 1944, however, they were still in use when World War II ended. At the end of the war they were all retired.

A variation of the 75mm Gun Motor Carriage M3 was the 57mm Gun Motor Carriage T48. Fifty of the T48s were built in 1942-1943 using the half-track (as modified to mount the modernized French 75 gun) to mount the gun, recoil and top carriage of the 57mm Antitank gun M1. After the U.S. Army tested and rejected this unit, the British accepted them under Lend-Lease. The British then requested and received permission to hand them off to the Russians, and what the Russians did with them is unknown.

Another requirement for a half-track self-propelled cannon was for one mounting the new 105mm Howitzer M2 issued in September 1941. Using an armored half-track with modifications similar to those for the 75mm Gun Motor Carriage M3, a unit mounting the barrel, recoil and top carriage of the 105mm Howitzer M2 was built. Despite the fact that the howitzer could bend the half-track's frame firing at high angles of elevation, 324 of these units were built in 1942 as the 105mm Howitzer Motor Carriage T19.

The 105mm howitzer half-track served adequately as a training vehicle, and a small number of them were deployed to North Africa in 1942. The half-tracks proved to be an unstable carriage for the 105mm howitzer, which adversely affected its normally excellent accuracy. The 105mm Howitzer Motor Carriage T19 was retired from all service in 1943, and the half-tracks were salvaged by removing their howitzers.

In the fall of 1941, the U.S. Army Armored Force requested a half-track mounted 75mm howitzer. This unit was easily designed by mounting the barrel, recoil and top carriage of a 75mm Pack Howitzer M3 on an armored half-track with modifications similar to those for the 75mm gun model. This unit was adopted as the 75mm Howitzer Motor Carriage T30, and the first of the 500 built was delivered in December 1941.

The half-track 75mm howitzer T30 was first used in North Africa in 1942, and was found to be a useful but unspectacular weapon. It was also used as a training vehicle. It was used in combat in ever declining numbers in Sicily and then in Italy, and was retired by 1944. The remaining units were salvaged by removing their 75mm howitzers.

In mid-1940, the U.S. Armored Forces began using the new armored half-track to transport its standard U.S. Army 81mm infantry mortars, and this soon developed a requirement for an armored half-track modified to carry one mounted so it could be fired from the vehicle. This was a very simple project, and before the unit was adopted in October as the 81mm Mortar Carrier M4, early production units were already in service.

The 81mm Mortar Carrier M4 was called a carrier because it was perceived that it would be used primarily to transport the mortar, which would normally be fired on the ground. Because of this, the M4 was designed so the mortar fired over the rear end of the vehicle.

An early 1941 production U.S. Army 75mm Gun Motor Carriage M3 with the original type gun shield of which very few ever were used in combat.

The body arrangement of a U.S. Army 81mm Mortar Half-Track Carrier M4.

A U.S. Army 75mm Gun Motor Carriage M3 in action, firing as field artillery in Sicily in 1943.

A U.S. Marine Corps U.S. Army 75mm Gun Motor Carriage without winch in action in the Pacific Theater of Operations in 1943.

The 81mm Mortar Carrier was first used in North Africa in 1942-1943. In combat, it was found that the mortar was fired from its mount in the half-track as often or more than it was fired dismounted on the ground. Because of this, the fact that the mortar could only be fired from the vehicle after it had been turned around (so its rear end faced the enemy) proved to be a serious deficiency: It delayed the time it took to get the mortar firing. The 600 81mm Mortar Carriers M4 were declared limited standard in 1943; however, a few of them were still in service late in World War II.

An improved design called the 81mm Mortar Carrier M21 was adopted in 1943, in which the mortar fired over the front of the half-track. This was a limited standard and limited production unit. Although this unit was used in combat, combat evaluations showed the half-track mounted 81mm mortar was not nearly as mobile as the same mortar carried in a half-ton trailer behind a Jeep. By 1944, anybody who wanted to employ an 81mm mortar in a half-track was doing it by building a simple wooden firing platform for it in the back of a regular half-track. By 1944, the half-track mounted 81mm mortar had been largely discarded as unneeded and unwanted.

All these half-track artillery weapons were built as emergency expedient weapons, and the U.S. Army always considered them as such. Within their limitations, however, they proved an interim solutions until self-propelled artillery weapons on full-track chassis replaced them.

A U.S. Army 105mm Howitzer Motor Carriage T19 in action in Sicily in 1943. These self-propelled 105mm howitzers were withdrawn from combat service at the end of the Sicilian Campaign.

A U.S. Army 75mm Howitzer Motor Carriage T30 in Sicily in 1943. This self-propelled howitzer was only used in the late phases of the North African Campaign, Sicily, and Italy.

The interior body arrangement of the U.S. Army 81mm Mortar Half-Track Carrier M21.

A U.S. Army 105mm Howitzer Motor Carriage T19 in action in North Africa in early 1943.

RA PD 45973

The U.S. Army 57mm Gun Motor Carriage T48.

MODEL: 57mm Gun Motor Carriage T48

WEIGHT: Fighting: 19,800 lbs.

DIMENSIONS: Length: 20 ft., 4-3/4 in. Height: 7 ft., 4-5/8 in. Width: 7 ft., 2-1/2.

CANNON: Modified 57mm Gun M1 Antitank. Range: 10,860 max, 1,000 yds., Antitank. Ammunition: Fixed HE, AP and APC. Projectile Weight: 6.3 to 7.3 lbs.

TRAVERSE: 27-1/2 degrees R&L. Elevation: +15 degrees, -5 degrees. Fires from tracks Min. Time to emplace: None; can fire while moving.

BASIC CHASSIS: Modified Half-Track Personnel Carrier M3.

NORMAL ROAD SPEED: 45 mph max

CREW: 5

RA PD 46079

The U.S. Army 75mm Gun Motor Carriage M3.

MODEL: 75mm Gun Motor Carriage M3

WEIGHT: Fighting: 20,000 lbs.

DIMENSIONS: Length: 20 ft., 4-3/4 in. Height: 7 ft., 10 in. Width: 7 ft., 2-1/2 in.

CANNON: Modified 75mm Gun M2 (Modified M1897). Range: 13,600 yards max., 1,000 yards Antitank. Ammunition: Fixed HE, AP, APC and chem. smoke. Projectile Weight: 13 to 15 lbs.

TRAVERSE: 19 degrees L, 21 degrees R. Elevation: +29 degrees, -10 degrees. Fires from tracks. Min. time to emplace: None; can fire while moving.

BASIC CHASSIS: Modified Half-Track Personnel Carrier M3.

NORMAL ROAD SPEED: 45 mph max

CREW: 5

RA PD 54014

The U.S. Army 75mm Howitzer Motor Carriage T30.

MODEL: 75mm Howitzer Motor Carriage T30

WEIGHT: Fighting: 19,500 lbs.

DIMENSIONS: Length: 19 ft., 7-3/4 in. Height: 8 ft., 0-3/4 in. Width: 7 ft., 2-1/2 in.

CANNON: Modified 75mm Pack Howitzer M3. Range: 9,600 yards max. Ammunition: Semifixed or fixed HE, Heat and chem. smoke. Projectile Weight: 13.3 to 14.7 lbs.

TRAVERSE: 22-1/2 degrees R&L. Elevation: +50 degrees, -9 degrees. Fires from tracks. Min. time to emplace: None; can fire while moving.

BASIC CHASSIS: Modified Half-Track Personnel Carrier M3.

NORMAL ROAD SPEED: 45 mph max

CREW: 5

The U.S. Army 81mm Half-Track Mortar Carrier M4.

MODELS: 81mm Mortar Half-Track Carriers M4 and M21
WEIGHT: Fighting: 18,500 lbs.
DIMENSIONS: M4: Length: 20 ft., 1-1/2 in. Height: 7 ft., 5 in. Width: 7 ft., 3-1/2 in.; M21: Length: 19 ft., 8-1/4 in. Height: 6 ft., 0-1/2 in. Width: 7 ft., 2-1/2 in.
CANNON: Standard Infantry 81mm Mortar M1. Range: 100 yards min. to 2,655 yards max. Ammunition: Semi-fixed 81mm mortar. Projectile Weight: Light: Approx. 8 lbs.; Heavy: Approx. 12 lbs.

MORTAR WEIGHT: 136 lbs. complete. Traverse: 5 degrees R&L. Elevation: +40 degrees to +85 degrees. Fires from half-track or off half-track.
BASIC CHASSIS: M4: Modified Half-Track Car M2; M21: Modified Half-Track Personnel Carrier M3.
NORMAL ROAD SPEED: 45 mph max
CREW: 6
MODEL DIFFERENCES: M4: Mortar fires to rear; M21: Mortar fires over front.

The U.S. Army 81mm Half-Track Mortar Carrier M21.

The U.S. Army 105mm Howitzer Motor Carriage T19.

MODEL: 105mm Howitzer Motor Carriage T19

WEIGHT: Fighting: 20,000 lbs.

DIMENSIONS: Length: 19 ft., 9-1/2 in. Height: 7 ft., 8 in. Width: 7 ft., 2-1/2 in.

CANNON: Modified 105mm Howitzer M2. Range: 11,700 yards max. Ammunition: Semifixed HE, Heat, WP and chem. smoke, M2 Howitzer Series only. Projectile Weight: 28 to 33 lbs.

TRAVERSE: 20 degrees R&L. Elevation: +35 degrees, -5 degrees. Fires from tracks. Min. time to emplace: None, but firing while moving not recommended.

BASIC CHASSIS: Modified Half-Track Personnel Carrier M3.

NORMAL ROAD SPEED: 45 mph max.

CREW: 6

Chapter 18
Full-Tracked Self-Propelled Artillery

During World War I, the U.S. Army began experimenting with mounting artillery weapons on full-tracked tractor chassis to increase their mobility. The early efforts were primitive and not very successful, but the 1919 Westervelt Board Report recommended continued development. Development continued, but nothing worth adoption was built until just before the U.S. Army entered World War II.

In 1941, a U.S. Army Armored Force requirement led to the construction of three experimental self-propelled cannon on modified M3 Grant medium tank chassis. One mounting a 3-in. Antiaircraft Gun M1918 and one mounting the newer 3-in. Antiaircraft Gun M2 were for antitank use; the third mounted the new 105mm Howitzer M2 as a self-propelled light field artillery piece. The ones mounting the 3-in. antiaircraft guns led directly to the development of the 3-in. Gun Motor Carriage M10 tank destroyer by proving the chassis could mount the powerful cannon. The version mounting the 105mm howitzer was developed into the 105mm howitzer motor carriage "Priest," one of the most successful self-propelled artillery weapons of World War II.

The M7 Priest mounted the barrel, recoil and top carriage of the 105mm Howitzer M2 in the chassis of the M3 Grant medium tank

in a new open top hull. The British gave it the name "Priest" when they saw its towering compartment mounting a cal. .50 Browning Machine Gun M2-HB, which looked like a church pulpit, and the name was used by the U.S. Army in World War II.

When the U.S. Army adopted the M7 Priest in April 1942, it had been in production for several months. Early production units were already in the hands of troops, and they liked it.

The first M7 Priests to see combat were Lend-Leased to the British, who used them in North Africa in the summer of 1942. They proved it to be an excellent weapon, and the U.S. Army personnel with the British were very satisfied with its performance. By the summer of 1942, the M7 Priest had been designated as the standard weapon for the field artillery battalions of U.S. Army armored divisions. Production of the M7 Priest continued until February 1945, by which time all requirements for them had been filled, and a new self-propelled 105mm howitzer to replace it was going into production. In all, some 3,000 M7 Priests were built; they remained in U.S. Army service long after World War II.

As an auxiliary unit for the M7 Priest, the U.S. Army developed the Armored Trailer M8 in 1942. It was intended to carry ammunition. This proved to be only a marginally useful unit. How-

A U.S. Army 75mm Howitzer Motor Carriage M8 moving in Northern Europe in the winter of 1944-1945.

A U.S. Army 155mm Gun Motor Carriage M40 in action in the Pacific Theater of Operations in the summer of 1945.

A U.S. Army 105mm Howitzer Motor Carriage M7 with the fording gear used in amphibious landings.

A U.S. Army 155mm Gun Motor Carriage M12 firing at fortifications in northern Germany in the spring of 1945. The 155mm gun is at full recoil.

Although the comparison is inappropriate, this photo of a German 8.8cm FLAK 36, the vaunted "88" dual-purpose antiaircraft antitank gun, and a U.S. Army 105mm Howitzer Motor Carriage M7 was widely used in 1943.

A battery of four U.S. Army 155mm Gun Motor Carriages M12 in action in France in the fall of 1944.

The U.S. Army Cargo Carrier M30 used with the U.S. Army 155mm Gun Motor Carriage M12 to carry its ammunition. Fully loaded with forty rounds of 155mm gun ammunition, this vehicle weighed about 45,600 pounds.

The experimental U.S. Army 240mm Howitzer Motor Carriage T90 firing in late 1945. The chassis of this self-propelled 240mm howitzer was developed from that of the Heavy Tank M26.

A U.S. Army 75mm Howitzer Motor Carriage M8 in action in Germany in early 1945. Note the pile of empty cartridge cases and ammunition containers in the left foreground.

The U.S. Army Armored Trailer M8 originally built to carry the ammunition for the U.S. Army 105mm Howitzer Motor Carriage M7. This trailer weighed 2,640 pounds and could carry 2,200 pounds.

ever, it saw limited service in World War II since it could be used to carry many calibers of ammunition. It saw little service after World War II.

The M7 Priest was used everyplace the U.S. Army fought in World War II, and it was always considered an excellent weapon. Its basic 1941 design never changed, and it defied improvement.

The second full-tracked self-propelled artillery piece the U.S. Army developed in World War II was the 155mm Gun Motor Carriage M12. It mounted the barrel, recoil and top carriage of the 155mm GPF Gun M1918Al on a much modified M3 Grant medium tank chassis equipped with a massive trail spade on its rear end to stabilize the heavy gun when it fired. The requirement for the M12 originated in early 1941, and a prototype was built by the U.S. Army Rock Island Arsenal late that year. To carry the gun's ammunition, the Cargo Carrier M30 was built on the M3 Grant medium tank chassis at the same time.

The 155mm Gun Motor Carriage M12 and its Cargo Carrier M30 were extensively, if hastily, tested, and the U.S. Army adopted them in March 1942. A production order for 100 sets of this materiel was issued, and they were completed by March 1943.

As soon as it was available, the 155mm M12 received a lot of publicity as it was the most powerful self-propelled field gun in existence at the time. The American public was very impressed with it. U.S. Army public relations gave it the name "King Kong" for the movie ape, but this name never did stick well. During the operations in North Africa in 1942-1943, U.S. Army Intelligence found the enemy was also impressed with them and expected to see them in combat.

Unfortunately, most of the M12s had been placed in U.S. Army Depot Storage as soon as they had been built! The U.S. Army Ground Forces Command had no requirement for this powerful weapon, and neither did the U.S. Army Armored Force Command! It took over a year for anybody to see the weapon's potential, and, except for a few in training commands which were often seen in public relations demonstrations, they languished in storage.

Then U.S. Army personnel, planning for the D-Day invasion and fighting in northern France, decided a couple of battalions of M12s would be useful for fighting German fortifications and heavy armored vehicles. In 1943, six battalions of artillery equipped with the M12 were organized, equipped and trained, and all of them were in action in France by July 1944.

Once in action, the M12 proved to be an outstanding weapon. In addition to being an excellent field artillery weapon for all targets, its fire could devastate any German pillbox and demolish Panther and Tiger tanks at ranges over 1,000 yards. Every available M12 unit was engaged in the war in Northern Europe when World War II ended, and it was a weapon greatly feared by the enemy.

At the end of World War II, the M12s were pretty badly worn, and there was no supply of the venerable 155mm M1918A1 guns to make overhauling the M12s worthwhile. With new self-propelled 155mm guns available to replace them, the M12 was declared obsolete and retired.

In 1942, the U.S. Armored Force initiated a requirement for a self-propelled 75mm pack howitzer for use in its infantry cannon companies. A number of prototypes, all either impractical and/or overdesigned, were built on M3 Stuart light tank chassis. Then

A U.S. Army 155mm Gun Motor Carriage M12 at a U.S. Army Field Artillery training center in 1943.

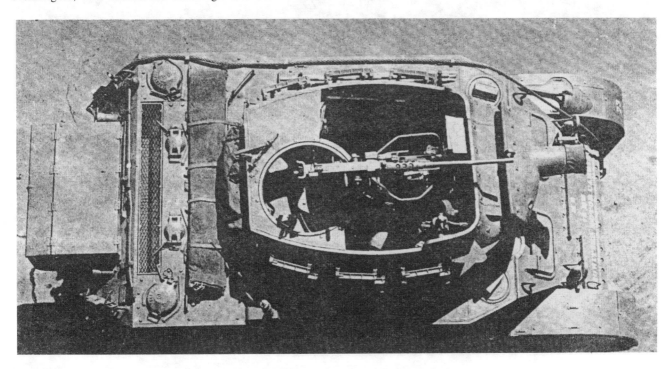

Top view of a U.S. Army 75mm Howitzer Motor Carriage M8 showing its open top turret.

The prototype U.S. Army 105mm Howitzer Carriage T32 with the U.S. Army Medium Tank M3, on which it was based, at Aberdeen Proving Ground in Maryland in January 1942. The T32 was developed into the U.S. Army 105mm Howitzer Motor Carriage M7.

A U.S. Army 105mm Howitzer Motor Carriage M7 towing an Armored Trailer M8 in North Africa in early 1943.

A top view of a U.S. Army 155mm Gun Motor Carriage M12. Note the trail spade raised behind the 155mm gun's breech in traveling position.

somebody suggested it would be possible to simply mount a 75mm pack howitzer in a Stuart with a modified turret.

A prototype was quickly built by mounting a specially modified 75mm pack howitzer mount in a much modified Stuart light tank turret. It was adopted in September 1942 as the 75mm Howitzer Motor Carriage M8 to be built on the chassis of the new M5 Stuart light tank with a new open top turret. Some 1,000 were built before the requirement for them was filled in January 1944 when production was stopped.

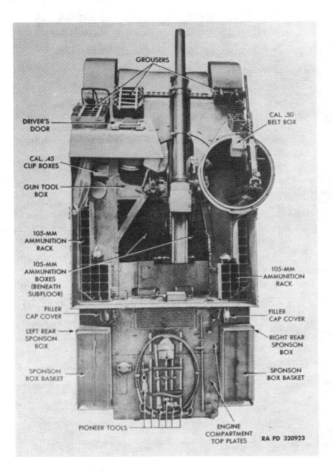

Top view of the U.S. Army 105mm Howitzer Motor Carriage M7 showing its interior arrangement.

The M8 self-propelled 75mm pack howitzer was first used in combat by armored units in Italy in mid-1943. It was successful, and it saw much service in both the European and Pacific Theaters of War. The M8's 75mm pack howitzer turret was used to construct the LVT(A)-4 tracked landing vehicle as a cannon armed vehicle.

Early in 1944, the U.S. Army began building a M4 Sherman medium tank armed with a 105mm howitzer to fill the same Armored Force requirement as the M7 Priest self-propelled 105mm howitzer. Between April 1944 and May 1945, over 3,000 M4 Shermans were built with 105mm howitzers, and many were issued to U.S. Army Armored Forces units. They were very effective for fighting almost anything but an enemy tank, and they continued in service with the U.S. Army long after World War II.

While the U.S. Army fully recognized the advantages of self-propelled field artillery, the high mobility and effectiveness of its regular towed field artillery prevented the introduction of additional models from receiving a very high priority. However, the development of new self-propelled artillery weapons continued.

The first of the improved self-propelled artillery weapons was the 8-in. Howitzer Motor Carriage M40 adopted in July 1943. This unit mounted the barrel, recoil and top carriage of the standard

The experimental U.S. Army 8-in. Gun Motor Carriage T93 emplaced in 1945. The chassis of this 8-in. self-propelled gun was developed from the Heavy Tank M26.

U.S. Army 8-in. Howitzer M1 on the chassis of an M4 Sherman medium tank with a heavy trail spade on its rear end to stabilize the howitzer when it fired. Production of this weapon was delayed in favor of higher priority projects until 1944, and then the unit went into production, using the latest improved wide-track Sherman M4 chassis. The fast-moving pace of the last months of World War II kept any units armed with this weapon from seeing action. However, it proved an excellent weapon, and the U.S. Army retained it after World War II.

Since the standard 8-in. Howitzer M1 and 155mm Gun M1 shared the same carriage, one of the first 8-in. Howitzer Motor Carriage M40 was fitted with a 155mm gun barrel. This conversion was very successful and was adopted as the 155mm Gun Motor Carriage M43 in March 1945.

Due to the urgent requests from the European Theater of Operations for more self-propelled 155mm guns, one battery of the new M43s arrived there in time to see action in the last weeks of the war. Additional units were sent to the Pacific Theater of War, but they arrived too late to see much action there. The 155mm Gun Motor Carriage M43 was an excellent weapon, and it was retained by the U.S. Army long after World War II.

When the excellent M24 Chaffee light tank was adopted, U.S. Army Ordnance began building self-propelled artillery weapons on its chassis. Only two of the many field artillery experimental types went into production.

A U.S. Army 155mm Gun Motor Carriage M40 on the march in Germany in the spring of 1945.

A U.S. Army 105mm Howitzer Motor Carriage M7 on the move in northern France in the summer of 1944. The M7 was the primary artillery weapon of U.S. Army armored divisions.

The experimental U.S. Army 240mm Howitzer Motor Carriage T90 in marching order and loaded on a railroad flat car for shipment. The U.S. Army required all its mobile equipment to be able to be shipped on a standard width U.S. railroad flat car.

The first was the 105mm Howitzer Motor Carriage M37 adopted in January 1945 as a replacement for the M7 Priest self-propelled 105mm howitzer. The M37 used the same 105mm howitzer used in the M4 Sherman medium tank, and it had a tower mount for a cal. .50 Browning Machine Gun M2-HB, which resembled the one in the M7 Priest. Some 316 M37s were built, mostly after World War II, and none saw combat in World War II, although the U.S. Army retained them long after the war.

The second self-propelled field artillery weapon using the M24 Chaffee light tank chassis was the 155mm Howitzer Motor Carriage M41. This unit — which mounted the barrel, recoil and top carriage of the standard U.S. Army 155mm Howitzer M1 on a M24 Chaffee chassis with a trail spade to stabilize the howitzer when it fired — was a low priority production project because of the capabilities of the regular towed 155mm Howitzer M1. Some 250 155mm Howitzer Motor Carriages M41 were built during and after World War II, so they did not see action in the war. This excellent weapon was retained by the U.S. Army long after World II.

The last self-propelled field artillery project the U.S. Army began in World War II was one to mount the huge 8-in. Gun M1 and 240mm Howitzer M1, giving these super heavy field artillery

A U.S. Army 105mm Howitzer Motor Carriage M7 in action in Germany in 1945. Note that the man on the right in the vehicle is using a telephone to receive firing data.

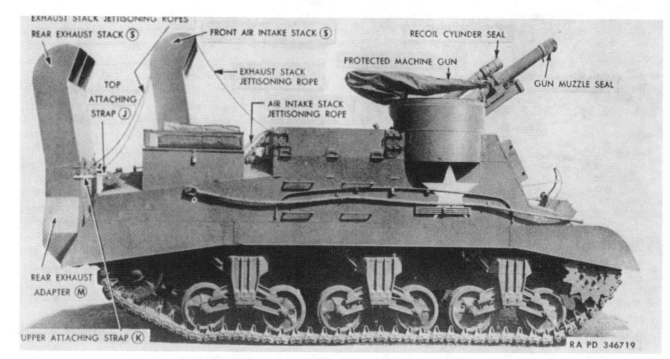

A U.S. Army 105mm Howitzer Motor Carriage M7B1 with fording gear for amphibious operations.

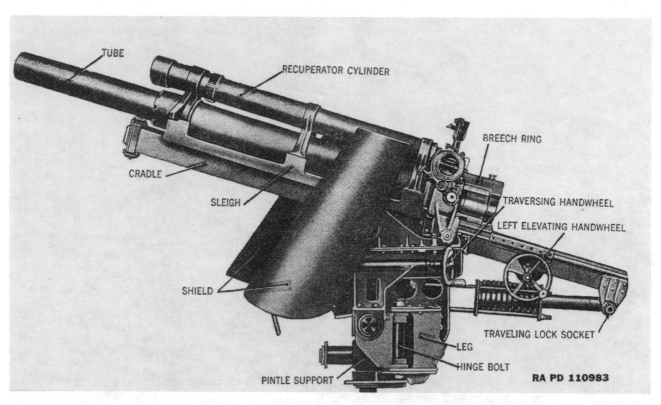

The modified barrel, recoil and top carriage of the standard U.S. Army 105mm Howitzer M2 as used in the U.S. Army 105mm Howitzer Motor Carriage M7.

weapons additional mobility. Their chassis were based on the new M26 Pershing heavy tank chassis. The 8-in. Gun Motor Carriage T-93 and 240mm Howitzer Motor Carriage T92 were both adopted in March 1945 as limited procurement items.

The first unit was delivered in July 1945, and in all, two T92s and five T93s were built. None of these saw action in World War II, but they were extensively tested and proven reasonably practical; however, neither of these huge self-propelled guns ever got past the field trial experimental stage.

The chief problem with the T92 and T93 was their weights: They both weighed over sixty-five tons! In the judgment of the U.S. Army Ground Forces Command, the U.S. Army Corps of Engineers and practically everybody else, they were much too heavy for the roads and bridges they would have to use in a combat zone. The verdict was, "if you can't move them, you can't use them," and they were retired several years after World War II.

A U.S. Army 155mm Gun Motor Carriage M12 under test at Aberdeen Proving Ground in Maryland in 1942.

A U.S. Army 155mm Gun Motor Carriage M12 with its cargo carrier M30 under test at Aberdeen Proving Ground in Maryland in 1942.

The U.S. Army 75mm Howitzer Motor Carriage M8.

MODEL: 75mm Howitzer Motor Carriage M8

WEIGHT: Fighting: 34,571 lbs.

DIMENSIONS: Length: 16 ft., 4 in. Height: 9 ft., 1-1/4 in. Width: 7 ft., 7-1/2 in.

CANNON: 75mm Howitzer M2 or M3 (Interchangeable). Range: 9,489 yds. max. Ammunition: Semifixed or fixed HE, Heat and chem. smoke for Pack Howitzer Series. Projectile Weight: 13.3 to 14.7 lbs.

TRAVERSE: 360 degrees. Elevation: +40 degrees, - 20 degrees. Fires from tracks. Min. time to emplace: None; can fire while moving.

ADDITIONAL ARMAMENT: 1 cal. .50 Browning Machine Gun M2-HB.

BASIC CHASSIS: Modified Light Tank M5.

NORMAL ROAD SPEED: 26 mph max

CREW: 4

The U.S. Army 105mm Howitzer Motor Carriage M7.

MODEL: 105mm Howitzer Motor Carriage M7 and M7B1

WEIGHT: Fighting: M7: 50,634 lbs.; M7B1: 56,470 lbs.

DIMENSIONS: Length: 20 ft., 3-1/2 in. Height: 9 ft., 4-1/2 in. Width: 9 ft., 8 in.

CANNON: Modified 105mm Howitzer M2. Range: 11,400 yards max. Ammunition: Semifixed HE, Heat, WP and chem. smoke; M2 Howitzer Series only. Projectile Weight: 28 to 32 lbs.

TRAVERSE: 12-1/4 degrees L, 25-1/2 degrees R. Elevation: +32-1/2 degrees, -5 degrees. Fires from tracks. Min. time to emplace: None; can fire while moving.

ADDITIONAL ARMAMENT: 1 cal. .50 Browning Machine Gun 174-HB.

BASIC CHASSIS: Medium Tank M3 or M4.

NORMAL ROAD SPEED: 25 mph max

CREW: 7

MODIFICATIONS: M7: Medium Tank M3 chassis with air-cooled radial engine. M7B1: Medium Tank M4 chassis with air-cooled radial engine.

194

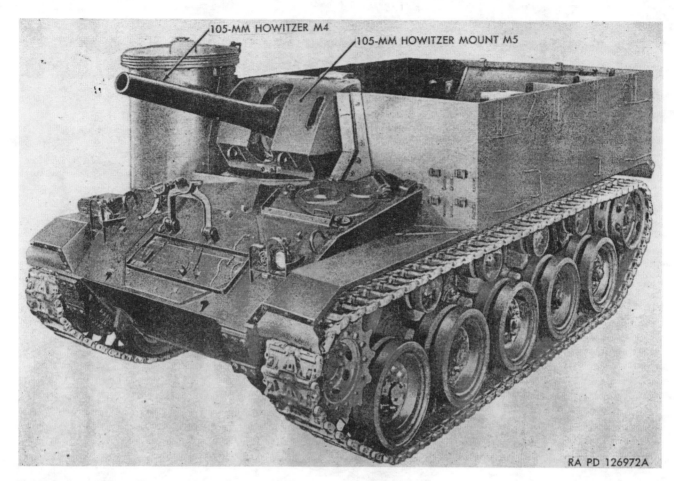

The U.S. Army 105mm Howitzer Motor Carriage M37.

MODEL: 105mm Howitzer Motor Carriage M37
WEIGHT: Fighting: 46,000 lbs.
DIMENSIONS: Length: 19 ft., 4 in. Height: 8 ft., 9 in. Width: 9 ft., 10 in.
CANNON: 105mm Howitzer M4. Range: 12,205 yds. max. Ammunition: Semifixed HE, Heat, WP and chem. smoke, M2 Howitzer Series only. Projectile Weight: 28 to 33 lbs. Traverse: 22-1/2 degrees R&L. Elevation: +43 degrees, -10 degrees. Fires from tracks. Min. time to emplace: None, can fire while moving.

ADDITIONAL ARMAMENT: 1 cal. .50 Browning Machine Gun M2-HB.

BASIC CHASSIS: Modified Light Tank M24.

NORMAL ROAD SPEED: 35 mph max.

CREW: 7

The U.S. Army 155mm Gun Motor Carriage M12.

MODEL: 155mm Gun Motor Carriage M12
WEIGHT: Fighting: 55,536 lbs.
DIMENSIONS: Length: 21 ft., 9 in. Height: 8 ft., 10 in. Width: 8 ft., 3 in.
CANNON: Modified 155mm Gun M1918. Range: 15,200 yards max, 18,700 yards with supercharge. Ammunition: Separate loading HE, AP, WP and chem. smoke, for M1918 gun only. Projectile Weight: 95 to 100 lbs. Traverse: 14 degrees R&L. Elevation: +30 degrees, -5 degrees. Fires from tracks with firing spade emplaced. Min. time to emplace: 15 min.

BASIC CHASSIS: Medium Tank M3 with radial air-cooled engine.

NORMAL ROAD SPEED: 25 mph max.

CREW: 6

NOTE: Accompanied by Cargo Carrier M30, which carries ammunition.

The U.S. Army 155mm Howitzer Motor Carriage M41.

MODEL: 155mm Howitzer Motor Carriage M41
WEIGHT: Fighting: 43,000 lbs.
DIMENSIONS: Length: 19 ft., 4 in. Height: 8 ft., 0 in. Width: 9 ft., 5 in.
CANNON: Modified 155mm Howitzer M1. Range: 16,355 yards max. Ammunition: Separate loading HE, WP and chem. smoke, M1 Howitzer Series only. Projectile Weight: 95 lbs. Traverse: 17 degrees L, 20 degrees R. Elevation: +45 degrees, -5 degrees. Fires from tracks with firing trail spade emplaced. Min. time to emplace: 5 min.
BASIC CHASSIS: Modified Light Tank M24.
NORMAL ROAD SPEED: 35 mph max.
CREW: 12

The U.S. Army 155mm Gun Motor Carriage M40.

MODEL: 155mm Gun Motor Carriage M40

WEIGHT: Fighting: 82,000 lbs.

DIMENSIONS: Length: 29 ft., 8 in. Height: 10 ft., 5-3/4 in. Width: 10 ft., 4 in.

CANNON: Modified 155mm Gun M1. Range: 25,715 yards max Ammunition: Separate loading HE and APC for M1 gun only. Projectile Weight: 95 to 100 lbs. Traverse: 18 degrees L&R. Elevation: +55 degrees, -5 degrees. Fires from tracks with firing trail spade emplaced. Min. time to emplace: 15 min.

BASIC CHASSIS: Modified Medium Tank M4 with HVSS suspension.

NORMAL ROAD SPEED: 25 mph.

CREW: 8.

The U.S. Army 8-in. Howitzer Motor Carriage M43.

MODEL: 8-in. Howitzer Motor Carriage M43

WEIGHT: Fighting: 83,000 lbs.

DIMENSIONS: Length: 24 ft., 1 in. Height: 10 ft., 5-3/4 in. Width: 10 ft., 4 in.

CANNON: Modified 8-in. Howitzer M1. Range: 18,510 yards max. Ammunition: Separate loading HE. Projectile Weight: 200 lbs. Traverse: 16 degrees L, 18 degrees R. Elevation: +52 degrees, -0 degree. Fires from tracks with firing trail spade emplaced. Min. time to emplace: 15 min.

BASIC CHASSIS: Modified Medium Tank M4 with HVSS suspension.

NORMAL ROAD SPEED: 25 mph max.

CREW: 8

Chapter 19
Rocket Field Artillery

Despite the outstanding success of the "Bazooka" 2.36-in. shoulder-fired rocket launcher introduced in 1942, the World War II U.S. Army was slow and reluctant to adopt rocket field artillery. The U.S. Army had made limited use of rocket field artillery before the Civil War and found it unsatisfactory. From then until the late 1930s, the only rockets the U.S. Army used were pyrotechnic signal devices, but they did not use many of them.

During the rearmament period of the late 1930s, there was worldwide consideration given to rocket artillery. It always featured the fact that the rockets and launchers for them would cost less than regular artillery weapons and ammunition, and that they could be built in much less time. These discussions failed to mention the problems with artillery rockets, including their lack of range and accuracy. Until the development of the Bazooka, the U.S. Army had little or no interest in rocket field artillery.

After observing the use of rocket artillery by the British, Russians and Germans, the U.S. Armed Forces decided to begin building them for specialized uses. The British had instigated the U.S. production of rockets under Lend-Lease in 1941, and their technology was the starting point for the U.S. Armed Force's.

By 1942, considerable American scientific and manufacturing resources were being devoted to rockets, and the Bazooka was the first spectacular result of this. The development of air-to-ground aircraft rockets was a priority item, and both the U.S. Army Air Force and the U.S. Navy Air Force had their own programs. The U.S. Navy also had programs to develop rockets for shore bombardment, but the U.S. Army still had little or no interest in field artillery rockets.

A U.S. Army 4.5-in. Multiple Rocket Launcher T27 being demonstrated in Northern Europe in late 1944.

In 1942, the U.S. Army observed the use of rocket artillery with some interest. One type was the Russian "Katayusha" type truck-mounted multiple rocket launcher. Another was the German "Nebelwerfer" multiple rocket launchers. The U.S. Army captured and tested German Nebelwerfer in North Africa in 1942.

The tests of the Nebelwerfer did little to inspire the U.S. Army's interest in field artillery rockets. They were not only inaccurate short-range weapons, but they could be dangerous. The rockets were erratic in flight. In some cases they could fall well

GIs loading a pair of U.S. Army 4.5-in. Multiple Rocket Launchers T27 mounted in the back of a U.S. Army 2-1/2-ton 6x6 truck before going into action in Northern Europe in late 1944.

A U.S. Army 7.2-in. Multiple Rocket Launcher M17 mounted on a U.S. Army Medium Tank M4 being loaded in the Pacific Theater of Operations in mid-1945. The tankers could quickly and easily jettison the M17 launcher after firing its rockets.

A GI loading a U.S. Army 4.5-in. Multiple Rocket Launcher T34 mounted on a U.S. Army Medium Tank M4. The T34 launcher was designed so the tankers could quickly and easily jettison it after its rockets had been fired.

On the left is a U.S. Army 4.5-in. spin stabilized rocket; on the right is a U.S. Army 4.5-in. fin stabilized rocket with its fins extended as the rocket leaves the launcher tube.

U.S. Army 4.5-in. Multiple Rocket Launcher T34 going into action in Northern Europe in late 1944. These T34s mounted as shown on U.S. Army Medium Tanks M4 were probably the most used U.S. Army World War II artillery rocket launchers. They were used in Italy, France and Northern Europe in 1944 and 1945.

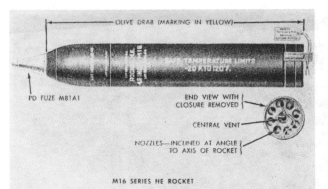

*The U.S. Army spin stabilized rocket M16 series. **WEIGHT:** 42.5 lbs. avg.; **VELOCITY:** 830 feet-per-second from a ground launcher; **RANGE:** 5,200 yds. max. This rocket is normally fired from short tube launchers but may be fired from modified long tube launchers. It is fired by electrical ignition through contact rings on the rear of the rocket body. As a field artillery rocket, only an impact point fuse is used. Its effect is similar to that of a standard U.S. Army 105mm Howitzer projectile.*

A U.S. Army 4.5-in. Multiple Rocket Launcher T34 mounted on a U.S. Army Medium Tank M4 firing in northern France in 1944.

short of their intended targets or turn in flight, and either of these problems could endanger friendly troops.

However, early in 1943, the U.S. Army had established preliminary requirements for rocket field artillery. They were very stringent with regards to overall reliability and accuracy.

The first U.S. Army field artillery rockets were a type not developed for field artillery use. In mid-1943, the 4.5-in. "Flying Bazooka" was adopted by the U.S. Army Air Force. This used very unaerodynamic 10-foot launching tubes to fire folding fin sta-

A U.S. Army quarter-ton Truck 4x4 "Jeep" mounting two U.S. Navy 4.5-in Automatic Rocker Launchers Mark 7 (U.S. Army T45). This experimental unit was not used in combat in World War II.

bilized air-to-ground rockets, and it enjoyed some success. It first saw service in Italy and China-Burma-India in late 1943.

More of the 4.5-in. Flying Bazookas were sent to Italy than the U.S. Army Air Corps could use, and some attempts were made there to employ them as rocket field artillery. In 1944-1945, the U.S. Army Ordnance Department developed several multiple launchers for the 4.5-in. fin stabilized rockets, which were used in combat, and several more of this type were built from surplus aircraft launcher tubes in the field. A single tube launcher for the 4.5-in. fin stabilized rocket was also developed for use by infantry units.

From the time the 4.5-in. fin stabilized rocket for the Flying Bazooka was adopted, the U.S. Army Air Force was not satisfied with its accuracy. In a serious effort to improve it, an interchangeable spin stabilized rocket was developed. It used a system of offset rocket nozzles to spin the rocket and stabilize it as the rifling in a gun stabilizes its projectile. This unit was perfected in 1944 and worked reasonably well, but before it could be put in wide service, an entirely new rocket and launching system developed by the U.S. Navy made the Flying Bazooka obsolescent. This made large numbers of the 4.5-in. spin stabilized rockets available for field artillery rocket use, and launchers for them were used in combat in late 1944-1945.

In 1943, the U.S. Navy developed a 4.5-in. fin stabilized rocket for anti-submarine use, and quickly found out it was also very useful for shore bombardment in amphibious operations. This 4.5-in. Navy rocket, which had fixed shrouded fins, was fired from an "automatic" launcher.

The U.S. Marine Corps adopted the U.S. Navy 4.5-in. rocket and its automatic launcher for mounting on light trucks and LVT tracked landing vehicles in 1944, and used it on a number of their amphibious operations in 1944-1945 with success. The U.S. Army adopted this rocket and launcher in 1945, and a Jeep mounting two of their design saw very limited service in the War in 1945.

A U.S. Army 4.5-in. Multiple Rocket Launcher T66 firing in Germany a few days before the end of World War II. Note the back-blast and rocket smoke, which instantly reveal the launcher's position when it is fired, one of the great problems with rocket artillery.

The U.S. Army 4.5-in. Multiple Rocket Launcher T44. This 108-tube launcher was designed to be assembled in and fired from the well deck of a U.S. Army 2-1/2-ton 6x6 Amphibious Truck DUKW (shown), the well deck of an LVT landing vehicle tracked or the well deck of a small U.S. Navy landing craft. It was intended to give shore bombardment during amphibious operations. A limited production of 250 were built in 1944-1945, and some of these were employed in U.S. Army and U.S. Marine Corps amphibious operations in the Pacific Theater of Operations in 1945. This unit was only marginally successful, and was retired shortly after World War II ended.

The U.S. Army 7.2-in. Multiple Rocket Launcher T32. This open crate launcher mounted on the bed of a standard U.S. Army 2-1/2-ton 6x6 truck was designed to fire only the improved U.S. Army model 7.2-in. long-range rockets. Its design was inspired by the success of the Russian truck-mounted "Katayusha" multiple rocket launchers. Only a few prototypes of this launcher were built, and when testing after World War II proved they were not satisfactory for U.S. Army use, they and the project were scrapped. None were ever used in combat in World War II.

203

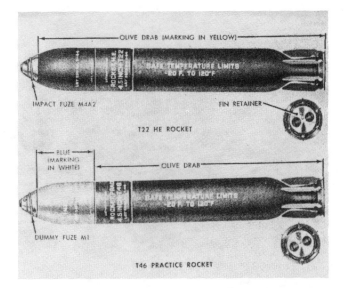

The U.S. Army 4.5-in. folding fin stabilized rocket M8 series. WEIGHT: 38.5 lbs avg.; VELOCITY: 850 feet-per-second from a ground launcher. RANGE: 4,200 yds. max. This rocket is suitable for long tube launchers only. It is fired by electrical ignition through "pigtail" connections. An impact fuse is used only for field artillery. Its effect is similar to that of a standard U.S. Army 105mm howitzer projectile.

The last, and largest, rocket adopted for artillery rocket use by the U.S. Army in World War II was the U.S. Navy's 7.2-in. fin stabilized type. The Navy had originally developed this rocket for anti-submarine use in 1943, and then quickly adapted it for use as an amphibious assault shore bombardment weapon. In 1945, the U.S. Army adopted two launchers for the U.S. Navy 7.2-in. bombardment rocket in 1945, and both were given "combat tests" late in World War II.

All of the World War II U.S. Army artillery rockets were electrically fired from multiple rocket launchers, and electrical firing boxes had to be developed for them. These were battery powered. The legend was that the first type used in Italy was field improvised by a U.S. Army ordnance man who had built similar devices to fire special effects for Hollywood movies. These "electrical firing boxes" could fire their launcher's rockets three ways: one at a time, in a sequential "ripple" of one every second or so, or all in one salvo. Ripple fire or single fire was most desirable because it had a minimum effect on the launcher's accuracy, making the fire more effective on the desired target.

Because of the accuracy limitations of World War II rockets, the U.S. Army found them only effective in area fire and useless in firing at point targets. When they were to be used their fire missions were assigned and directed by the local U.S. Army Field Artillery fire control and direction system.

With the firing data given them, the field artillery rocket launchers were pointed at the target and given the elevation necessary for the rockets to reach it. This done, they would cut loose their rockets when ordered to do so, and there was no possibility of correcting their fire once it started. In most cases the field artillery rocket launchers only fired one or two loads and moved away from

their firing location because of the danger of enemy artillery locating it and firing back.

Although the U.S. Army and U.S. Marine Corps made some effective use of rocket field artillery in World War II, it was never very extensive because of the experimental nature of the weapons. In addition, their use was not necessary since the U.S. Army had all the conventional field artillery it needed, and its more accurate fire was far more effective than rocket fire.

During World War II, U.S. Army rockets fired in combat in the European Theater of Operations were fired either by units composed of technicians from the U.S. Army rocket development facilities and any other local troops available or by regular U.S. Army field artillerymen assigned the task. The U.S. Army had formed a number of Rocket Field Artillery Battalions before the end of World War II, but only two saw combat: one on Okinawa and the other in the Philippines. The U.S. Marine Corps also formed a number of rocket field artillery units, which it used in the last of its World War II campaigns.

At the end of World War II, the U.S. Army considered rocket field artillery still in the experimental and developmental stage. No existing type of rocket or launcher was considered entirely satisfactory, although a number remained in service after the end of the war. Nevertheless, the further development of rocket field artillery continued.

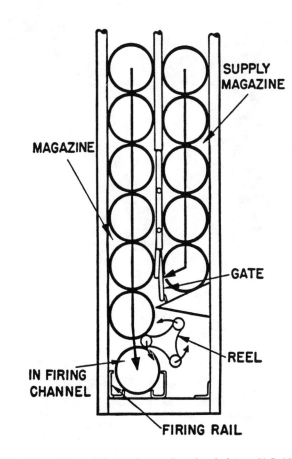

The disposition of the twelve rockets loaded in a U.S. Navy 4.5-in. Automatic Rocket Launcher Mark 7 (U.S. Army T45).

204

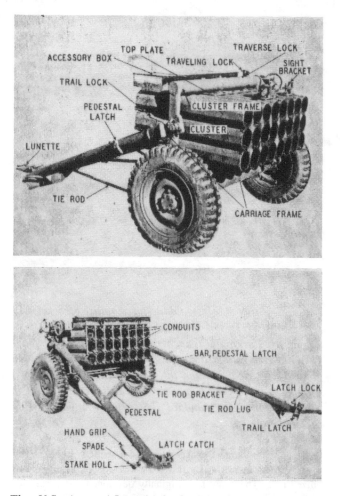

The U.S. Navy 4.5-in. fin stabilized barrage rocket.
WEIGHT: *30 lbs.* **VELOCITY:** *400 feet-per-second;*
RANGE: *1,100 yds. max. This rocket is fired in the U.S.
Navy 4.5-in. Automatic Rocket Launcher Mark 7 (U.S. Army
T45) only. It is fired by electrical ignition through contact
rings on the rocket's tail fin shroud. Only a point impact fuse
is used. Its effect is similar to a standard U.S. Army 75mm
gun or howitzer high-explosive shell.*

FUZE LINER
FUZE
PROPELLER
FUZE DETONATOR & BOOSTER
BODY BOOSTER
HEAD
HIGH EXPLOSIVE
FIBER DISK
ADAPTER
BLACK POWDER IGNITER
PROPELLANT
IGNITER LEAD WIRES
2.25-IN. MOTOR
SHORTING CLIP
SHORTING CLIP RING
FIN SHROUDS
NOZZLE
DRYING BAG
FIBER DISK
NOZZLE
REAR SHROUD (GROUND CONTACT)
FRONT SHROUD (POSITIVE CONTACT)
RA PD 113295

ACCESSORY BOX — TOP PLATE — TRAVELING LOCK — TRAVERSE LOCK — SIGHT BRACKET
TRAIL LOCK
PEDESTAL LATCH
CLUSTER FRAME
CLUSTER
LUNETTE
TIE ROD
CARRIAGE FRAME

CONDUITS
BAR, PEDESTAL LATCH
TIE ROD BRACKET
LATCH LOCK
PEDESTAL
TIE ROD LUG
TRAIL LATCH
HAND GRIP
SPADE
LATCH CATCH
STAKE HOLE

The U.S. Army 4.5-in. Multiple Rocket Launcher T66.
WEIGHT: *1,200 lbs. unloaded, 2,220 lbs. with rockets.*
LENGTH: *120 in.;* **WIDTH:** *62 in.;* **HEIGHT:** *43 in.*
RANGE: *5,000 yds apprx. This twenty-four-tube rocket
launcher was designed to fire the U.S. Army 4.5-in. spin stabilized rocket as a rocket field artillery weapon. It was a
self-contained unit with azimuth and elevation aiming provisions and electric firing gear for the rockets. It was
designed to be normally towed by a U.S. Army three-quarter-ton 4x4 Weapons Carrier and could be towed by a Jeep.*

*A limited production run of 500 T66 launchers were built in
1944-1945, and they saw limited use in Northern Europe
and the Pacific Theater of Operations in 1945. This
launcher was retained in service by the U.S. Army after
World War II.*

A U.S. Army 75mm Howitzer armed Landing Vehicle Tracked LVT(A)-4 mounting two U.S. Navy 4.5-in. Automatic Rocket Launchers Mark 7 (U.S. Army T45) on its stern. The U.S. Army and U.S. marine Corps used this system in 1945 amphibious operations.

The U.S. Army 4.5-in. Multiple Rocket Launcher T27. This lightweight eight-tube launcher for the U.S. Army 4.5-in. fin stabilized rocket was developed in 1944. It was intended to be fired either from the ground or from the bed of a truck such as the U.S. Army 2-1/2-ton 6x6. A limited production run of 912 of these launchers was made in 1944-1945, including their electrical firing boxes and other accessories. After limited combat use in World War II, particularly in Northern Europe, this launcher was retired shortly after World War II.

The U.S. Army 4.5-in. Multiple Rocket Launcher T34. This sixty-tube launcher was designed to mount on the turret of the U.S. Army Medium Tank M4 to provide bombardment firepower for offensive tank actions. The tank could quickly and easily jettison the launcher after its rockets had been expended. A limited production run of 850 of these launchers was built in 1943-1944, and this launcher saw considerable use in Italy and the European Theater of Operations in 1944-1945. This launcher was retired shortly after the end of World War II. It is reported that T34 launchers modified to be fired from the ground were used in very limited numbers in combat as field expedient bombardment rocket artillery.

The U.S. Army field improvised Jeep-mounted 4.5-in. rocket launcher. This model of twelve-tube rocket launcher was designed and built in France in late 1944 to provide highly mobile rocket fire support for U.S. Army armored units. A small number of these launchers were built, and they saw some combat use in Germany in 1945. This design was never adopted by the U.S. Army on an official basis, and the existing units were scrapped shortly after the end of World War II.

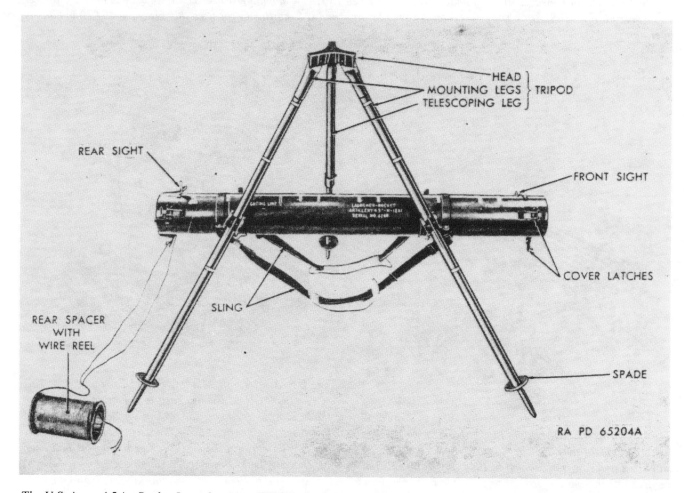

The U.S. Army 4.5-in. Rocket Launcher M12. **WEIGHT:** 22 lbs.; **TUBE LENGTH:** 48 in.; **VELOCITY:** 830 feet-per-second; **RANGE:** 5,300 yds. max., 500 yds at point targets. This lightweight launcher was made to fire both the fin and spin stabilized U.S. Army 4.5-in. rockets. It was intended to be used in the same manner and situations as the U.S. Army 4.2-in. Chemical Mortar M2. This launcher could be used singly, however, in its limited combat use it was used in groups as a barrage firing rocket launching system. Although it was retained by the U.S. Army after World War II, it was never considered a satisfactory weapon.

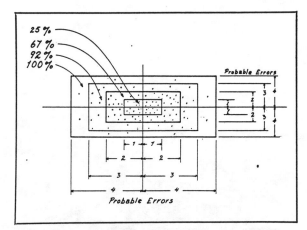

Dispersion pattern showing typical distribution of 100 shots.

TABLE OF DISPERSION
FOR M16 ROCKETS (SPIN-STABILIZED)

Range (yards)	Range Dispersion (8 probable errors) (yards)	Lateral Dispersion (8 probable errors) (yards)
1,000	900	105
2,000	815	210
3,000	720	310
4,000	580	420
5,000	380	520
5,200	340	550

This dispersion data for the 4.5-in. spin stabilized rocket published shortly after World War II shows their accuracy was not nearly as good as any conventional artillery, and only suitable for area targets.

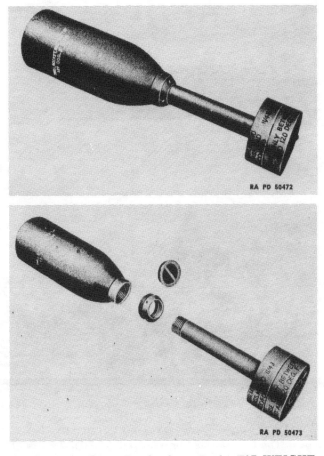

The U.S. Navy 7.2-in. Bombardment Rocket T37. **WEIGHT:** *61 lbs.* **VELOCITY:** *160 feet-per-second:* **RANGE:** *230 yds. max. This rocket is fired from the U.S. Army 7.2-in. Multiple Rocket Launcher M17 mounted on the U.S. Army Medium Tank M4. It is fired by electrical ignition through contact rings on the rocket's tail fin shroud. Only point impact fused high-explosive rockets were used for field artillery use. The effect of this rocket is about the same as that of a standard U.S. Army 105mm howitzer HE Shell. At the end of the war, improved field artillery versions of this rocket, which weighed 52 pounds and had a 3,430-yard range, were under field test.*

U.S. Marine Corps "Rocketeers" on Iwo Jima, firing U.S. Navy 4.5-in. Automatic Rocket Launchers Mark 7 (U.S. Army T45) mounted on U.S. Marine Corps International one-ton 4x4 M2-4 trucks.

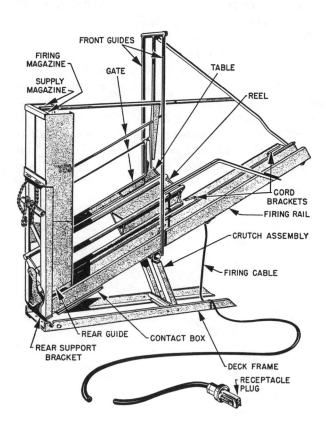

The U.S. Navy 4.5-in. Automatic Rocket Launcher Mark 7 (U.S. Army T45). *This twelve-round launcher was designed by the U.S. Navy for use as an anti-submarine weapon mounted on U.S. Navy small craft. It was then adapted for mounting on U.S. Navy small landing craft to deliver fire support during amphibious operations. Then the U.S. Marine Corps adapted it to mount on their LVT landing vehicles tracked and on their light trucks for use in amphibious operations. The U.S. Army developed a system of eight of these launchers to mount in the well deck of the U.S. Army 2-1/2-ton 6x6 amphibious truck DUKW, as well as a system mounting a pair of them on the back of a Jeep or one-ton truck.*

This launcher fires its twelve rockets from its gravity-fed magazine either singly or in one long burst. The mounting for these launchers is fixed, and they could be fired only in the direction of the enemy since precision aiming was not provided for. When required for installation in or on boats or vehicles, a blast shield was provided.

The production of these launchers was over 10,000 with some 2,000 going to the U.S. Army. Vehicles mounting these launchers saw considerable service with both the U.S. Army and U.S. Marine Corps in the Pacific Theater of Operations in 1944 and 1945, particularly in amphibious landing operations.

Although the U.S. Army discontinued the use of this launcher shortly after the end of World War II, the U.S. Navy continued to use it long after World War II.

The U.S. Army Bomb Rocket Launcher T103. This experimental trough-type rocket launcher was built on the carriage of a standard U.S. Army Pack Howitzer M3 to launch either U.S. Army 100-pound or 250-pound General Purpose Aircraft Bombs fitted with a special rocket motor and fired at ground targets. The inspiration for this unit was a similar one developed by the Japanese and used in their Pacific Theater of Operations defenses.

A very small number of these units were combat tested in the Philippines in 1945 and found totally unsatisfactory in respect to range and accuracy. The project had been dropped by the time World War II ended.

A GI loads a field-improvised and constructed 4.5-in. twelve-tube fin stabilized rocket launcher in Germany in the spring of 1945.

The U.S. Army 7.2-in. Multiple Rocket Launcher M17 (T40). This twenty-round armored launcher mounted on the turret of a standard U.S. Army Medium Tank M4 to give short-range fire support in amphibious operations. The tankers could easily and quickly jettison the launcher after its rounds had been expended. This launcher was developed with the difficulty of overcoming Japanese beach obstructions and barbed wire entanglement in mind.

A limited production run of 582 of these M17 launchers were built in 1944-1945, and a very limited number saw combat use late in the war. This unit was retained by the U.S. Army after the end of World War II.

Chapter 20
Light Antiaircraft Weapons

The U.S. Army recognized the need for light antiaircraft weapons for attacks from low flying enemy aircraft in World War I. A program was begun to develop them, which provided many uses in World War II.

The first U.S. Army light antiaircraft weapons were machine guns mounted on antiaircraft mounts. In 1922, the U.S. Army adopted the water-cooled cal. .50 Browning Machine Gun M1921 described as "suitable for either antiaircraft or ground fire use." Many M1921 Browning .50's were used on a high tripod mount adapted for antiaircraft use. Although the M1921 Browning was obsolescent by World War II, a number were used in the Philippines and elsewhere in 1941-1942.

In 1932, the U.S. Army adopted an improved version of the cal. .50 Browning; any of the three models were easily converted to any other model. The models adopted were the cal. .50 Browning Aircraft Machine Gun M2, the cal. .50 Browning water-cooled Machine Gun M2, and the air-cooled cal. .50 Browning Machine Gun M2-HB, which is still in U.S. Armed Forces use today.

The Browning water-cooled cal. .50 was intended for use as an antiaircraft weapon. For this use, it was provided with a heavy antiaircraft mount and antiaircraft sights. By 1938, special U.S. Army truck-transported antiaircraft units armed with this weapon

A U.S. Army cal. .50 Multiple Machine Gun Carriage M51 emplaced to defend the Rhine River bridge at Remagen, Germany.

A U.S. Army cal. .50 Browning water-cooled Machine Gun M2 on Mount M2 in firing position with the U.S. Army Desert Training Command in California in 1942.

were in service; they were equipped with a simple fire control and direction system to acquire targets and give firing data on them to the guns. Although this system was used into 1943, and its fire control and direction system was used with light antiaircraft weapons for the rest of World War II, the use of the .50 Browning changed during the war.

The development of motorization in the U.S. Army brought about a need for self-propelled antiaircraft protection, and to fill it, water-cooled cal. .50 Brownings on antiaircraft mounts were mounted in the backs of trucks. This use precluded the use of the fire control and direction equipment, and the guns had to rely on antiaircraft sights and tracer ammunition fire. Although this measure was employed into 1943, it was wasteful and impractical to employ a truck for just one cal. .50 antiaircraft gun, so the guns were fired more and more often from the ground at flying "targets of opportunity."

Although the water-cooled .50 Browning was an excellent weapon capable of more sustained fire than an air-cooled .50, combat use proved the weight and complications of the water-cooled gun were not necessary because of the limited time targets were within range. The cal. .50 water-cooled Browning became obsolescent in 1943, and was not employed by the U.S. Army after World War II.

Before World War II, the air-cooled Browning .50 M2-HB was being issued to units with an antiaircraft adapter for its low tripod. At the same time, a number of vehicle mounts that could be used for antiaircraft fire were being developed, and in World War II, large numbers of U.S. Army tanks and trucks were fitted with .50 M2-HBs for both antiaircraft and local defense. While vehicle-mounted .50 M2-HBs proved useful, they were not what the U.S. Army wanted for cal. .50 Browning light antiaircraft weapons.

In 1941, the U.S. Army tested one of the new Martin twin .50 Browning aircraft turrets mounted on a half-track. Tests proved this was potentially a very effective antiaircraft weapon, but it was obvious that aircraft use requirements would make it impossible to

A U.S. Army cal. .50 Browning water-cooled Machine Gun M2 on Mount M2 in firing position in Italy in the winter of 1943-1944.

use this turret. This led to a requirement for a twin .50 Browning power turret designed for ground use only.

The W.L. Maxon Company quickly developed a self-contained twin .50 Browning power turret to meet the requirement for one suitable for mounting on vehicles. While it was obviously related to the aircraft-type power turret, it was a design well adapted for ground use. It tested better than anyone could have predicted, and its development went very quickly.

In late 1941, the U.S. Army adopted the "Maxon Mount" as the Twin cal. .50 Machine Gun Mount M33. It mounted two cal. .50 Browning Machine Guns M2-HB. It was a compact fully self-contained unit complete with a small gasoline engine motor-generator to power it. It was equipped with the brand new U.S. Navy Mark IX aircraft reflex gun sight to be used in conjunction with tracer fire. The unit weighed 1,500 pounds, so it could be mounted on any motor vehicle with a one-ton capacity.

By early 1942, the Maxon twin .50 mount had been mounted on a standard U.S. Army half-track with its armor sides made to fold part way down so as not to interfere with the unit's field-of-fire. This unit was adopted in early 1942 as the Multiple Gun Motor Carriage M13 (on the White half-track) and M14 (on the International Harvester half-track). Production began at once, and half-tracks with Maxon twin .50 power turrets were in the hands of troops by mid-1942.

The Maxon twin .50 mount on half-tracks first saw action in North Africa in 1942-1943. It was completely successful; however, a major modification of the twin .50 unit caused it to become obsolete in 1944, and it was retired by the end of World War II.

As soon as the twin .50 Maxon Mount was in production, people began to suggest it would be much more effective if it mounted four guns. At the same time, the vastly expanded production of cal. .50 Brownings was sufficient to supply the number required for this use without affecting any other requirements. The Maxon Mount was quickly redesigned to accommodate four cal. .50 Browning Machine Guns M2-HB, and was adopted as the Multiple Machine Gun Mount M45. This quad .50 Maxon Mount added a shield to protect the gunner. It was in production in 1943.

A well-camouflaged quad .50 machine gun U.S. Army Multiple Gun Motor Carriage M16 in action at Anzio, Italy.

A U.S. Army 40mm Automatic Antiaircraft Gun M1 firing at a ground target in Italy in 1944.

A crewman with a ten-round clip of ammunition for his U.S. Army 37mm Automatic Antiaircraft Gun M1 in the Pacific Theater of Operations in the fall of 1944.

A U.S. Army 40mm Automatic Antiaircraft Gun M1 covers a road during the Battle of the Bulge in Belgium in late 1944. The 40mm gun was surprisingly effective against lightly armored vehicles.

A twin cal. .50 machine gun Multiple Gun Motor Carriage M13. A very few of these units were used in combat in North Africa in 1942-1943 before they were replaced with self-propelled quad .50 machine gun half-tracks.

One of the first applications of the quad .50 Maxon mount was to mount it on a half-track as had been done with the twin .50 Maxon mount. This unit was adopted in mid-1943 as the Multiple Gun Motor Carriage M16 (on the White half-track) and M17 (on the International Harvester half-track), Both of these were in the hands of troops in 1943. They were soon used in combat and proved very effective, and they remained in service after World War II.

While the half-track-mounted Maxon quad .50 was an ideal mobile antiaircraft weapon, it was also suitable for use in a less mobile form. To achieve this, the quad .50 Maxon mount was adapted to mount in a special Mount Trailer M17, a modification of a motor-generator set trailer. This combination was designated the Multiple cal. .50 Machine Gun Carriage M51, and it was also in service in 1943. The M51-towed quad .50 Maxon mount was very useful and effective, and it remained in U.S. Army use long after World War II.

The U.S. Army Airborne Command initiated a requirement for a lightweight version of the quad .50 Maxon mount, and one was designed in late 1943. This unit consisted of the quad .50 Multiple Machine Gun Mount M45C, a model without the heavy shield, and

a special lightweight Trailer M20 combined as the Multiple cal. .50 Machine Gun Trailer Mount M55. This unit was in the hands of airborne troops in early 1944. Its use in World War II was limited as it required either a cargo aircraft or glider to carry it into action, however, it remained in U.S. Army service long after World War II.

World War II combat records show the quad .50 Maxon mount was very effective against low flying hostile aircraft. When the threat of enemy air attack declined late in the war, they were often used to fire on enemy ground troops, and they could be devastatingly effective in this role.

In World War I, the U.S. Army tested such weapons as the 37mm Maxim machine gun for antiaircraft use. This weapon fell between the light machine guns and the heavy cannon types used against hostile aircraft flying at intermediate altitudes. As a result, the U.S. Army had a requirement for such an automatic antiaircraft gun. John M. Browning, inventor of the cal. .50 machine gun and many other U.S. Army weapons, began working on one about 1922. He had a prototype 37mm automatic gun firing shortly before his death in 1925, and then the Colt Patent Firearms Company took over its development in association with the U.S. Army Ordnance Department.

Although the U.S. army requirement for a 37mm automatic gun was fairly urgent, its development was slow due to the many technical problems associated with the development of the gun, its carriage and ammunition. The Browning 37mm Automatic Antiaircraft Gun M1 was finally adopted by the U.S. Army in 1938, and immediately put into production by Colt and the U.S. Army Watervliet Arsenal.

A top view of the U.S. Army Combination Gun Motor Carriage M15A1.

The U.S. Army Combination Gun Mount M42 used in the Combination Gun Motor Carriage M15.

A U.S. Army Combination Gun Motor Carriage M15A1 in action in Northern Europe in the fall of 1944.

A U.S. Army 40mm Automatic Antiaircraft Gun M1 set up for action in a town in Northern Europe in late 1944.

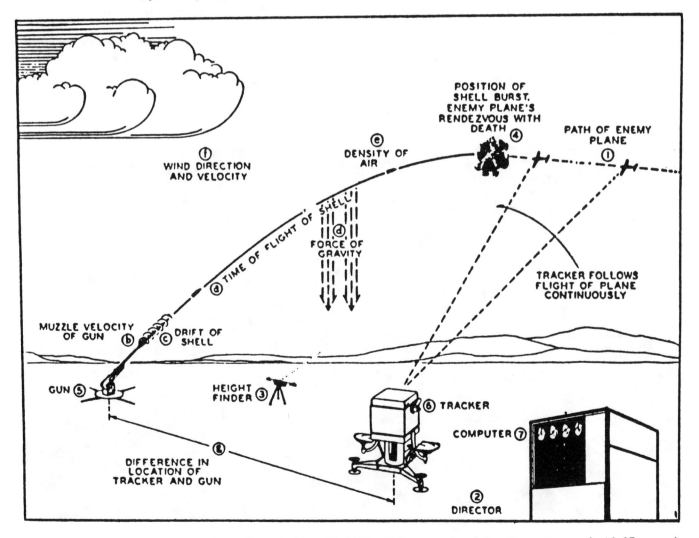

This U.S. Army training diagram shows the typical late World War II fire control and direction system used with 37mm and 40mm ground-mounted antiaircraft guns. If available, radar input could be added through the computer.

The U.S. Army 40mm Automatic Antiaircraft Gun M5 in firing position. This airborne weapon was a very limited production item.

The 37mm Automatic Antiaircraft Gun M1 was mounted on a two-axle trailer with wheels that elevated so the gun could be emplaced on the ground. The mount was manually loaded and aimed by soldiers sitting on either side of the gun. It used either its own optical sights or fire direction from off the mount, and tracer ammunition was used to correct aim. This weapon first went into U.S. Army service in 1939, and it was used in the Defense of the Philippines and other places in 1941-1942. However, at the time the U.S. Army entered the war, its known deficiencies were being corrected.

By the time U.S. Army troops went into action in North Africa in November 1942, the improved 37mm Automatic Antiaircraft Gun M1A1 had been adopted and was in service. The major changes in the M1A1 model were cartwheel "speed ring" sights replacing the original optical sights, and power traverse and elevation units to complement the original manual controls so the gun could be aimed by an off-carriage fire control and direction system. These new sights and fire control system provisions made the M1A1 37mm gun much more effective against high-speed hostile aircraft. The M1A1 37mm automatic antiaircraft gun remained a standard weapon until the U.S. Army retired it shortly after the end of World War II.

The U.S. Army Armored Force Command developed a requirement for a self-propelled mount for the 37mm automatic antiaircraft gun in 1941, and to fill it the U.S. Army Ordnance Department experimentally mounted one on the back of an armored half-track without the armor body aft of the drivers compartment. This mount used the original M1 gun and had no provisions for off-mount fire control. Its fire against high-speed low-flying aircraft was not nearly as effective as desired.

Then somebody, another of the legion of forgotten World War II U.S. Army geniuses, suggested mounting a pair of cal. .50 Browning machine guns with the 37mm automatic gun so the 37mm could use the Brownings' tracer fire to aim with before it opened fire. This was tried with a 37mm automatic gun with cartwheel antiaircraft speed ring sights, and it worked very well.

In early 1942, the U.S. Army adopted the 37mm Combination Gun Mount M42 with a 37mm Automatic Antiaircraft Gun and top carriage with two cal. .50 Browning water-cooled Machine Guns M2 mounted with it, and this was mounted on an open back armored half-track. A large box shield was provided to protect the guns and gunners, and it rotated with them. The unit was adopted

A camouflage draped quad .50 machine gun U.S. Army Multiple Gun Motor Carriage M16 firing at a ground target in northern France in the fall of 1944.

GI gunners practice firing a U.S. Army 40mm Automatic Antiaircraft Gun M1 at the U.S. Army Desert Training Center in California in 1942.

The original version of the U.S. Army Combination Gun Motor Carriage M15 with cal. .50 water-cooled machine guns and no gun shield. A number of this version were used in North Africa in 1942-1943, after they had been equipped with a gun shield, and they were later converted to mount cal. .50 air-cooled machine guns.

An early manufacture U.S. Army 37mm Automatic Antiaircraft Gun M1 in a firing demonstration in 1940.

The limited production U.S. Army 40mm Automatic Antiaircraft Gun M5 in traveling order.

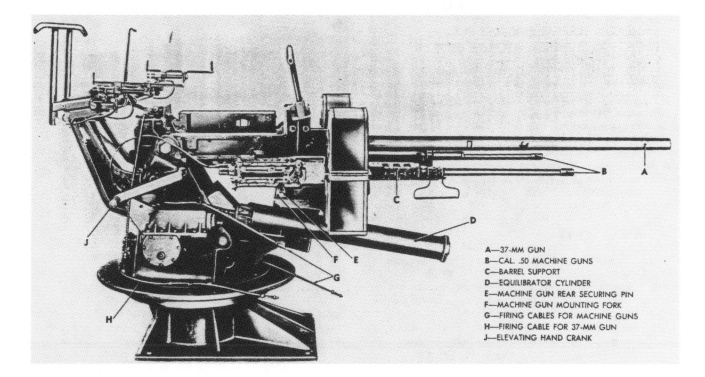

A—37-MM GUN
B—CAL. .50 MACHINE GUNS
C—BARREL SUPPORT
D—EQUILIBRATOR CYLINDER
E—MACHINE GUN REAR SECURING PIN
F—MACHINE GUN MOUNTING FORK
G—FIRING CABLES FOR MACHINE GUNS
H—FIRING CABLE FOR 37-MM GUN
J—ELEVATING HAND CRANK

The U.S. Army Combination Gun Mount M54 used in the Combination Gun Motor Carriage M15A1.

in early 1942 as the Multiple Gun Motor Carriage M15, and it first saw service in North Africa in 1942.

Combat use proved the mount did not require the water-cooled .50 Brownings since they fired at flying targets in very short bursts, which did not heat them much. The M42 mount was reequipped with air-cooled cal. .50 Browning Machine guns M2HB, and the existing mounts were retrofitted with them. The whole self-propelled mount remained the M15, and it saw service during and after World War II.

In late 1943, reports from U.S. Army troops in the field led to an improvement of the 37mm automatic gun, cal. .50 Browning combination mount. In the original M42 combination mount, the cal. .50 Brownings had been mounted above the 37mm automatic gun, and tests showed the fire of the guns would be better "harmonized" so their trajectories better matched if they were below it.

Improved sights were also developed, and the huge box shield was made lower and less confining. By 1944, all these and other minor changes had been incorporated in the Combination Mount M54, which was mounted on a modified armored half-track as the Combination Gun Motor Carriage M15A1. The M15A1 was an effective unit used in World War II, and it was retained after the war.

Production of all the models of the 37mm automatic antiaircraft gun was completed in 1944, with all anticipated U.S. Army requirements for them filled. Late in the war, when the threat of air attack declined, the 37mm automatic antiaircraft guns were often fired very effectively at ground targets. The 37mm automatic gun was considered obsolete at the end of World War II; however, a number of them, mounted on half-tracks, were used in Korea.

The 37mm automatic gun became obsolete because the U.S. Army had adopted the 40mm Bofors automatic gun to replace it. The Bofors 40mm was developed in Sweden in the early 1930s. It was proven a very effective antiaircraft weapon in the Spanish

A U.S. Marine Corps field improvised twin 20mm Oerlikon automatic antiaircraft gun used in the Pacific Theater of Operations in 1943. The U.S. Armed Forces never adopted a 20mm antiaircraft gun for ground use in World War II, although they were used on practically every American ship of every type.

Civil War of the late 1930s, and by 1940 it was in use in the British, German and French armies. Shortly after the fall of France in 1940, the British were preparing to have the gun manufactured for them in the United States.

However, in the late 1930s, both the U.S. Army and U.S. Navy had procured 40mm Bofors guns and found they were potentially very effective antiaircraft weapons. The British request to have them manufactured in the United States was made part of the Lend-Lease program, and the U.S. Army and U.S. Navy both expressed the intention of adopting the gun.

The British government assisted the United States government in obtaining manufacturing rights for the gun, and it became a joint U.S. Army-U.S. Navy project. Before the gun could be put in production in the United States, its design had to be reengineered to suit American manufacturing and related standards. Initially, the priority was for the U.S. Navy's water-cooled shipboard mount for the gun, so the U.S. Army deferred their needs until the Navy's could be met.

The U.S. Army wanted to adopt the air-cooled version of the 40mm Bofors automatic antiaircraft gun used by the British Army. The gun and mount were reengineered to American standards by Chrysler Corporation and Firestone Tire and Rubber Corporation, and in December, 1940, the U.S. Army adopted the Bofors as the 40mm Automatic Antiaircraft Gun M1. However, because of U.S. Navy requirements, the U.S. Army only received a limited number of their M1 40mm Bofors guns before 1943.

The 40mm Bofors had a higher muzzle velocity and longer effective range than the co-standard 37mm automatic gun. It was also larger and heavier than the 37mm gun. The 40mm Bofors had "cartwheel" speed ring antiaircraft sights as well as provisions for power control with off-carriage fire control and direction equip-

ment. Because of its long range, the most effective fire of the 40mm Bofors was delivered with off-carriage control.

The 40mm U.S. Army Bofors was an excellent weapon, but by the time substantial numbers of units armed with it went into combat in late 1943 and early 1944, the threat of enemy aircraft attack was on the decline. This led to its employment against ground targets, where it proved effective. It was also effective against lightly armored vehicles.

Production of the 40mm Bofors was very high because of the U.S. Navy's need for them, and by early 1944, the existing and anticipated U.S. Army requirement for them had been filled.

At about the time U.S. Army 40mm Bofors production stopped, a special model was produced for airborne use. This was the limited production 40mm Automatic Gun M5 (Airborne). This weapon had a very light carriage, making it suitable for cargo aircraft or glider transportation. This single axle mount was only suitable for trucks towing short distances at low speeds, but it met the requirement. When this design had been adopted in late 1943, it was designated as both an antiaircraft and antitank weapon, and it had no provisions for off-carriage power fire control.

After a series of experiments, the U.S. Army adopted the Bofors self-propelled Twin 40mm Gun Motor Carriage M19 in 1943. This adapted the U.S. Navy's twin 40mm Bofors mount for mounting on the modified chassis of the new U.S. Army M24 Chaffee light tank. By the time this powerful weapon was ready for production, the threat from hostile aircraft attack had declined so much that the production was given little priority. Few, if any, M19s saw action in World War II; however, it was an excellent weapon and its production continued after the end of the war.

A U.S. Army 37mm Automatic Antiaircraft Gun M1 in firing position in Alaska in 1942.

The U.S. Army 40mm Automatic Antiaircraft Gun M5 as the U.S. Army Airborne Command configured it for glider transport. The unit shown included the gun action and mount with one trail; its barrel and three other trails were transported on a second trailer.

Both the 40mm Bofors towed M1 model and the self-propelled M19 twin mount were retained by the U.S. Army long after World War II.

Although 20mm light antiaircraft guns were used by the British, German, Japanese and other combatants in World War II, the U.S. Army never adopted one. Two different types of 20mm automatic guns were used by the U.S. Armed Forces in World War II: the U.S. Navy shipboard-type 20mm Oerlikon gun and the U.S. Army Air Force 20mm aircraft gun. While the U.S. Army experimented with light antiaircraft mounts for both, none were ever adopted, and there were several reasons for this.

A primary reason the U.S. Army never adopted a 20mm antiaircraft gun was because it believed that its family of cal. .50, 37mm and 40mm antiaircraft weapons was all it required, and this was born out by their proven effectiveness. In order to use 20mm antiaircraft weapons safely over friendly troops, a self-destroying element was required by the U.S. Army, something such as a self-destroying tracer element to explode the projectile in flight so it would not explode when it fell in friendly areas, and no such ammunition was developed in World War II.

The U.S. Army did test an enlarged version of the .50 Browning Maxon mount, which mounted four 20mm Hispano-Suiza aircraft automatic guns. It was never adopted because it was very large and clumsy, and the reliability and ruggedness of the 20mm gun it mounted did not meet U.S. Army Ground Forces requirements.

The U.S. Army did use U.S. Navy 20mm Oerlikon guns on practically all its Transportation Corps ships and other vessels, and reports indicate a few were emplaced on shore to protect forward area harbors. The U.S. Army never authorized the use of the 20mm Oerlikon on land.

The U.S. Marine Corps, a part of the U.S. Navy, occasionally did emplace shipboard 20mm Oerlikons on shore for local antiaircraft defense, but this required construction of a heavy base for the mount. The Marines also tried to employ the 20mm Oerlikon shipboard gun in landing operations, but they could never devise a practical way of doing this. The Marines also tried mounting twin 20mm Oerlikons on the carriage for the U.S. Army standard 37mm Automatic Gun M1. While this system worked and a few field constructed units were employed in combat areas, it was tested by the U.S. Army and never adopted since the cal. .50 Maxon quad mount filled the same role.

Postwar evaluations of U.S. Army light antiaircraft weapons stressed the large amount of effort devoted to them from World War I until 1943. In 1943, Allied air power began to dominate the skies, and the requirement for light antiaircraft weapons rapidly declined. So did their development. This led to efforts to make use of available light antiaircraft weapons for ground combat, and as a result of this, much was said about the dual purpose use of them and their mounts in the future.

The U.S. Army 40mm Automatic Antiaircraft Gun M1 on the march and prepared to fire from its wheels.

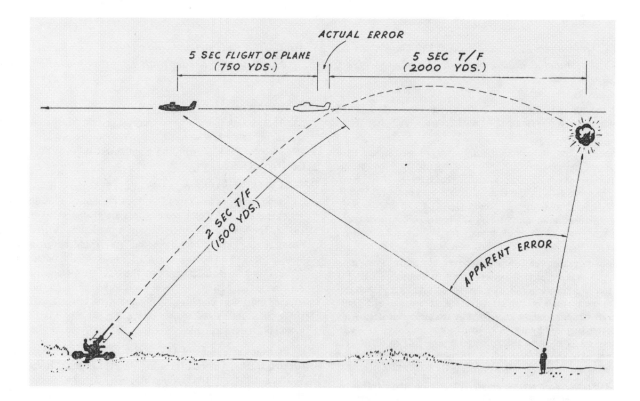

This U.S. Army World War II training diagram depicts the difference between actual error and apparent error of a 40mm anti-aircraft gun firing at a 300 mph aircraft at 1,500 yards range. This shows the problem U.S. Army antiaircraft radar fire control solved by the end of 1944.

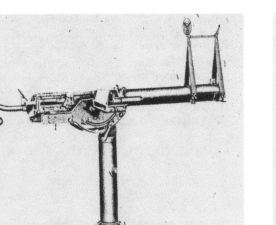

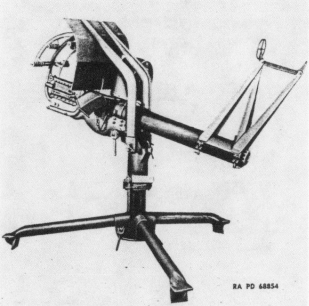

The U.S. Army cal. .50 Browning water-cooled Machine Gun M2 on Mount M2.

The U.S. Army cal. .50 Browning water-cooled Machine Gun M2 on Mount M3.

MODEL: Cal. .50 Browning Water-Cooled Machine Gun M2 and Antiaircraft Mounts M2 and M3

WEIGHTS: Machine Gun only: 121 lbs.; Machine Gun with Mount M2: 506 lbs.; Machine Gun with Mount M2 with armor shield: 623 lbs.; Machine Gun with Mount M3: 646 lbs.

DIMENSIONS: Length of Machine Gun only: 5 ft., 6 in.; Height of Machine Gun on Mount: M2: 4 ft., 6 in.; M3: 3 ft., 6 in. Emplacement requires a 6 ft. 10 in. diameter clear circle on ground.

TRAVERSE: 360 degrees. Elevation: Mount M2: +60 degrees, -15 degrees; Mount 3: +90 degrees, -15 degrees.

AMMUNITION: Any standard U.S. Army cal. .50 machine gun type.

RATE OF FIRE: 450 rounds per minute in bursts, 100 to 150 rounds per minute sustained.

RANGE: Antiaircraft approx. 2,000 ft.; Horizontal: 7,200 yards max.

ACCESSORIES: 200 round cal. .50 Ammunition Chest M2, weight: 95 lbs. filled; cal. .50 Water Chest M3 complete with hoses, weight: 139.5 lbs. filled with 8 gallons of water.

NOTE: The above mounts may be modified to mount the cal. .50 Browning Machine Gun M2-HB by installing a counterweight for the weight of the water-cooled .50 machine guns' water jacket.

These mounts are impractical for use with the air-cooled cal. .50 Browning Aircraft Machine Gun AN-M2.

The U.S. Army cal. .50 Browning water-cooled Machine Gun M2 on Mount M2 with armor gun shields.

U.S. Army cal. .50 Twin Machine Gun Mount M33.

MODELS: Cal. .50 Twin Machine Gun Mount M33 and Cal. .50 Multiple Machine Gun Mount M45

WEIGHTS: M33: 1,500 lbs. without armor; M45: 1,468 lbs. without armor, 2,396 lbs. ready for action.

DIMENSIONS: Length: 6 ft., 4.8 in. Height: 4 ft. 7 in. with guns level. Width: 6 ft. 9.5 in. with ammunition chests. Base diameter: 3 ft., 5.375 in.

TRAVERSE: 360 degrees. Elevation: +90 degrees, -10 degrees.

ARMAMENT: M33, 2, and M45, 4 cal. .50 Browning Machine Guns M2-HB; Weight: 85 lbs. each; Length: 5 ft., 5.125 in. Rate of Fire: 125 rounds per minute each in bursts, 25 rounds per minute sustained. Ammunition: All types standard U.S. Army cal. .50 machine gun.

OPERATION: Self-contained, power-operated mounts with electric motor-generator set incorporated. The mounts will elevate, depress or traverse at rates up to 60 degrees per second.

RATES OF FIRE: M33: 250 rounds per minute in bursts, 50 rounds per minute sustained; M45: 500 rounds per minute in bursts, 100 rounds per minute sustained.

MODEL VARIATION: The Multiple Machine Gun Mount M45C, which is Multiple Machine Gun Mount M45 without the gun shield.

The U.S. Army cal. .50 Multiple Machine Gun Mount M45.

The U.S. Army 37mm Automatic Antiaircraft Gun M1.

MODEL: 37mm Automatic Antiaircraft Gun M1

WEIGHT: 6,124 lbs.

DIMENSIONS: Length: 20 ft., 1 in. Height: 6 ft., 0 in. Width: 5 ft., 9-1/2 in.

RANGE: Antiaircraft: 11,883 ft. with self-destroying tracer. Horizontal: 8,875 yards max.

RATE OF FIRE: Rounds per minute in bursts: 120; in prolonged fire: 20.

AMMUNITION: Fixed HE and HE with self-destroying tracer, M1 Automatic Gun Series only. Projectile Weight: 1.34 lbs. Ammunition Feed: 10 round clips.

CARRIAGE: Type: 4-wheel folding. Traverse: 360 degrees. Elevation: +85 degrees, -0 degrees. Fires emplaced with wheels raised. Min. time to emplace: 2 min., 12 min. with antiaircraft fire control equipment.

NORMAL TOWING SPEED: 25 mph max.

MODIFICATIONS: M1: Manual traverse and elevation. M1A2: Manual and power remote control traverse and elevation.

The U.S. Army Combination Gun Motor Carriage M15.

MODEL: Combination Gun Motor Carriage M15 and M15A1 (Antiaircraft)

WEIGHT: Fighting: 20,800 lbs.

DIMENSIONS: Length: 20 ft., 3-1/2 in. Height: 7 ft., 8 in. Width: 7 ft., 2-1/2 in.

GUN MOUNT: Modified 37mm Automatic Antiaircraft Gun M1 with two cal. .50 Browning Machine Guns M2-HB. Ammunition: Fixed HE, HE with self-destroying tracer, M1 Automatic Gun Series only and cal. .50 Machine Gun. Projectile Weight: 37mm: 1.34 lbs. Traverse: 360 degrees. Elevation: +85 degrees, -5 degrees. Fires from half-track. Min. time to emplace: None; can fire while moving.

BASIC CHASSIS: Half-Track Personnel Carrier M3.

NORMAL ROAD SPEED: 40 mph max.

CREW: 7

MODIFICATIONS: M15: Half-Track M3 and Combination Gun Mount M42 with .50 MGs above 37mm gun. M15A1: Half-Track M3 and Combination Gun Mount M54 with .50 MGs below 37mm gun.

NOTE: In 1943, these units were used with cal. .50 Browning Machine Guns M2 water-cooled, which were later replaced on all combat units.

The U.S. Army 40mm Automatic Antiaircraft Gun M1.

MODEL: 40mm Automatic Antiaircraft Gun M1

WEIGHT: 5,549 lbs.

DIMENSIONS: Length: 18 ft., 9-1/2 in. Height: 6 ft., 7-1/2 in. Width: 6 ft., 0 in.

RANGE: Antiaircraft: 12,600 ft. with self-destroying tracer. Horizontal: 9,475 yards max.; Antitank: 500 yards.

RATE OF FIRE: Rounds per minute in bursts: 120; in prolonged fire: 20.

AMMUNITION: Fixed HE, HE with self-destroying tracer and APC. Projectile Weight: 1.9 to 2.1 lbs. Ammunition Feed: 4 round clips.

CARRIAGE: Type: 4-wheel folding. Traverse: 360 degrees. Elevation: +90 degrees, -11 degrees. Fires emplaced with wheels off ground. Min. time to emplace: 2 min., 12 min. with antiaircraft fire control equipment.

NORMAL TOWING SPEED: 35 mph max.

NOTE: Fires with either manual or power remote control traverse and elevation.

RA PD 137741

The U.S. Army 40mm Twin Automatic Gun Motor Carriage M19.

MODEL: 40mm Twin Automatic Gun Motor Carriage M19

WEIGHT: Fighting: 37,000 lbs.

DIMENSIONS: Length: 17 ft., 1 in. Height: 9 ft., 11 in. Width: 9 ft., 4 in.

CANNON: Modified 40mm Automatic Gun M2, Twin Mount. Range: Antiaircraft: 12,600 with S.D.T. Horizontal: 9,475 yards max. Ammunition: Fixed HE, HE with self-destroying tracer and APC. Projectile Weight: 1.9 to 2.1 lbs. Traverse: 360 degrees. Elevation: +86 degrees, -3 degrees. Fires from tracks. Min. time to emplace: None; may fire while moving.

BASIC CHASSIS: Modified Light Tank M24.

NORMAL ROAD SPEED: 35 mph max.

CREW: 6

The U.S. Army 40mm cal. . 50 Multiple Machine Gun Carriage M51.

MODEL: cal. .50 Multiple Machine Gun Carriage M51
WEIGHT: 8,600 lbs. combat loaded.
DIMENSIONS: Length: 16 ft. 0 in; Width: 8 ft. 0-1/2 in;
Height: 7 ft. 2 in

NORMAL TOWING SPEED: 35 mph max.
NOTES: Fires from trailer emplaced with firing jacks.
The M51 materiel consists of a cal. .50 Multiple
Machine Gun Mount M45 mounted on a Trailer M17.

The U.S. Army Multiple cal. . 50 Machine Gun Trailer Mount M55 (Airborne)

MODEL: Multiple cal. .50 Machine Gun Trailer Mount M55 (Airborne)

WEIGHT: 3,040 lbs. combat loaded

DIMENSIONS: Length: 9 ft. 0 in; Width: 6 ft. 11 in. over ammunition chests; Height: 5 ft. 3 in on wheels, 4 ft. 8 in on ground emplaced.

NOTES: Fires from trailer on wheels with firing jacks or from ground with wheels removed.

The M55 mount consists of a cal. .50 Multiple Machine Gun Mount M45C on a Trailer M20.

The U.S. Army Multiple Gun Motor Carriage M13 and M14.

MODEL: Multiple Gun Motor Carriage M13 and M14

WEIGHT: Combat Loaded: 19,800 lbs.

DIMENSIONS: Length: 21 ft. 4 in.; Height: 7 ft. 3 in; Width: 7 ft. 3 in.

ARMAMENT: 2 cal. .50 Browning Machine Guns M2-HB in a cal. .50 Twin-Machine Gun Mount M33.

CHASSIS: M13: Half-Track Car M2;   M14: Half-Track Car M5

NORMAL ROAD SPEED: 45 mph max.

NOTE: These units withdrawn from combat service in 1943.

The U.S. Army Multiple Gun Motor Carriage M16 and M17.

MODEL: Multiple Gun Motor Carriage M16 and M17

WEIGHT: Combat Loaded: 19,800 lbs.

DIMENSIONS: Length: 21 ft. 4 in.; Height: 7 ft. 8-1/2 in.; Width: 7 ft. 3 in.

ARMAMENT: 4 cal. .50 Browning Machine guns M2-HB in a cal. .50 Multiple Machine Gun Mount M45.

BASIC CHASSIS: M16: Half-Track Car M2; M17: Half-Track Car M5.

NORMAL ROAD SPEED: 45 mph max.

Chapter 21
Heavy Antiaircraft Guns

The U.S. Army recognized there would be a need for antiaircraft guns about 1900. Although it had fixed antiaircraft guns well before World War I, that war made mobile antiaircraft guns essential. The U.S. Army fought the war with an assortment of borrowed and improvised antiaircraft guns, and designed and built a number of its own. One of these was its first modern antiaircraft gun, and it remained in service until early World War II.

In 1917, the U.S. Army completed the design of a 3-in. trailer-mounted antiaircraft gun, and it was adopted and put in production in 1918. It was an advanced design for the time, and production problems delayed its introduction until 1918, and so it was designated the 3-in. Trailer Mount Antiaircraft Gun Model 1918.

The 3-in. M1918 proved very successful for such an early design. It was one of the few weapons kept in production after the end of World War I until the U.S. Army's anticipated requirement for them had been built. A number of improvements were made in it in the 1920s, and when a new 3-in. antiaircraft gun was introduced in the late 1920s, it became a substitute standard weapon.

A U.S. Army SCR-584 antiaircraft radar emplaced in northern Europe in the winter of 1944-1945. The SCR-584 remained in service long after World War II.

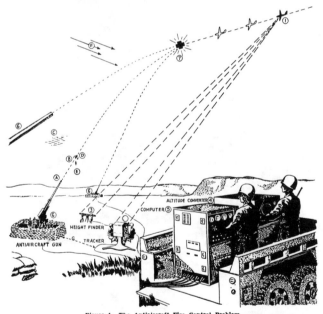

Figure 1. The Antiaircraft Fire Control Problem.
HOW TO HIT AN ENEMY PLANE AT 5 MILES—Solved Instantly By the Electical Gun Director
THE PROBLEM
An enemy bomber is sighted 5 miles away, 3 miles high, flying fast. He's within range of your 90 mm. anti-aircraft battery. A shell will take perhaps 20 seconds to reach him, but meanwhile he'll have flown nearly 2 miles. How could you possibly tell where to aim to hit such a speeding target?
HOW THE GUN DIRECTOR SOLVES IT
Enemy plane ① is spotted and followed by Tracker ② and Height Finder ③, which feed information into Altitude Converter ④ and Computer ⑤. Swiftly the Computer plots the plane's distance, course and speed—aims the gun ⑥ and sets the fuse of the shell to burst at a calculated point ⑦ for a hit.
This electrical brain—the Computer—thinks of everything. It figures on: A, muzzle velocity of gun; B, shell drift to the right due to its spin; C, air density; D, time of shell's flight; E, downward pull of gravity; F, direction and velocity of wind; G. even the distance between Tracker and gun!

This U.S. Army training diagram shows the difficult fire control and direction of antiaircraft guns firing at high flying aircraft.

Many 3-in. M1918s were in service when the U.S. Army was preparing for World War II in the late 1930s. A number of them were used in the Defense of the Philippines in 1941-1942, however, its primary use was as a training weapon until was retired as obsolete in 1943.

The 1919 U.S. Army Westervelt Board Report on existing and future artillery weapons said the 3-in. M1918 was a suitable antiaircraft gun, but that work on an improved design should begin at once. It also noted that the antiaircraft gun would also be employed as an antitank gun in future wars, a prediction based on observations made in World War I.

Since fire control and direction equipment is essential to the employment of antiaircraft guns, the U.S. Army began devoting considerable effort to this problem in World War I. This materiel began with French equipment adopted in World War I, and this was much improved in the 1920s. The development centered on a three-meter optical height (range) finder and an improved fire direction instrument based on one invented by the British Vickers-Armstrong Company. Considerable work was done on improving sound location and searchlight materiel, both of which originated in World War I.

In thee 1920s, the U.S. Army concentrated on the integration of antiaircraft fire control and direction equipment, and a system of electrical data transmission to transmit its firing data to the guns. Although the work proceeded at a careful stately pace, major improvements were made.

Work begun on an improved 3-in. antiaircraft gun also proceeded, and in 1925 the prototype existed. Since military aircraft were rapidly improving, this improved gun had become the highest

A U.S. Army 90mm Antiaircraft Gun M2 firing from its wheels in training exercise in late 1943.

A battery of four U.S. Army 120mm Antiaircraft Guns M1 firing in training in 1945.

U.S. Army 90mm Antiaircraft Guns M1 emplaced to defend a rear area base in 1943.

A U.S. Army 90mm Antiaircraft Gun M1 in action in southern England in the late summer of 1944.

priority development program in the U.S. Army Ordnance Department.

In 1927, the U.S. Army adopted the 3-in. Antiaircraft Gun M1. Its twin detachable bogie carriage, which ran on pneumatic rubber-tired wheels, was very advanced for the time. So was its folding firing platform system and its use of "equilibrator" barrel springs, which allowed its barrel to be mounted near its breech to permit firing at high elevations.

The new 3-in. M1 also included a very advanced fire control and direction system. This integrated the optical height finder, the director with additional data provided from the searchlight, and sound locator equipment. It had a data transmission system, which delivered the firing data to the guns, and it also ran a unit on the gun, which set the time fuses of antiaircraft shells to burst at the desired altitude (range) above the guns.

From its introduction, the 3-in. Antiaircraft Gun M1 was considered an excellent weapon. Massive antiaircraft maneuvers held by the U.S. Army proved it could do what they wanted it to as well or better than any other system then in existence.

However, in the 1930s, the development of military aircraft advanced with great speed, and the basic antiaircraft firing problem changed with them. Aircraft speeds jumped from just over 100 mph to 200-250 mph, and their operating altitude rose from under 14,000 feet to over 20,000 feet. In 1932, the U.S. Army adopted an improved fire control and direction system, and through the 1930s, its capabilities were able to keep up with the advances in aircraft performance.

When the U.S. Army Air Corps adopted the revolutionary Boeing B17 "Flying Fortress" heavy high-altitude bomber in the mid-1930s, the U.S. Army developed a requirement for an improved antiaircraft gun and fire control and direction to counter aircraft in its class. U.S. Army Ordnance Technical Intelligence reports had been carefully watching foreign antiaircraft gun development, and particular the German's 8.8cm guns first introduced in World War I. Reports on the latest, the German 8.8cm Flak 36 (Model 1936, the legendary "88" of World War II) and the new British 3.7-in. mobile antiaircraft gun, led the U.S. Army to consider the development of more powerful antiaircraft guns.

A U.S. Army 120mm Antiaircraft Gun M1 firing in training in 1945.

On the left is a U.S. Army sound locator, on the right a sixty-in. antiaircraft searchlight; these units were used to camouflage the existence of U.S. Army antiaircraft radar in early World War II.

The U.S. Army experimental 4.7-in. Antiaircraft Gun T1, the prototype of the U.S. Army 120mm Antiaircraft Gun M1, under test at Aberdeen Proving Grounds in Maryland in mid-1942. The lack of an urgent U.S. Army requirement for this gun delayed its production until nearly the end of the war.

An emplaced U.S. Army 3-in. Antiaircraft Gun M2 near Pearl Harbor, Hawaii in late December 1941.

In 1938, the U.S. Army issued requirements for the development of new 90mm and 120mm antiaircraft guns in anticipation of future aircraft developments. The development of the 120mm gun was a low priority project, but the development of the 90mm gun was a priority project and something of a military secret. The 90mm gun was to fire a new caliber ammunition that had been under development for several years, and initial work on an antiaircraft gun to fire it was already well into the design stage. The prototype 90mm Antiaircraft Gun T1 was under test in 1938, and modifications and improvements suggested by testing soon made it the T2 model 90mm antiaircraft gun.

In March 1940, the U.S. Army adopted the T2 as the 90mm Antiaircraft Gun M1, and ordered it put in production. The 90mm M1 gun had a very compact single bogie carriage, which could be hooked directly to a towing truck or to a simple limber, which hooked to the prime mover. Its fire control and direction system and its firing data transmission system were all improved models.

The 90mm M1 gun was much used in World War II, and it was an excellent weapon. During the war, a power loading unit was developed for it, and this was applied to many of them. It also received the necessary instruments and modifications so it could also fire as a field artillery gun early in World War II. This gun's 90mm ammunition was the standard for all U.S. Army World War II 90mm guns.

At the same time the 90mm M1 gun was introduced, a completely new and revolutionary antiaircraft fire control and direction system was introduced. As a result of development begun about 1932, the U.S. Army first tested a practical radar for antiaircraft fire control and direction in 1938! Experiments proved this very secret development was more effective than anybody believed possible, and, in high secrecy, its development proceeded.

By the end of 1938, the U.S. Army Signal Corps had adopted the SCR-268 Radar antiaircraft fire control and direction system. It immediately went into production, and units were in the hands of antiaircraft units of the U.S. Army by mid-1941.

The SCR-268 antiaircraft radar was continuously improved and used until the end of World War II. Unfortunately, by about 1943, the enemy had developed ways of jamming it, which reduced its effectiveness.

Because the development of radar was highly secret, the U.S. Army camouflaged it. A flurry of press releases on the improvement of sound locators and searchlights stressed their improvement. Actually, radar had made these obsolete for antiaircraft fire control and direction, but radar was a secret until the U.S. Army announced its existence in mid-1943.

When the U.S. Army entered World War II on Dec. 7, 1941 it had 803 3-in. and 171 90mm antiaircraft guns, and large shortages of radar and all other fire control anti-direction equipment. Production of the 3-in. M1 gun wound up in 1942. However, it served until the end of the war, particularly in the Pacific Theater of Operations. The production of the 90mm M1 gun was a very high-priority program, while the development of the 120mm gun was still a low priority item.

After having fought the very effective German "88" in North Africa in 1942-1943, the U.S. Army issued a requirement for the design of a new carriage for the 90mm antiaircraft gun. The new design was to be a multi-purpose carriage for antiaircraft or field artillery use, capable of firing from its wheels as an antitank gun. This concept actually had been originated in mid-1941, but the urgency of producing the existing 90mm M1 delayed its becoming a requirement until 1942.

In May 1943, the U.S. Army adopted the 90mm Antiaircraft Gun M2 with a multi-purpose carriage. It was a very flexible design that traveled on two axles, which did not have to be dismounted to use it as an antitank gun. It had all the antiaircraft fire data transmission gear of the 90mm M1 gun, complete provisions for firing as a field

U.S. Army 3-in. Antiaircraft Guns M2 in action in a late 1930s night firing exercise.

artillery piece, and provisions for special direct aiming optical sights for antitank use. It also had a power loader, which photographs indicate was sometimes removed in the field. The 90mm Antiaircraft Gun M2 was a very effective and successful weapon.

The production of 90mm antiaircraft guns was stopped in early 1944 with all current and anticipated U.S. Army requirements for them having been filled. Both the M1 and M2 models remained in U.S. Army service long after World War II, in no small way due to two remarkable pieces of their system, which made them about the most effective antiaircraft guns ever used.

These two pieces were the Variable Time Fuse (also known as the VT or proximity fuse) introduced in 1943 and the vastly improved SCR-584 Radar antiaircraft fire control system introduced about the same time. Another element of this improved system was the M9 Fire Director, the first electronic computer type used by the U.S. Army.

The VT fuse was a miniaturized radar unit that caused a shell fitted to it to detonate when it was close enough to its target to destroy it. This was another very secret development, and it was first used by the U.S. Navy for shipboard antiaircraft guns to be fired only when it would fall into the water if its self destroying element failed to function when it failed to find a target.

The SCR-584 antiaircraft radar was a vastly improved model based on a combination of British and American developments. It was much easier to use than older model radars, as well as being more compact and mobile. Its biggest advantage over older types may have been the difficulty the enemy had in jamming it. It was first used in combat at Anzio, Italy in February 1944, when it proved so effective that it broke up the German's heavy air attacks on the confined beachhead. Like all World War II radars, this one was improved during and after World War II, and it remained in service long after the end of World War II.

The M9 electronic fire director went into service in 1943, and it was the link that converted the SCR-584 Radar's data into the firing data supplied to the guns. It made these firing data calculations both faster and more accurately than the older electro-mechanical directors, and this made antiaircraft gun fire more effective because of rapid response.

The combination of the VT fused ammunition, SCR-584 Radar and M9 director was first used by the U.S. Army against the German V-1 "Buzz Bomb" bombardment of southern England shortly after D-Day, June 6,1944. It had been withheld from U.S. Army use until then because of the danger of an unexploded shell with one falling in enemy-held territory. The system shot down and/or detonated some ninety percent of the Buzz Bombs fired at, and that was an unbelievable kill ratio for antiaircraft guns then or now.

The VT fuse was used for U.S. Army antiaircraft guns for the rest of World War II with similarly great effect. During the Battle of the Bulge in 1944, it was introduced in field artillery fire, and by causing the shells to detonate in the air above their targets, this proved very effective.

While all this development was going on, the work on the 120mm antiaircraft gun had slowly proceeded. A handful of prototypes had been built in 1942, but it had not yet gone into production. Then the U.S. Army Air Force adopted the high speed, high altitude Boeing B29 "Superfortress" heavy bomber, and the U.S. Army made the requirement for it more urgent since the enemy might develop similar aircraft.

In early 1944, the U.S. Army adopted the 120mm Antiaircraft Gun M1, the "stratosphere gun." Production facilities were available to get it into production very quickly, and by the end of the year, U.S. Army Antiaircraft Battalions were being equipped with it.

The 120mm M1 gun was nearly twice the size and weight of a 90mm antiaircraft gun. Its projectile and a separate metallic cartridge case with its propellant were fed into the huge gun by a power loader. Its fire control system used the SCR-584 Radar and an M10 electronic director, which was similar to the M9 but suitable for use with the gun.

By the time the 120mm M1 gun was available, it was evident the enemy did not and would not have aircraft it was designed to fight. Only 550 of the guns were built, many of them completed after World War II, and none were sent overseas in World War II. The weapon was retained in U.S. Army service long after the end of World War II.

A tremendous amount of effort was expended on antiaircraft weapons and everything that went with them in World War II. However, post-war evaluations suggested that the best means for defeating hostile aircraft was to have air superiority, and this led to an argument between the U.S. Army Ground Forces and U.S. Army Air Force, which raged from the end of World War II to long after.

A battery of four U.S. Army 3-in. Antiaircraft Guns M2 in a late 1930s training exercise.

A U.S. Army 90mm Antiaircraft Gun M1 going into action in a training exercise in the fall of 1941.

The U.S. Army 90mm Antiaircraft Gun M2 emplaced so it can fire as either an antitank gun, a field artillery gun or an antiaircraft gun.

This U.S. Army training diagram shows how the U.S. Army SCR-584 antiaircraft radar worked with antiaircraft guns. "A" is an electric generator; "B" is the SRC-584 radar; and "C" is the fire director that provides firing data to "D" director, which transmits it to "E," the guns.

A battery of four U.S. Army 90mm Antiaircraft Guns M1 practice firing at the U.S. Army Desert Training Center in California in 1942.

The U.S. Army SCR-268 antiaircraft radar. The SCR-268 was in service when the U.S. Army entered World War II in 1941, and was still in use in improved form in 1945. It was retired at the end of World War II.

A U.S. Army 90mm Antiaircraft Gun M1 going into action at the U.S. Army Desert Training Center in California in 1942.

The U.S. Army 3-in. Antiaircraft Gun M1918.

MODEL: 3-in. Antiaircraft Gun M1918

WEIGHT: 14,085 lbs.

DIMENSIONS: Length: 19 ft., 2 in. Height: 9 ft., 11 in. Width: 6 ft., 5 in.

RANGE: Antiaircraft: 23,700 ft. max.; Horizontal: 12,140 yards max.

RATE OF FIRE: Rounds per minute in bursts: 20; in prolonged fire: 10.

AMMUNITION: Fixed HE and Shrapnel, M1918 Series only. Projectile Weight: 15 lbs.

CARRIAGE: Type: Trailer. Traverse: 360 degrees. Elevation: +10 degrees to +85 degrees. Fires from trailer with outriggers and jacks. Min. time to emplace: 15 min.

NORMAL TOWING SPEED: 10 mph max.

The U.S. Army 3-in. Antiaircraft Gun M2.

MODEL: 3-in. Antiaircraft Gun M2

WEIGHT: 15,915 lbs.

DIMENSIONS: Length: 25 ft. Height: 10 ft. 0 in. Width: 6 ft. 9 in.

RANGE: Antiaircraft: 31,200 ft. max. Horizontal: 15,400 yards max.

RATE OF FIRE: Rounds per minute in bursts: 20; in prolonged fire: 10.

AMMUNITION: Fixed HE and Shrapnel, M2 Gun series only. Projectile Weight: 15 lbs.

CARRIAGE: Type: Folding 2 bogie. Traverse: 360 degrees. Elevation: + 85 degrees, -1 degree. Fires emplaced only. Min. time to emplace: 30 min. including antiaircraft fire control system.

NORMAL TOWING SPEED: 25 mph max.

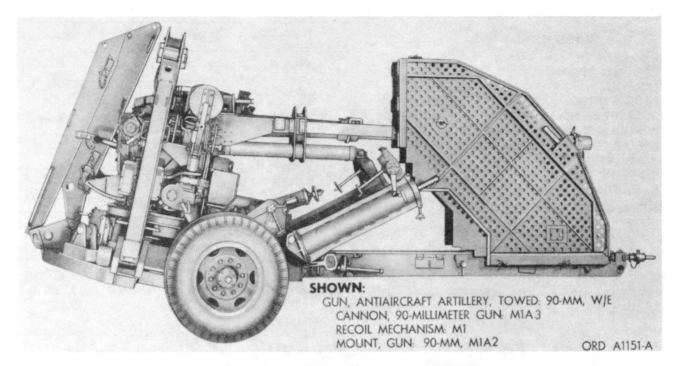

SHOWN:
GUN, ANTIAIRCRAFT ARTILLERY, TOWED: 90-MM, W/E
CANNON, 90-MILLIMETER GUN: M1A3
RECOIL MECHANISM: M1
MOUNT, GUN: 90-MM, M1A2

ORD A1151-A

The U.S. Army 90mm Antiaircraft Gun M1 in traveling position.

The U.S. Army 90mm Antiaircraft Gun M1 in firing position.

MODEL: 90mm Antiaircraft Gun M1
WEIGHT: 19,000 lbs.
DIMENSIONS: Length: 20 ft., 11 in. Height: 8 ft., 9 in. Width: 7 ft., 1 in.
RANGE: Antiaircraft: 34,000 ft. max. Horizontal: 18,900 yards max.
RATE OF FIRE: Rounds per minute in bursts: 22; in prolonged fire: 10.

AMMUNITION: Fixed HE, APC, HVAP and chem. smoke, M1 gun series only. Projectile Weight: 23 to 24 lbs. (HVAP: 16.8 lbs.)
CARRIAGE: Type: Folding single bogie. Traverse: 360 degrees. Elevation: +80 degree, -5 degrees. Fires emplaced. Min. time to Emplace: 30 min. including antiaircraft fire control equipment.
NORMAL TOWING SPEED: 30 mph. max

The U.S. Army 90mm Antiaircraft Gun M2 in traveling position.

MODEL: 90mm Antiaircraft Gun M2

WEIGHT: 32,300 lbs.

DIMENSIONS: Length: 29 ft., 7 in. Height: 10 ft., 1 in. Width: 8 ft., 7 in.

RANGE: Antiaircraft: 34,000 ft., max.; Horizontal: 18,900 yards max.; antitank: 1,000 yards.

RATE OF FIRE: Rounds per minute in Bursts: 22; in prolonged fire: 10.

AMMUNITION: Fixed HE, APC, HVAP and chem. smoke, M1 series only. Projectile Weight: 23 to 24 lbs. (HVAP: 16.8 lbs.)

CARRIAGE: Type: Folding 2 bogies. Traverse: 360 degrees. Elevation: +80 degrees, -10 degrees. Fires on wheels, off wheels and emplaced. Min. time to emplace: on wheels (for antitank use): 3 min.; off wheels (for horizontal use): 7 min.; Emplaced (for antiaircraft fire): 30 min. including antiaircraft fire control equipment.

NORMAL TOWING SPEED: 30 mph. max.

The U.S. Army 90mm antiaircraft Gun M2 in firing position.

FUZE SETTER

The U.S. Army 120mm Antiaircraft Gun M1.

MODEL: 120mm Antiaircraft Gun M1

WEIGHT: 61,500 lbs.

DIMENSIONS: Length: 30 ft., 9 in. Height: 10 ft., 4 in. Width: 10 ft., 3-1/2 in.

RANGE: Antiaircraft: 47,400 ft. max. Horizontal: 27,100 yards.

RATE OF FIRE: Rounds per minute in bursts: 12; in prolonged fire: 6.

AMMUNITION: Separate loading HE. Projectile Weight: 50 lbs.

CARRIAGE: Type: Folding 2 bogie. Traverse: 360 degrees. Elevation: +80 degrees, -5 degrees. Fires emplaced. Min. time to emplace: 40 min. including anti-aircraft fire control equipment.

NORMAL TOWING SPEED: 25 mph max.

Chapter 22
Armored Bulldozers

The commercial crawler tractor with a bulldozer attachment came into the U.S. Army Corps of Engineers use in the 1930s. In World War II, it proved a most useful piece of earth-moving equipment, and it was used everywhere, even in combat. To work under fire, such as filling enemy trenches or covering dug-in emplacements, made armoring bulldozers a necessity. In 1941-1942, the U.S. Army Corps of Engineers developed "Tankdozers" and "Armored Bulldozers," which could work under enemy fire. Both of these were accessory kits to be applied to existing vehicles to enhance their capability in offensive combat.

The Tankdozer was a kit that added a bulldozer blade to a standard U.S. Army M4 series medium tank. A number of kits were tested, all adaptations of standard crawler tractor bulldozer units, and a hydraulically operated one from La Plante Choate Manufacturing Company was adopted in 1942. Some 1,400 Tankdozer kits were manufactured in World War II; these were applied to M4 Shermans with the original narrow track without affecting the tank's turret or main gun.

Tankdozers were used more in the European Theater of Operations than in the Pacific Theater of Operations because of the availability of tanks on which to mount the bulldozer kits. Although the Tankdozer was not as good an earthmover as a regular bulldozer, it was still very useful, and it was retained by the U.S. Army long after World War II.

To make it possible for the U.S. Army Combat Engineers to use their bulldozers under enemy fire, the U.S. Army Corps of Engineers developed an armor cab kit for a standard crawler tractor. This made the Armored Bulldozer one of the only unarmed offensive combat weapons of World War II!

The bulldozer armored cab was one of a series developed by the U.S. Army Corps of Engineers in 1942. Others fit such equipment as graders, scrapers, etc., but the one for the bulldozer was the only one seeing much use. The armor was light, but it offered protection from small arms fire and shell fragments. The bulldozer blade offered additional protection; this contributed to the armored bulldozer's success.

The Crawler Tractor Armored Cab Kit could be applied to any of the Caterpillar, International Harvester or Allis Chalmers standard for the U.S. Army Corps of Engineers. It was adopted in late 1942, extensively used for the rest of World War II, and retained after the war.

The Armored Bulldozer proved very useful in both the European and Pacific Theaters of Operations. In addition to filling trenches and burying enemy fortifications, it proved very useful in clearing streets for tank movement in street fighting.

In 1943-1944, the U.S. Army Corps of Engineers experimented with a series of fully armored crawler tractor bulldozers. The armor made these too heavy to perform satisfactorily, and the idea was dropped. None were produced or used in combat in World War II.

A U.S. Army Corps of Engineers armored bulldozer in action in Italy in 1944. The cab armor resisted small arms fire and shell fragments, and the heavy steel of the bulldozer blade, although not armor, also would.

A U.S. Army Corps of Engineers armored bulldozer in operation in the Battle of Manila in the Philippine Campaign in 1945.

A U.S. Army Medium Tank M4 with a Bulldozer M1 in operation in Northern Europe in the winter of 1944-1945.

The U.S. Army Medium Tank M4 with the Bulldozer M1
adopted by the U.S. Army Corps of Engineers in 1944. The
bulldozer blade was raised and lowered by a hydraulic cylinder unit on the front of the tank; the power unit and controls were inside the tank. The bulldozer added
approximately 8,000 pounds to the weight of the tank.

A U.S. Army Medium Tank M4 with an early non-standardized bulldozer in operation in Northern Europe in the
winter of 1944-1945.

The U.S. Army Corps of Engineers' Armored Bulldozer.

MODEL: Earth Moving Crawler Tractor, Diesel, Armored, No. 1 and No. 2. "Armored Bulldozers"

VARIATIONS: No. 1 on a 46 to 60 hp tractor: Caterpillar D6, Allis-Chalmers HD7W or International Harvester TD-9.

No. 2 on a 61 to 90 hp tractor; Caterpillar D7, Allis-Chalmers HD10W or International Harvester TD-18.

WEIGHT: Tractor with bulldozer and cab armor: No. 1: approx. 25,000 lbs., No. 2: apprx. 35,000 lbs.

DIMENSIONS: (Approx): No. 1: Length: 15 ft. Width: over tracks: 6 ft., 6 in.; over bulldozer: 8 ft., 6 in. Height: 9 ft., 6 in. No. 2: Length: 20 ft., 6 in. Width: over tracks: 9 ft., 6 in., over bulldozer: 13 ft., 6 in. Height: 9 ft., 6 in.

NOTE: Armored bulldozer shown is being tested in 1943.

Appendix 1

U.S. Army World War II Materiel Classifications And Models

U.S. Army orders and regulations defined the classifications and models of materiel as follows:

STANDARD: Adopted materiel preferred for issue.

SUBSTITUTE STANDARD: Adopted materiel, often older models, with satisfactory military characteristics approved for issue in place of Standard materiel.

LIMITED STANDARD: Older Standard of Substitute Standard materiel with less than satisfactory military characteristics available for issue only if Standard or Substitute Standard materiel is unavailable.

LIMITED PROCUREMENT: Materiel, often special purpose, not adopted in any Standard category with satisfactory military characteristics and available for issue.

EXPERIMENTAL: Developmental materiel not available for issue for field use by troops.

OBSOLETE: Antiquated and/or superseded materiel no longer suitable for military use to be disposed of. Obsolete materiel may be retained for museum, historical, instructional or engineering collections, or for decorative purposes at posts, camps, stations and other approved places.

REMANUFACTURED: Materiel worn out in service sent to a manufacturing facility for reconditioning, including incorporating any or all improvements and/or modifications to bring it up to the latest standards for such materiel.

OVERHAULED: Materiel worn by service, reconditioned to its original as manufactured condition. Overseas depot overhaul facilities often added improvements and/or modifications to bring overhauled materiel to improved military standards.

Model Designations

Materiel with "M" model numbers was that adopted for production and issue to troops. Materiel with "T" model numbers was experimental and/or developmental. Materiel with "T" model numbers could be placed in limited and full production, and such materiel was usually assigned an "M" model number to replace its "T" model number.

When an "A" model designation is added to materiel with an "M" model number, it indicates a significant difference and/or change from the original "M" model has been introduced in its production. When an "E" designation is added to materiel with either an "M" or "T" model designation, it indicates a major change in the materiel for experimental purposes.

When the prefix "AN" precedes a "M" or "T" model number, it designates materiel made for use by both the U.S. Army and U.S. Navy and that it is produced by either or both services.

Unfortunately, the above model designations were not always carefully followed due to wartime production and supply urgent conditions. Major changes and/or modifications made in remanufacture and/or overhaul were frequently not recorded due to urgent wartime conditions. Although confusing at times, this had no significant effect on the issue or use of the materiel, and the resulting condition remained in effect long after World War II.

Appendix 2

U.S. Army World War II Abbreviations And Terms

The World War II U.S. Armed Forces had its own language, a collection of slang names, terms and official nomenclature. The abbreviations and official nomenclature for ordnance materiel were well standardized.

The following example of standard abbreviations and terms is from the U.S. Army Ordnance School, Aberdeen Proving Grounds, text OS93, Handbook Of Ordnance Materiel, June 1944 edition:

List of Abbreviations

AA ....antiaircraft
AAF.............................Army Air Forces
allow......................................allowable
amm or ammn.....................ammunition
AN..................................Army Navy
AP...............................armor piercing
APC ....armor-piercing capped
approx or apprx ....approximate
AT...antitank
auto ....automatic
BAR.............Browning automatic rifle
BC ....battery commander
BE..................................base ejection
BI..................................base ignition
cal ....caliber
cml or chem............................chemical
COE......................cab-over-engine
comb ....combination
cont.......................................continuous
cyl..cylinder
dep ....depression
diam or dia..............................diameter
dir ....director
dist char ...distinguishing characteristics
DP.....................................deck piercing
dt...dual tires
DTS ....data transmission system
ea ....each
eff ....effective
elec ....electric, electrical
elev ....elevation
equip.......................................equipment
F..Fahrenheit
FA ....field artillery
flex...flexible
FM ....Field Manual
f/s or fps........................feet per second
frag ....fragmentation
gal ....gallon

gen ....generator, generating
GPF.................Grand Puissance Filloux
grad ....graduations
HB ....heavy barrel
HE...............................high explosive
horiz.....................................horizontal
how ....howitzer
hp ....horsepower
hv .... heavy
I...incendiary
ID.................................Inside diameter
In ....inch
inst ....instrument
kw ....kilowatt
L...left
lb ....pound
lb/sq In ....pounds per square Inch
load ....loading
LS ....limited standard
Lt ....light
LWB ....long wheelbase
mag ....magazine
max ....maximum
mech ....mechanism, mechanical
MG................................ machine gun
mi .... miles
min ....minimum
misc ....miscellaneous
Mk ....mark
mod .... modification, modified
mph..........................miles per hour
No ....number
obs ....obsolete
ord...ordnance
oz ....ounce
p..page
pan ....panoramic
PD..........................point detonating
pdr...pounder

pert.......................................pertinent
port...portable
quad ....quadrant
quan ....quantity
qt...quart
R .... right
RCS................. remote control system
rd..round
rd/min ....rounds per minute
rpm....................revolutions per minute
S .... standard
SCR...................... Signal Corps Radio
SDT.................shell-destroying tracer
semiauto...................semiautomatic
sep..separate
shrap..shrapnel
slid ....sliding
SMG ....submachine gun
SNL.........Standard Nomenclature List
SS...........................substitute standard
subcal...................................subcaliber
SWB ....short wheelbase
sys...system
T......................tentative (experimental)
tel ....telescope
TM ....Technical Manual
trav ....traverse
V...volt
vel ....velocity
vert ....vertical
vol...volume
W .... wheel
W/ .... With
W/o ....without
yd ....yard
' or ft...foot
" or in..Inch
o .... degree

Conclusion

During the five years of World War II, during which the ordnance materiel described in this book was used, the "war production" of the United States rose from one of the smallest to the largest of any nation in the world. In a 1946 preliminary report, Munition For The Army, prepared by the Historical Section of the U.S. Army Chief of Ordnance, this production was summarized:

87,235 tanks

36,069 artillery pieces

48,816 self-propelled weapons

For the above, some 283 million rounds of artillery ammunition and huge quantities of maintenance and spare parts were produced. This prodigious production was made possible by the unique mass production capabilities of the civilian industries of the United States, which were converted to "war production." Their mass production capability was based on as much standardization as possible with as much parts interchangeability as possible and incorporating the most advanced manufacturing technology as possible.

These capabilities of American industry not only made the huge wartime production totals possible, they also made it the overall best of any nation in World War II.

Acknowledgements

The author's interest in World War II tanks and artillery began with his service in World War II and continues to the present. Over this period of fifty years, countless people have contributed to his knowledge of it, and, with the exception of Col. George B. Jarrett to whom this book is dedicated, it would be impossible to name them.

A huge number of official and semi-official U.S. Armed Forces publications, reports and other documents were the source of much of the data and information in this book. A selected sample of these will be found in the Selected Bibliography.

The author wishes to thank the many U.S. Armed Forces associates and instructors who suggested that all publications — even though instructions with them said previous issues should be destroyed — be saved because they could contain information not included in the new editions. This proved a very sound suggestion, and the author has always followed it.

The photographs and illustrations used in this book are all from the World War II era. Unless otherwise credited, they are all from official U.S. Armed Forces sources.

Selected Bibliography

In his fifty years of accumulating information on this subject, the author has consulted hundreds, if not thousands, of published and unpublished sources. The following is a selection of key published sources. Such sources as unpublished official reports, etc. have not been included because many, if not most, are very difficult or impossible to access today.

Official Publications

U.S. Army Technical Manuals

TM 9-1900, Ammunition General, June 1945

TM 9-1901, Artillery Ammunition, June 1944 and Sept 1950

TM 9-1950, Rockets General, July 1945 and July 1950

TM 9-2005, Ordnance Materiel General, 4 vols., Dec 1942 to Jan 1943

TM 9-2300, Artillery Materiel And Associated Equipment Feb 1944, May 1949

TM 9-2305, Fundamentals Of Artillery Weapons, Sept 1947

TM 9-2800, Standard Military Motor Vehicles, March 1943, Sept 1943, TBl Feb 1945, Oct 1947

U.S. Army Ordnance School Manuals

OS 9-18, Ammunition General, 3 vols, 1942

OS 9-63, Handbook Of Ordnance Materiel, Aug 1943, June 1944

U.S. Army Office Of The Chief Of Military History series The United States Army In World War II

Constance McLaughlin Green, Harry C. Thomson and Peter C. Roots, The Ordnance Department: Planning Munitions For War, 1955

Harry C. Thomson and Lida Mayo, The Ordnance Department: Procurement And Supply, 1960

Lida Mayo, The Ordnance Department: On Beachhead And Battlefront, 1968

Blanche D. Coll, Jean E. Keith and Herbert H. Rosenthal, The Corps Of Engineers: Troops And Equipment, 1958

Leo P. Brophy, Wyndham D. Miles and Rexmond C. Cochrane, The Chemical Warfare Service: From Laboratory To Field, 1959

Brooks E. Kleber and Dale Birdsell, The Chemical Warfare Service: Chemicals In Combat, 1966

Miscellaneous Publications

Lt. Cdr. Buford Rowland and Lt. William B. Boyd, U.S. Navy Bureau Of Ordnance In World War II, n.d. (1953)

Modern Ordnance Materiel, Raritan Arsenal Publications Division, Feb 1943

Report 206, Weapons Mounts For Secondary Armament, Detroit Arsenal (G. 0. Noville & Associates) 1957

Ordnance Data Sheets, U.S. Army Office of the Chief of Ordnance, 1944 to 1946

ORD 3 series SNLs (Standard Nomenclature Lists), U.S. Army Service Forces Ordnance Supply Catalogs, 1943-1947

Semi-official Publications

Maj. Gen. G. M. Barnes, *Weapons of World War II*, 1947

James Phinney Baxter 3rd, *Scientists Against Time*, 1946

John E. Burchard (ed), *Rockets, Guns and Targets*, 1948

Lt. Gen. Levin H. Campbell, *The Industry-Ordnance TEAM*, 1946

Lt. Col. William C. Farmer, *Ordnance Field Guide*, 3 vols, 1944-1945

Maj. Theodore C. Ohart, *Elements of Ammunition*, 1946

Serial Publications

Army Ordnance magazine, 1920-1948

Field Artillery Journal, 1940-1947

Special Reference

Shelby L. Stanton, *Order Of Battle, U.S. Army, World War II*, 1984

Index